Advance Praise for
ExtraVeganZa

We should give thanks every day for people like Laura Matthias:
People who live purposeful, meaningful lives, in harmony with nature,
contributing to a worldwide awakening of small production, organic farming.
These farms are our future, and our past. Support your local heroes!

— Medeski Martin & Wood, *recording artists*

I feel very fortunate to have been a guest at Laura's dinner table on
many occasions. I am always delighted with her ability to create delicious
gourmet meals using the most honest and healthy ingredients. Laura's
food is a unique blending of her own innovative style with traditional
vegetarian favorites, a recipe for many successful and exciting meals!

—Andy Cunningham, *owner of Green Cuisine vegetarian restaurant*

Great ideas and healthy recipes that nourish both the soul and the environment
at the same time! Laura Matthias's cookbook is for anybody looking for
creative new ways to use the bounty of local, organic and seasonal produce
that's right in our backyard, and exemplified at Phoenix Organic Farm.

—Derek James Laframboise, *Chef*

If every community had a person as passionate and resourceful as Laura,
the impact would be felt globally. Laura has taken the ideal and made it
a reality. Locally producing nutritious, organic, vegan food for the
community is one of the most proactive ways to be part of the solution.

—Brendan Brazier, *vegan, professional endurance athlete,*
bestselling author on performance nutrition, and formulator of VEGA

It comes as no surprise to those of us who know her that Laura Matthias has created the exceptional cookbook you hold in your hands. A boon for food lovers, *ExtraVeganZa* is loaded with delicious recipes, tantalizing visuals and a farmer's sense of cooking with the seasons. Hats off from one chef to another!

—HEIDI FINK, *chef, food writer and cooking class instructor, former Executive Chef of ReBar Modern Foods*

ExtraVeganZa: Original Recipes from Phoenix Farm (my new kitchen bible!) is a manifestation of everything that Laura Matthias represents. The recipes carry with them the magic that I have witnessed in Laura's kitchen time and time again. They are simple yet classy and loaded with the earthy, delicious, whole elements of nature's gifts that we all long to reconnect with and savor. From choosing your ingredients, to enjoying the very last bite, these recipes will nourish and ground you, inspire your senses and make you want to cook the way nature and your body intended. Salute!

—ALICE BRACEGIRDLE, *creator of* "BellyFit - Stronger Women. Stronger World."

ExtraVeganZa

ORIGINAL RECIPES *from* PHOENIX ORGANIC FARM

For Spicy K

ExtraVeganZa

ORIGINAL RECIPES *from* PHOENIX ORGANIC FARM

LAURA MATTHIAS

NEW SOCIETY PUBLISHERS

Cataloging in Publication Data:
A catalog record for this publication is available from the National Library of Canada.

Cover design by Diane McIntosh. Cover and interior: Savory photos by Jessica Ouellette. Dessert photos by Jennifer Klementti. Interior design by Greg Green and Teresa Lynne.

Printed in Canada.
First printing April 2006.

New Society Publishers acknowledges the support of the Government of Canada through the Book Publishing Industry Development Program (BPIDP) for our publishing activities.

Paperback ISBN-13: 978-0-86571-551-6
Paperback ISBN-10: 0-86571-551-3

Inquiries regarding requests to reprint all or part of *ExtraVeganZa* should be addressed to New Society Publishers at the address below.

To order directly from the publishers, please call toll-free (North America) 1-800-567-6772, or order online at www.newsociety.com

Any other inquiries can be directed by mail to:
New Society Publishers
P.O. Box 189, Gabriola Island, BC V0R 1X0, Canada
1-800-567-6772

New Society Publishers' mission is to publish books that contribute in fundamental ways to building an ecologically sustainable and just society, and to do so with the least possible impact on the environment, in a manner that models this vision. We are committed to doing this not just through education, but through action. We are acting on our commitment to the world's remaining ancient forests by phasing out our paper supply from ancient forests worldwide. This book is one step toward ending global deforestation and climate change. It is printed on acid-free paper that is 100% old growth forest-free (100% post-consumer recycled), processed chlorine free, and printed with vegetable-based, low-VOC inks. For further information, or to browse our full list of books and purchase securely, visit our website at: www.newsociety.com

NEW SOCIETY PUBLISHERS   www.newsociety.com

Contents

Foreword

By John Robbins

I WONDER, SOMETIMES, how anyone manages to live a healthy life today. There are so many things out-of-balance in the modern world. But then there are people like Laura Matthias, who has given us inspiring recipes from Phoenix Organic Farm.

She gives me hope, and not just because her life is in alignment with the earth, though it is and that is wonderful. What impresses me is that in this book she has given the rest of us something we deeply need in order to restore balance to our lives.

I can't tell you how to solve anyone else's problems. But I can tell you this: enjoy this book, use her recipes and make them your own, and you will accomplish several things.

You will celebrate a delicious and Earth-friendly way of eating that brings you and your loved ones happiness and health.

And your body will thank you for the rest of your life.

John Robbins is considered to be one of the world's leading experts on the dietary link between the environment and health. He is the founder of EarthSave International, a non-profit organization supporting healthy food choices, preservation of the environment, and a more compassionate world. The recipient of the 1994 Rachel Carson Award, he is also the author of *Diet For A New America* and *Healthy At 100*.

Acknowledgments

T HERE ARE SO MANY PEOPLE that I would like to acknowledge for their support and time in helping to make this book a reality. First, I would like to give a special thank you to Judy Matthias and Janice Meier for all of the time they put into taking care of my son, Kinkade, while I worked on recipes, photo shoots and editing. Judy was also invaluable in providing metric conversions for all of my recipes and Janice tested numerous recipes for me and proofread everything! Yeah for Grandmas!

Many people helped to test recipes and came to recipe sampling parties: Alice Bracegirdle, April Caverhill, Leah Chisholm, Evelyn Crete, Todd Harmer, Laryl Males, Geoff Matthias, Judy Matthias, Kinkade Matthias, John McWilliams, Janice Meier, Mike Meier, Paul Meier, Brian Mullin, Leslie Palmer, Alison Patterson, Chris Patterson, Gillian Player, Wendy Sequin, Kim Shortreed-Webb and David Stuss—your efforts were greatly appreciated.

Many WWOOFers on our farm have spent countless hours growing and harvesting the wonderful food that, in a moment's notice, I have been able to quickly harvest for a recipe or photo shoot. They have also provided great feedback on the outcome of many of my recipes as well. Some of our longer-term WWOOFers deserve mention: Daniel (Scotland), Cathy (Australia), Romain (France), Roupen (Montreal), Jamie Leigh and Jamie Leigh (both of Ontario), Patrick (Germany), Lyndsay (Scotland), Tomo (United Kingdom), Steph and Babs (Switzerland), Nick (Ontario), Hannah (USA) and John (United Kingdom). Mynah Meagher, Lindsay Miller and Leah Chisholm deserve special note for their role as WWOOFers-turned-employees whose ongoing assistance on the farm has been invaluable.

To all of the lovely and patient folks who passed through or established themselves at Phoenix Farm during my recipe-testing trials and hectic kitchen presence, a resounding thank you: Alice Bracegirdle, Anne-Marie Madden, John

McWilliams, Paul Meier, Hamish Nicolson and David Stuss.

To Jennifer Klementti and Jessica Ouellette who persevered through countless hours of photoshoots and food preparation, and whose wonderful photographs grace this book – many, many thanks!

Thank you to all of the staff at New Society Publishers who have done an outstanding job of supporting and promoting my cookbook, and to Diane McIntosh for her gorgeous and talented cover design.

And a special thanks to Nola, LeeAnn and James, for their suggestions for an all-star title. However, final credit must go to Geoff Matthias who came up with ExtraVeganZa!

Finally, to Kinkade for being the inspiration behind it all.

And to anyone I might have forgotten, you are the most important as you graciously provided your behind-the-scenes support!

Introduction

IN 2003 I WAS LIVING IN VICTORIA, BC, working part time as a field biologist and gardening small plots of land cultivating food for my family and friends. I was forever trying to conjure up ways to create an ideal living opportunity in the country, while creating a unique and sustainable way of life that would enhance the lives of those immediately surrounding me and within my own community. At the time my son, Kinkade, was three years old, and I was increasingly seeking a move from the city center to the country. Being a field biologist by trade, my job takes me to different locations frequently, so I felt no need to conduct my day-to-day life right in the city.

The opportunity auspiciously arose for me to co-purchase a beautiful piece of land on the Saanich peninsula that had been farmed organically some years earlier. I jumped at the chance, and before I knew it I was moving into a unique and funky home in the country. The house and land needed a lot of work, but I was very keen and got started right away.

When I arrived with my family just days before Christmas, the house was cold, dark and dirty. We huddled in front of the woodstove for warmth and used it to cook our meals as well. Assessing our immediate environs, we saw so many things that needed to be done: stacking wood for the winter, fixing pipes and plumbing, upgrading septic tanks, replacing boilers and old woodstoves, clearing debris, getting storm windows installed, sanding and finishing floors, repainting the interior and exterior of the house—the list went on and on. I found myself thinking: "What have I done?" And this list only applied to the house!

But, with considerable help from of friends and family, we managed to plug away at our ever-growing lists and achieve some semblance of order. With so many good people working on the house during that winter, I was free to prepare the outdoors for a summer garden and farm market.

I had worked on organic farms before, and had grown food for myself and my family for many years, but never had I had a market stand, which involved making all of the decisions about and planning for the harvest of crops, not to mention handling all of the marketing as well. The farmland had been as good as abandoned for the past few years, and most of it was fallow or covered in weeds. I began ripping out weeds, creating beds, establishing compost piles and installing fences and irrigation, all the while trying to imagine how many people would come to our small farm-gate market stand, how much produce they would buy and what type of food they would actually be interested in purchasing. A summer of experimentation and learning was ahead of me.

I had a few small greenhouses set up in which to plant seedlings, and I ordered many different varieties of organic seeds to try a bit of everything so that I could determine what grew well in the different soils we had in the fields. I was in full swing by April and, to my delight, had our market stand open by the middle of the month. There were many busy, long days, but at night, listening to the cacophony of sounds coming from the tree frogs in the creek and the Canada geese and trumpeter swans in the back fields, it all seemed worth it and I was satisfied. Each night I came home to my own orchestral serenade.

During that time, I was constantly considering other plans for the farm as well. I had so many ideas that I was unsure of where to focus my energy. I finally decided that opening a Bed and Breakfast would be a great way to utilize our home and to enhance the lifestyle that was daily developing on the farm. I was excited about the prospect of having a home-based business, as well as creating a cozy atmosphere for my guests. In addition, I was delighted at the idea of being able to use farm-fresh, organically grown produce from our farm for the breakfasts I would serve my guests. Creating enticing, organic meals was a unique and marketable avenue for this new business venture.

As the summer progressed, however, I realized I would need far more help on the farm. Not only was there so much to do, but because of the overwhelmingly positive response at the market stand, I often sold out completely. I had visions of using more farmland and planting more crops so that I would be able to keep up with the demand, but I knew I wouldn't be able to do it on my own. Having started to sell some of our more unique market items to local restaurants, this only increased the demand for our produce.

It became increasingly difficult to balance the work demands of running a full-fledged farm, marketing and selling produce, working part-time as a field biologist, setting up a B&B business and staying at home with my young son on a relatively full-time basis, not to mention trying to fit in the writing and testing of recipes for a cookbook! I did have incredible support from family and friends who provided much needed help by spending time with my son when I had managed to double-book myself—which seemed to happen a fair bit—but I realized I needed more hands on the farm.

I decided to look into the WWOOF program, which stands for Worldwide Opportunities on Organic Farms. I had heard about the program before, but wanted more details on what was involved as a host farm. Typically, people register with a country's WWOOF organization and they search through the listings of host farms looking for a region they may want to visit. The farm workers usually work about 30-35 hours per week in exchange for accommodation, three meals a day and experience working on an organic farm. I decided to register as a host farm and before I knew it calls came pouring in from keen travelers who were looking for an educational and interesting farm experience with the added benefits of participating in family life and meeting new people.

I had many wonderful farm helpers visit us and work on our farm that first summer. There were folks from Europe, Asia, the United States and many areas of Canada who offered us their hands in the field and their stories around the dinner table. I realized what a valuable tool the WWOOF program was for me as a farmer, as well as for those looking for farm experience.

With this increase in help, I started to expand the farm ventures. I was given several rare Light Sussex chickens, in hopes of controlling the insects in the garden beds as well as assisting in the preparation of new garden areas for future use. The chickens were amazingly good at this, and they brought a certain country feel with them that added to the general atmosphere. Soon after, a family of three black cats came to live at the farm—mother Tula and her two kitten daughters, Brentwood and Woodleigh. They added their own spice to the farm, and it is wonderful to see them all wrestling and playing and learning to hunt mice in the fields.

The deeper involved I became in farming, the more questions arose about the best way to do things, like preparing beds, mulching crops and developing

techniques for irrigation. The more I learned, the more questions I had, and the more I discovered that everyone had a differing opinion on just about everything! There were many areas on the property that had great growing potential for gardens, but they needed to be prepared. Many of the areas were fallow and covered in grasses or weeds, and I wondered what the best way would be to turn in the land and get rid of the weeds and weed seeds, while at the same time maintaining an ecologically sound process. Being an organic farmer, I was not interested in using any sort of herbicides, and the expense of purchasing a tractor and all the necessary equipment seemed prohibitive, to say nothing of the reliance on fossil fuels that that would create. Somehow, the idea of using pigs for this task was unveiled—yes, pigs!

Folks on the farm had thought to look into the possibility of using pigs as permanent rototillers, composters and fertilizers, as well as serving double duty as our friends. I thought this was an interesting idea, as pigs are known to be wonderfully skilled in these chores. However, I was concerned about how big they would get, how much food they would eat, whether they would escape and how friendly would they be with our small child. We did some research and decided on a breed of pigs called Tamworth. We learned that they did not grow quite as fast as the typical pink wiener pigs that most farms and factories use for meat supply. Plus, they had a thick, hairy coat to keep them warm in a cool climate and were known for being great rooters and diggers. Just what we needed! There was a place on Vancouver Island that bred this type of pig and we got on the waitlist to buy two piglets from the next litter of pigs. We decided we wanted female pigs, as they do not get as big as the males. In October our piglets were born and we eagerly awaited the end of November when we could pick them up.

It was quite a memorable morning bringing the two piglets to the farm. The girls we got were absolutely gorgeous, one a dark redhead, and the other an orangey-brown-haired girl. We decided to name them Paprika and Nutmeg, as their colors were indicative of these spices.

We gathered as much information as possible about pig raising and what to expect having our own piglets. The books gave the impression that one needed to leave the pigs alone for sometime so they could adapt to their new surroundings after being traumatized by transport, and slightly nervous. But when I gently picked up our little piglets and placed them in their new pen, full of grass and roots and bugs and fresh air and a clean, warm straw-bale shelter that had been constructed for them with a heat-lamp to keep them warm through the winter, they were in absolute heaven! They ran around squealing, their tails spinning around in what as far as I could tell was utter joy. They began rooting and digging up the ground instantly, emitting squeals of sheer delight. I was overjoyed as well!

Within a few days they were completely used to the comings and goings from their pen, and would come happily snorting up to me when I came in to scratch their bellies or feed them dinner. They have also been very gentle with our son, who visits them on a daily basis. The pigs have proven to be fairly good rooters as well, turning in their new pen within the first couple of weeks, something we thought might take them months. It is amazing how a couple of animals can transform a field.

From the beginning, I'd had a vision of trying to maintain a relatively closed-loop system of energetics on the farm. I'd hoped to locally source as many things as possible that were needed on the farm, and in turn, sell our produce within our community to local restaurants and stores. I would try to save as many seeds as possible on my own farm and purchase other varieties from as local a source as possible. I presumed that this way the seeds would be adapted for the local climate, ensuring my support for another small business in the area. When we needed new tools or other farm implements, for example, we would go to the local family-operated store in our neighborhood to find the things we need.

After talking with several people about the idea of buying, selling, recycling and reusing as locally as possible, some interesting opportunities arose for the farm. A friend of ours owns a local bakery that makes wonderful certified organic breads and pastries. They grind their own grains into flours and use a wood-fired oven to bake their amazing products. Occasionally, there is leftover bread that cannot be resold or a batch of bread that hasn't risen enough. The bakery saves this bread in the freezer for us and, instead of going into the landfill, it is used as a supplementary certified organic food product for our pigs and chickens. In return, we compost the bran from the flour mill for them and promote their bakery products at our market stand.

Another friend of ours operates a small factory that produces soybean products. The leftover fiber that is strained out during the tofu-making process is called okara, which many organic farmers use as a source of organic matter and

The following are some suggestions for eating more sustainably and regionally:

- *Buy locally produced foods. Small farms often sell directly to the public from their roadside stands. Many local farmers sell their produce at farmers markets, which is a great way to meet the person growing your food.*

- *Buy organically grown food. Not only is organic food better for you, as there is no threat of filling your body with chemicals, but by supporting the farmers who grow it, you're also helping to maintain a healthy environment, soils and food systems in your community. By practicing crop rotation, composting, companion planting and mulching, you're helping to build and maintain the delicate soil structure for generations to come, while naturally keeping weeds and pests in check.*

- *Learn about the seasonal availability of foods. Appreciate when foods are in season and at the peak of taste and nutrition.*

- *Consider how far your food has traveled before it gets to your dinner table. Don't feel guilty about having something exotic or special now and again, but consider, for instance, whether you really need a banana every day when you could have a locally grown apple or pear.*

- *Support heirloom varieties; maintaining these seed resources is a critical part of agricultural diversity.*

nitrogen to enrich their soils. I was able to start using okara from our friend in this way, which was great for both him and me; he needed the tofu by-products removed and I needed a certified organic source of nitrogen and organic matter to help build and maintain the health of my soils on the farm. An added bonus— he runs a fabulous vegan restaurant in town. We now use the food waste from his restaurant to build our composts, and in turn he supports the farm by purchasing our produce. We also promote his soy products at our market stand. It has been fantastic to find these valuable local resources that might otherwise have gone to waste, and to be able to put them to great use on our farm.

As once again winter approached, and I had had a year of experience on the farm, I reflected on how beautiful each season had been. The trumpeter swans and Canada geese returned to their winter grounds in the lower fields, signaling the shorter and colder days, and the snow arrived in the new year officially laying our garden beds to rest. I heaved a sigh of relief.

That did not last long, however. The pigs were growing rapidly and needing new pens, which we created for them. Plans were made for the creation of a large greenhouse in the spring so that I could have more production over a longer growing season throughout the year. Slowly the greenhouse was erected and filled almost instantly with new seedlings ready to burst with life to produce food for the farm. I ordered many new varieties of heirloom and specialty seeds, as well as the tried and true favorites in preparation for another busy year at our farm. I decided to enlarge the market stand area, as the little stand that was there originally was proving too small to display all of the produce from the peak harvest season at the end of the summer. Some of the wonderful folks who had been WWOOFers the previous summer decided to stay on and become employees for the new season. We headed off again on another whirlwind summer of vegetable production, with new WWOOFers and farm workers from all around the globe there with us to witness the cycles of the growing season on the farm.

The Bed and Breakfast was officially opened in the spring and a wonderful assortment of travelers came through to stay with us. My son played a key part in maintaining the B&B, as he insisted on being the host and serving the guests their breakfast each morning. At the age of four, he already had a great work ethic and would wake up early to help me prepare breakfasts and keep me company. We would go out into the fields in the morning and pick fresh vegetables, berries, herbs and edible flowers for the guests to enjoy that day. At the end of breakfast, he insisted on clearing all the tables, even putting the dishes into the dishwasher. He has been an invaluable help and a key spokesperson for our guests!

That second spring season was fruitful and busy as I hosted workshops on the farm, ran the B&B, squeezed in biology work, enjoyed the company and invaluable assistance of dozens of traveling WWOOFers on the farm, tested and retested recipes for the cookbook, and had the kind support of so many wonderful members of our community who purchased fresh produce from the market stand every week. I realized there were so many cogs spinning in this engine of a farm and that they all played a vital part in making it run. I am thankful to everyone who played a role, however big or small. I look forward to the constant growth and learning on this farm, to the next B&B guests, to more wonderful traveling farm workers and to witnessing the ever-changing seasons at Phoenix Organic Farm.

- *Encourage your local schools to support and develop gardens and gardening as part of the curriculum. Pick a child an apple and she'll eat for a day; teach her to plant an apple tree and she'll eat for a lifetime. Teaching children about the connection between their food and where it actually comes from is an essential part of establishing a respect for agriculture and agricultural lands.*

- *Encourage school systems to supply healthy, organic and locally sourced foods where possible in their schools and cafeterias.*

- *If you plan to travel, consider joining the WWOOF program and stay on local farms where you can eat and grow organic foods, while learning about agriculture and farming practices.*

- *Volunteer on a farm to get a sense of the time and energy commitment that goes into growing your food.*

- *Plant a garden in your own backyard or in planter boxes on your balcony. It is very rewarding to pick and eat a head of lettuce that you grew yourself.*

- *Ask your local grocery store whether they sell local products and let them know you are interested in supporting local farmers through the purchasing power of your dollars.*

Part I

Savory Mainland

Spinach Balls

Chunky Black Bean Lime Dip

Divine Guacamole

Rebecca's Strawberry Salsa with Mango and Avocado

Shiitake Sake Pâté

Jerusalem Artichoke Hazelnut Pâté

Pumpkin Seed Yam Pâté

Diana's Artichoke Heart Dip

Sundried Tomato Olive Spread

Spinach Dip Served in a Bread Bowl

Edamame Beans with Lime

Olive Lemon Almond Spread

Garlic Bread

Spicy Stuffed Avocados

Spinach Hummus

Nutty Crackers

Tamari Toasted Nuts and Seeds

Dates and Dried Figs Stuffed with Toasted Walnuts and Pecans

Almond Stuffed Mushroom Caps

Raita with Soy Yogurt

Almond Rice Balls

Garbanzo Bean and Sundried Tomato Spread

Spinach Balls

Fresh spinach from the garden is so crisp and wonderful that I eat it as much as possible in the spring. We grow spinach throughout the year here at the farm, but it's really at the peak of its vitality in the spring. It is packed with calcium, phosphorous, iron, potassium and vitamin A. Adding almonds to this recipe boosts protein as well, creating a delectable and healthy appetizer.

INGREDIENTS:

1 bunch fresh spinach, washed and stems removed (1)

1 medium onion, chopped (1)

1 ¼ cups bread crumbs (310 ml)

1 ½ cup ground almonds (375 ml)

2 tbsp olive oil (30 ml)

2 tbsp tamari or soy sauce (30 ml)

½ cup brown rice flour (125 ml)

1 tsp dried dill (5 ml)

1 tsp onion powder (5 ml)

GARNISH: sprigs of fresh herbs, leafy greens, edible flowers

DIRECTIONS: 350°F (175°C); 30 MINUTES

Place the spinach and onion in a food processor and blend on high until a coarse paste begins to form. Add the bread crumbs, ¾ cups ground almonds, oil, tamari, rice flour, dill and onion powder, then blend again until all of the ingredients are thoroughly combined.

Fill a small bowl with water for wetting your hands while rolling the balls. Place the remaining ¾ cup of ground almonds on a large plate. Begin rolling the spinach mixture into small balls, then roll each ball in the ground almonds, thoroughly coating the outside of each ball. Place the finished balls on a lightly oiled cookie sheet. When the sheet is full, place it in a preheated oven and bake for 30 minutes. Remove from the oven and allow the balls to cool on the sheet. Place them in a serving bowl or on a platter and garnish with sprigs of fresh herbs, greens, and edible flowers. *Makes 15-20 balls.*

Chunky Black Bean Lime Dip

There are never any leftovers when I serve this delicious dip.
Packed with flavor and chunks of avocado and olives, this zesty dip
is a winner. Black beans grow in our West Coast climate, and I
have had great harvests from the bean plants in previous years.

DIRECTIONS:

Roast the red pepper over a gas flame or barbeque, turning it to gently brown the entire outer skin. If you do not have a gas flame, place the red pepper under a broiler in the oven for a few minutes, turning it occasionally to brown all sides. Be careful not to burn it! After the skin is browned, scrape off the skin, then remove the seeds and stem from the pepper. Place the pepper in a food processor along with the beans, tahini, tamari, cilantro and lime juice. Blend on high for several minutes until a creamy consistency starts to develop. Scoop the mixture into a bowl. Chop the avocado into small chunks, then stir the avocado and olives into the bean mixture. Serve with fresh bread or a bowl of tortilla chips for dipping. *Serves 4-6 as an appetizer.*

INGREDIENTS:

1 can black beans (400 ml)
1 red pepper (1)
2 tbsp tahini (30 ml)
juice of 2 limes
2 tbsp tamari or soy sauce (30 ml)
1 avocado, skin and pit removed (1)
½ cup black olives, pitted and sliced (125 ml)
¼ cup cilantro, chopped finely (60 ml)

Divine Guacamole

*For those who love things that are thick and chunky, this guacamole
was made for you! Although we don't grow our own avocados,
we do load this guacamole with our own sweet and flavor-packed
cherry tomatoes, green onions, garlic and jalapenos. Delicious!*

INGREDIENTS:

*2 large, ripe avocados, pits and skins
removed (2)*

2 tbsp lemon juice (30 ml)

½ tsp salt (2 ml)

*1 tsp tamari or soy sauce
(add more if desired) (5 ml)*

2 cloves garlic, finely minced (2)

*¾ cup cherry tomatoes, cut in halves (or
one large tomato, finely chopped) (175 ml)*

1 green onion, finely sliced (1)

*½ cup black olives, sliced
and pitted (125 ml)*

cayenne or chili powder, to taste

*1 jalapeno pepper, seeds and stem removed
and finely chopped (optional) (1)*

DIRECTIONS:

Place the avocado flesh into a bowl and mash with a fork until fairly smooth. Add the lemon juice, salt, tamari and garlic and mix thoroughly. Stir in the tomatoes, green onion, olives, cayenne/ chili and jalapeno. Spoon into a serving bowl and serve with crackers or tortilla chips.

Serves 4 as an appetizer.

Rebecca's Strawberry Salsa with Mango and Avocado

My friend Rebecca Jehn created this sublime appetizer. The stunning presentation and superb blend of flavors make this dish a sensation at a party. Trust me!

DIRECTIONS:

Combine all the salsa ingredients in a bowl and set aside. Prepare the mango and set aside. Prepare the avocado and place it in a bowl, gently stirring in the lime and salt. This will prevent the avocado from turning brown.

To serve, place the strawberry salsa in the centre of a platter, then place the mango chunks around the salsa and finally place the avocado pieces around the mango. The resulting platter adds a gorgeous splash of color to any meal or party. Serve with corn chips for dipping.

Serves 6-8 as an appetizer.

INGREDIENTS:

STRAWBERRY SALSA:

1 pint strawberries, sliced into small pieces (500 ml)

1 jalapeno pepper (1)

1 poblano pepper (1)

¼ cup diced red onion (60 ml)

1 orange pepper, seeds removed and finely diced (1)

juice of 1 lime

¼ tsp fine sea salt, to taste (1 ml)

½ cup cilantro, finely chopped (125 ml)

3 mangoes, chopped into small chunks (3)

4 avocados, chopped into small chunks (4)

juice of 1 lime

fine sea salt, to taste

Shiitake Sake Pâté

*The rich combination of sake, shiitakes and almonds is divine
in this pâté, and it is always a crowd pleaser. This is a wonderful
appetizer to serve at a gathering and is quite simple to make.*

INGREDIENTS:

1 cup almonds, ground (250 ml)
2 tbsp olive oil (30 ml)
*15 shiitake mushrooms, washed,
stems removed and sliced (15)*
1 small onion (1)
¼ cup sake (60 ml)
2 cloves garlic (2)
1 tsp Dijon mustard (5 ml)
1 medium potato (1)
2 tbsp tamari (30 ml)
2 tbsp nutritional yeast (30 ml)
1 tsp rosemary (5 ml)

DIRECTIONS: 350°F (175°C); 60 MINUTES

Grind the almonds in a blender until fine. Set aside.

On medium heat, sauté the mushrooms and onion in the oil for several minutes until the onions begin to soften. Place the mushrooms and onions in a blender and add the remaining ingredients. Blend until a creamy texture is achieved. You may need to use a spatula to scrape the sides of the blender down occasionally. When the mixture is fully blended, stir in the ground almonds and mix thoroughly.

Oil a loaf pan, pie plate or small casserole dish, and sprinkle rosemary around the inside of the dish on all sides and bottom so that it sticks to the oil. Pour in the blender mixture and gently give the dish a shake so that the mixture settles. Place the dish in a preheated oven and bake for about one hour. Remove from the oven and allow the pâté to cool before serving. Serve with a platter of crackers, slices of fresh bread and an assortment of olives or vegetable sticks.

Serves 6-8 as an appetizer.

Jerusalem Artichoke Hazelnut Pâté

*This savory pâté has a deep rich flavor, stemming from the
earthy artichokes and the distinct hazelnut flavors. Jerusalem artichokes
are relatively easy to grow and are often undervalued as a food source.*

DIRECTIONS: 350°F (175°C); 55 MINUTES

Grind the hazelnuts into a fine consistency and set aside. A food processor, hand mill or blender will do the trick.

Place all of the remaining ingredients, except the rosemary leaves, in a food processor and pulse until smooth. Add the hazelnuts and pulse again to combine them thoroughly. Oil a loaf pan or a pie dish with olive oil, and sprinkle rosemary leaves around the bottom and edges of the pan; they will stick to the oil. Scoop the mixture from the food processor into the pan and spread it evenly around the pan. Place the pan in a preheated oven and bake for about 55 minutes. Remove from the oven and allow the pâté to cool before serving. This pâté will keep for several days in the refrigerator, though it tends to dry out a little and is best served fresh. Try spreading it on crackers or using it as a filling for sandwiches.

Serves 4-6 as an appetizer.

INGREDIENTS:

1 cup hazelnuts, finely ground (250 ml)

2 cloves garlic (2)

½ cup Jerusalem artichokes, washed, unpeeled and chopped (125 ml)

2 tbsp nutritional yeast (30 ml)

2 tbsp olive oil (30 ml)

2 tbsp tamari (30 ml)

2 tbsp lemon juice, freshly squeezed (30 ml)

2 tbsp tahini (30 ml)

1 tsp rosemary (5 ml)

9

Pumpkin Seed Yam Pâté

This delightful, savory pâté is always a hit at parties.
Serve it with freshly made Nutty Crackers (pg. 17) or slices of bread.

INGREDIENTS:

1 cup pumpkin seeds,
finely ground (250 ml)
2 cloves garlic (2)
1 raw yam, peeled and sliced (1)
½ medium red onion (½)
2 tbsp nutritional yeast (30 ml)
2 tbsp live oil (30 ml)
2 tbsp tamari (30 ml)
2 tbsp lemon juice, freshly squeezed (30 ml)
¼ tsp sage, dried and crushed (1 ml)
1 tsp Dijon mustard (5 ml)
1 tsp rosemary (5 ml)

DIRECTIONS: 350°F (175°C); 55 MINUTES

Grind the pumpkin seeds into a fine consistency and set aside. A food processor, hand mill or blender will do the trick.

Place all of the remaining ingredients, except the rosemary leaves, in a food processor and pulse until smooth. Add the pumpkin seeds and pulse again to combine them thoroughly. Oil a loaf pan or a pie dish with olive oil, and sprinkle rosemary leaves around the bottom and edges of the pan; they will stick to the oil.

Scoop the mixture from the food processor into the pan and spread it evenly around the pan. Place the pan in a preheated oven and bake for about 55 minutes. Remove from the oven and allow the pâté to cool before serving. This pâté will keep for several days in the refrigerator, though it tends to dry out a little and is best served fresh. Try spreading it on crackers or using it as a filling for sandwiches.

Serves 4-6 as an appetizer.

Diana's Artichoke Heart Dip

My friend Diana makes this rich and sublime dip that exudes flavor.
It is exquisite when served with fresh French bread, and
can also be served on pasta or spread onto pizzas. Delicious!

DIRECTIONS:

In a medium saucepan, heat the olive oil, garlic, chili flakes, salt and artichoke hearts. Cover and simmer on low for about one hour. Remove from heat and blend about ½ of the mixture in a blender with the lemon juice until smooth, then stir the blended mixture into the remaining mixture in the pot. Mix the ingredients together thoroughly. Pour into a serving dish and chill. Serve with fresh bread. *Serves 4-6 as an appetizer.*

INGREDIENTS:

2-14 oz cans artichoke hearts (plain hearts will do, but if you use the marinated ones, drain the excess oil from the jars before using the hearts) (2-400 ml)

1 garlic bulb, peeled (1)

½ tsp chili flakes (2 ml)

5 tbsp olive oil (75 ml)

½ tsp fine sea salt (2 ml)

1 tbsp lemon juice, freshly squeezed (15 ml)

Sundried Tomato Olive Spread

This savory spread can be lathered on bread and crackers or stirred into a pot
of steaming pasta. It's quick and easy to make and absolutely delicious!

DIRECTIONS:

Place all ingredients in a food processor and blend until the ingredients become a paste. Spoon the spread into a serving bowl and serve with fresh slices of bread and crackers. *Serves 4-6 as an appetizer.*

INGREDIENTS:

½ cup pumpkin seeds, ground (125 ml)

1 cup Kalamata olives, pitted (250 ml)

1 cup sundried tomatoes (250 ml)

2-3 tbsp olive oil (30-45 ml)

1 tbsp medium-dry sherry (15 ml)

11

Spinach Dip Served in a Bread Bowl

*This zesty dip is a fabulous offering as a party hors d'oeuvre. Slice the
centre out of a round loaf of bread and place the dip in the loaf, using pieces of
the extracted bread to scoop out the dip. Crisp, fresh spinach is unbeatable,
and this is a great recipe to utilize spinach when it is in peak production.
I often make this for the folks working on the farm as a side dish for
lunch or dinner. It is quick and easy to make, and there are never any leftovers.*

INGREDIENTS:

⅓ cup red onion, finely diced (80 ml)
¾ cup soy mayonnaise (175 ml)
3 cloves garlic, diced (3)
1 tbsp tamari (15 ml)
1 tsp Dijon mustard (5 ml)
*1 bunch fresh spinach, stems removed
and finely chopped (1)*
*1½ tbsp lemon juice,
freshly squeezed (20 ml)*

DIRECTIONS:

Place the onion, soy mayo, garlic, tamari, mustard and lemon into a medium bowl and mix thoroughly. Stir in the spinach, then place in the refrigerator for an hour or so to allow the spinach to soften up and take on the flavors of the dip. When ready to serve, scoop the dip into the hollowed-out center of a round loaf of bread. Use the bread carved from the center to dip into the spinach mixture. *Serves 6-8 as an appetizer.*

Edamame Beans with Lime

Edamame beans are fresh soybeans, often eaten with the shell on. You can now find these in the freezer section of many local grocery stores. Edamame beans are rising in popularity, perhaps as a result of the fun derived from eating them. The idea is to steam the beans in the shell, then season the shells and pull the beans out of the shell with your teeth. This way you get the flavor off the seasoned shells, while leaving the tough shells behind. They're a great finger food for kids and adults alike, and a delicious and fun source of protein. You'll figure it out!

DIRECTIONS:

Place the edamame beans in a steamer with boiling water and steam the beans until they are a bright green color, about 5-8 minutes. Place the edamame beans in a serving bowl and drizzle with lime juice and oil, and sprinkle with salt. Serve immediately and have a second bowl on hand for the empty shells.

Variation: Add 1 tbsp (15 ml) fresh mint leaves, finely chopped.
Serves 2-4 as an appetizer.

INGREDIENTS:

17.6 oz package edamame beans, in shells (500 g)
¼ - ½ tsp fine sea salt (1-2 ml)
2-3 tbsp lime juice, freshly squeezed (30-45 ml)
2 tbsp olive or flax seed oil (30 ml)

13

Olive Lemon Almond Spread

A very tasty, yet simple appetizer to make in minutes.
This zesty spread is great served with warm fresh bread and crackers.

INGREDIENTS:

⅔ cup Kalamata olives, pitted (150 ml)
1 cup ground almonds (250 ml)
2 tbsp lemon juice, freshly squeezed (30 ml)
1 tbsp olive oil (15 ml)
1 cup fresh parsley, chopped (250 ml)
2 cloves garlic (2)

DIRECTIONS:

Grind the almonds in the food processor until fine. Combine the remaining ingredients in the food processor and blend on high for several minutes until all of the ingredients are thoroughly incorporated. Scoop into a serving bowl and serve with fresh bread and crackers. *Serves 4 as an appetizer.*

Garlic Bread

So simple to make and so delicious to eat. We enjoy this recipe very often on the farm. Serve it as an accompaniment to soups, salads or a full meal.

INGREDIENTS:

10 cloves garlic, diced (10)
½ cup olive oil (125 ml)
1 loaf bread (1)

DIRECTIONS: 350°F (175°C); 15-20 MINUTES

In a small bowl, place the olive oil and garlic and allow it to sit for 10-15 minutes. Slice a loaf of bread and set aside. I like to use a hearty loaf of bread but a baguette will work as well. Try olive bread or another flavored loaf.

Place the sliced loaf into a baking dish (keeping it in the shape of a loaf). Using a pastry brush, scoop out some garlic and oil and spread it between each slice of bread until all of the oil and garlic has been evenly distributed between the slices. Place the pan into a preheated oven on the middle rack and bake for 15-20 minutes. If you like your bread crispier, leave it in for an additional 5-10 minutes, but be careful not to burn the top of the bread. Remove from the oven and serve hot. *Serves 6-8 as an appetizer.*

Clockwise from bottom right:
Vegetable Kebabs (page 115),
Garbanzo Bean and Sundried
Tomato Spread (page 22),
Paul's Thai Noodle Salad (page 41),
Zesty Green Bean and Potato
Salad (page 45), Strawberry
Jalapeño Corn Muffins (page 121),
Lemon Lavender Spritzer (page 239),
Lemon Poppyseed Cake (page 154),
Almond Strawberry Spinach
Salad (page 50)

Mint Pea Lime Soup
(page 34) with Mom's
Basic Dinner Rolls
(page 132)

Nutty Crackers

*My son and I make these nutritious and crispy crackers and then
enjoy eating them together with a number of savory dips and spreads.*

DIRECTIONS: 350°F (175°C); 15 MINUTES

In a medium bowl, combine the flour, almonds, pumpkin seeds, sesame seeds and salt. Make a well in the centre of the mixture and pour the oil and water into the well, stirring rapidly to emulsify the liquids. Then slowly integrate the wet and dry ingredients together in the bowl, and use your hands to knead the dough into a ball. Cut the ball into two halves. Lightly flour a surface and roll half of the dough out with a rolling pin, using flour as necessary to keep it from sticking. Roll out the dough quite thin, then use cookie cutters to press out desired shapes for your crackers. If you do not have cutters, you can just cut out squares or triangles with a knife. Sprinkle some sesame seeds on a cookie sheet and place the crackers onto the sheet. Place the cookie sheet into a preheated oven and bake for about 15 minutes. Be careful not to overbake these delicious crackers. Keep an eye on them and take them out early if you think they might be getting overdone. Cool the crackers on a rack before serving. These crackers will keep for quite a long time in a sealed container.

INGREDIENTS:

2 cups whole spelt flour (500 ml)
⅔ cup almonds, finely ground (160 ml)
⅓ cup pumpkin seeds, finely ground (80 ml)
½ cup sesame seeds (125 ml)
1 tsp sea salt (5 ml)
½ cup olive oil or other natural oil (125 ml)
½ cup water (125 ml)

Tamari Toasted Nuts and Seeds

We often toast pumpkins seeds or almonds in our house, but any combination of seeds or nuts is delicious. If you're using different sized nuts, larger nuts should be toasted a bit longer than smaller ones. These are a great, nutritious snack for kids and adults alike.

INGREDIENTS:

1 cup each pumpkin seeds and almonds (250 ml)
1 tbsp tamari (15 ml)

DIRECTIONS:

In a large skillet, slowly dry toast the seeds and nuts on medium heat, stirring frequently to avoid burning. The pumpkin seeds will begin to pop and nuts will begin to brown slightly when they are just about done. Turn off the heat and pour the tamari over the seeds and nuts, stirring in the pan until they are dry. Pour into a serving dish and serve as a snack, or try sprinkling them on top of salads or steamed vegetables. *Serves 2-4 as an appetizer.*

Dates and Dried Figs Stuffed with Toasted Walnuts and Pecans

This is such a simple, healthy snack to make or whip up
when you're in need of a quick dessert. The sweet chewy fruit combined
with the crunchy toasted nuts is very satisfying. Kids love these!

DIRECTIONS:

In a small skillet, dry toast the walnuts and pecans on medium heat, stirring to ensure they do not burn on one side. When they begin to lightly brown, remove from heat and set aside to cool.

Slice the dates lengthwise along one side. Pull out the pit, but keep the date intact so that it stays in one piece. Slice the figs in the same fashion, cutting a slit in each one. Place a toasted nut inside each date and fig. press the sides of the dates and figs together to secure the nut inside. Serve on a platter as a snack or light dessert.

Serves 8-10 as an appetizer or snack.

INGREDIENTS:

10 medjhool dates (10)
10 whole walnuts (10)
10 dried figs (10)
10 whole pecans (10)

19

Almond Stuffed Mushroom Caps

These elegant little appetizers are a savory sensation and quick to disappear.

INGREDIENTS:

15-20 field mushrooms (15-20)
1 medium yellow onion, diced (1)
2 tbsp olive oil (30 ml)
1 cup almonds, finely ground (250 ml)
½ cup fresh parsley, chopped (125 ml)
2 tbsp tamari (30 ml)

GARNISH: several sprigs of parsley

DIRECTIONS: 350°F (175°C); 15-20 MINUTES

Wash the mushrooms and remove the stems from the caps. Set aside the caps, then dice the mushroom stems and set aside.

In a large, hot skillet, sauté the onion in the olive oil on medium heat, stirring occasionally. When the onions begin to lightly brown, stir in the ground almonds, mushroom stems, and parsley. Sauté for an additional 5 minutes, then stir in the tamari and cook for 2 minutes more. Remove from heat. Begin filling each mushroom cap with the almond stuffing, packing it in tightly with a spoon. Each cap will be stuffed quite full in a rounded mound over the top of the mushroom. Place prepared mushroom caps on an ungreased baking sheet and place in a preheated oven and bake for about 15-20 minutes. The mushrooms should be soft. Remove from the oven and place on a serving dish and serve immediately. Garnish with small sprigs of parsley on the side of the plate, or on top of each mushroom cap.

Serves 8-10 as an appetizer.

Raita with Soy Yogurt

*Raita is an East Indian side dish that is often served with curried dishes,
as it provides a refreshing juxtaposition to the spicy Indian flavors.
Made with soy yogurt, this variation on raita is an equally refreshing and
delicious accompaniment to a spicy meal. Try serving this raita with Curried
Potatoes and Vegetables (page 113), Spelt Chapatis (page 137) and steamed greens.*

DIRECTIONS:

In a large bowl, combine the soy yogurt, caraway, dill, lemon, salt and pepper. Stir in the chopped cucumber. Pour into a serving bowl and add the garnish on top. Keep chilled until ready to serve. *Serves 4-6 as an accompaniment.*

INGREDIENTS:

1½ cups soy yogurt, plain (375 ml)
1 tsp caraway seeds (5 ml)
1 tsp dried dill weed (5 ml)
3 tbsp lemon juice, freshly squeezed (45 ml)
1½ tsp fine sea salt (7 ml)
Several dashes ground black pepper
3½ cups cucumber, chopped
into small cubes (875 ml)

GARNISH: *sprigs of parsley and
edible flowers, such as Johnny Jump-ups
or nasturtiums*

Almond Rice Balls

*These tasty appetizers are quick to prepare and
they are great as a finger food at a party.*

DIRECTIONS: 350°F (175°C); 40 MINUTES

In a large bowl, combine the cooked rice, tahini, tamari, onion, garlic, dill and soy milk. Stir the ingredients thoroughly. Place the ground almonds on a plate. Roll small handfuls of the rice mixture into balls, then roll the balls in the ground almonds. Place the balls on a baking sheet and bake in a pre-heated oven for about 40 minutes. Remove from the oven and allow the balls to cool before serving. Place the balls on a platter of fresh parsley or dill and garnish with edible flowers. *Makes 20-25 balls.*

INGREDIENTS:

4 cups brown rice, cooked
and cooled (1,000 ml)
¼ cup tahini (60 ml)
2 tbsp tamari (30 ml)
¼ cup red onion, diced (60 ml)
3 cloves garlic (3)
1 tsp dill leaves, dried (5 ml)
¼ cup soy milk (60 ml)
¾ cup almonds, finely ground (175 ml)

GARNISH: *fresh parsley or dill,
edible flowers*

21

Garbanzo Bean and Sundried Tomato Spread

This colorful spread combines the wonderful summer flavors of sundried tomatoes and fresh basil. The garbanzo beans add a healthy source of protein as well. It is quick and easy to make and adds a beautiful splash of color to a meal. Try serving this spread with fresh pita bread, crackers, sliced baguette and an assortment of olives.

INGREDIENTS:

1 cup sundried tomatoes (250 ml)

14 oz can garbanzo beans, drained and rinsed (400 ml)

2 tbsp lemon juice, freshly squeezed (30 ml)

½ tsp fine sea salt (2 ml)

2 tbsp olive oil (30 ml)

¼ cup fresh basil, packed (60 ml)

2 tbsp tahini (30 ml)

3 cloves garlic (3)

DIRECTIONS:

Place all of the ingredients in a food processor and process on high until an even, smooth consistency is reached. This may take several minutes to ensure that the sundried tomatoes are thoroughly processed. Transfer to a serving bowl and garnish with fresh sprigs of basil. *Serves 4-6 as an appetizer.*

SOUPS

Spicy Peanut Lime Cilantro Soup

Spiced Red Lentil Soup

Cream of Spinach Celery Anise Soup

Spinach Orange Yam Soup

Sweet Pepper Coconut Corn Chowder

Potato Yam Leek Soup

Curried Squash Pear Soup

Tomato Garbanzo Spinach Soup

Ginger Oyster Mushroom Soup

Mint Pea Lime Soup

Sesame Shiitake Noodle Soup

Parsnip Potato Soup

Creamy Onion Soup

Carrot Red Pepper Mint Soup

Spicy Peanut Lime Cilantro Soup

*A deliciously warming winter soup
packed with protein and flavor!*

INGREDIENTS:

2 tbsp olive oil (30 ml)
4 cloves garlic, thinly sliced (4)
2 tbsp fresh gingerroot, grated (30 ml)
1 tsp chili flakes (5 ml)
1 leek including green stalk, diced (1)
*1 medium yam, peeled and
sliced into bite-sized pieces (1)*
2 carrots, thinly sliced (2)
1 celery stick, thinly sliced (1)
1 tsp coarse sea salt (5 ml)
1 tbsp tamari or soy sauce (15 ml)
⅔ cup crunchy peanut butter (160 ml)
4-5 cups water (1,000-1,250 ml)
1 cup green peas, fresh or frozen (250 ml)
juice of 1 lime
¼ cup cilantro, finely chopped (60 ml)

DIRECTIONS:

In a large saucepan, fry the garlic, ginger, cayenne, leeks, yam, carrot and celery in the oil on medium for 5-10 minutes, stirring occasionally to keep the vegetables from sticking to the pan. Add the salt, tamari, peanut butter and water. Stir the soup thoroughly until the peanut butter has dissolved in the liquid. Stir in the peas. Bring to a gentle boil. Turn the soup down to a simmer and cover for 15-20 minutes. Stir occasionally to make sure the soup does not stick to the pot. Remove from heat and stir in the cilantro and lime juice.
Serve hot. Serves 4.

Spiced Red Lentil Soup

*My friend Andee served me a dish similar to this one day, and
this became my re-creation of her recipe. It is a delicious and hearty
soup that is perfect after coming in from the cold on a winter day.*

DIRECTIONS:

In a large pot, heat the oil on medium heat and add the onions. Stir in the ginger and garlic. While these are cooking, grind the mustard and coriander seeds with a mortar and pestle, and add them to the pot as well. Stir in the turmeric, garam marsala, salt and red lentils. After a few minutes, add the water and bring to a boil. Once boiling, reduce to a low simmer and cover. Cook for about one hour. Stir the lentils occasionally to ensure that they are not sticking to the bottom of the pan. Remove from heat and stir in the green peas. Cover and allow the soup to sit for a few minutes to cook the peas. Serve warm with fresh bread.
Serves 6-8.

INGREDIENTS:

3 tbsp olive oil (45 ml)

1 medium onion, diced (1)

1 tbsp fresh gingerroot, grated (15 ml)

5 cloves garlic, finely chopped (5)

1 tsp brown mustard seeds (5 ml)

½ tsp each coriander seeds, garam marsala, turmeric (2 ml)

1 tbsp sea salt (15 ml)

2 cups red lentils, washed (500 ml)

6 cups water (1,500 ml)

1 cup green peas, frozen or fresh (250 ml)

25

Cream of Spinach Celery Anise Soup

The hint of anise in this creamy soup is superb and goes wonderfully with warm focaccia bread. Fresh garlic, onion, celery and spinach from our fields deliver an unparalleled quality to this lovely soup.

INGREDIENTS:

2-3 tbsp olive oil (30-45 ml)

1 medium onion, finely chopped (1)

9 sticks celery, thinly chopped (9)

3 cloves garlic, finely chopped (3)

1 tsp anise seeds, crushed (5 ml)

1 tbsp sea salt (15 ml)

½ tbsp tamari (7 ml)

4 cups vanilla or plain soy milk (1,000 ml)

1 bunch fresh spinach, cleaned, stems removed and chopped (1)

DIRECTIONS:

In a medium pot, fry the onion, celery, garlic and anise seeds in the olive oil on medium-low heat. Stir the ingredients so that they do not stick to the bottom of the pot. When the onions become translucent, stir in the salt, tamari and soy milk. Bring to a boil, then reduce to a simmer and cover for about 15 minutes. Remove from heat. Add the spinach and cover the soup again, allowing the spinach to wilt in the steam. Place half of the soup into a blender and blend on high until creamy and smooth. Pour this mixture back into the pot, stir and serve. *Serves 4.*

Spinach Orange Yam Soup

*A splash of sunshine in your meal, this gorgeous soup is full of sweet
and tangy flavors, and packed with vitamins and minerals!*

DIRECTIONS:

In a medium pot, fry the onion, yams, garlic and gingerroot in the oil on medium-low heat. Stir the ingredients so that they do not stick to the bottom of the pot. When the onions become translucent, stir in the salt, dill and water. Bring to a boil, then reduce to a simmer and cover for about 15 minutes. Remove from heat. Blend this mixture on high until a creamy and smooth consistency is reached. You may need to do this in two batches, depending on the size of your blender. Pour all of the blended soup back into the pot. Add the spinach and orange juice, and cover the soup, allowing the spinach to wilt in the steam. Serve immediately. *Serves 4.*

INGREDIENTS:

2 tbsp oil (30 ml)

1 medium onion, finely chopped (1)

2 medium yams, thinly sliced (2)

5 cloves garlic, finely chopped (5)

1 tbsp fresh gingerroot, grated (15 ml)

1 tbsp sea salt (15 ml)

¼ tsp dried dill weed (1 ml)

3 cups water (750 ml)

1 bunch fresh spinach (1)

⅓ cup orange juice,
freshly squeezed (80 ml)

Sweet Pepper Coconut Corn Chowder

The spicy medley of colors and flavors in this soup brightens and warms up many a day on our farm. There's nothing like fresh corn and sweet peppers, mixed with crisp leeks and carrots. A bundle of flavor from our hot peppers and garlic adds an unrivalled freshness to this cheerful soup.

INGREDIENTS:

2-3 tbsp oil (30-45 ml)

1 medium whole leek, finely diced (1)

3 medium carrots, thinly sliced (3)

3 cloves garlic, finely chopped (3)

⅛ tsp cayenne (optional) (0.5 ml)

1 jalapeno pepper, diced; stems and seeds removed (1)

14 oz can garbanzo beans (398 ml)

1 each medium red and yellow pepper, seeds and stems removed and thinly sliced (1 each)

1 tbsp coarse sea salt (15 ml)

2 cups corn kernels, fresh, frozen or canned (500 ml)

2-14 oz cans coconut milk (2-400 ml)

2 cups water (500 ml)

DIRECTIONS:

Thoroughly clean the leek before chopping. I find that slicing it lengthwise and rinsing the insides is an effective way to clean it.

In a medium pot, fry the leek, carrots, garlic, cayenne and jalapeno in the oil on medium-low heat. Stir the ingredients so that they do not stick to the bottom of the pot. When the leeks begin to soften, stir in the garbanzo beans, salt, red and yellow peppers, corn, coconut milk and water. Bring to a boil, then reduce to a simmer and cover for about 15 minutes. Remove from heat and serve immediately. *Serves 4.*

Potato Yam Leek Soup

This creamy soup has a wonderful, hearty garden flavor.
The yam is a delightful departure from the traditional potato leek
soup recipes, and mingles nicely with our farm vegetables.

DIRECTIONS:

In a large soup pot, sauté the leeks in the oil on medium heat. Add the potatoes, yams, garlic, dill and salt, stirring so that they do not stick to the bottom of the pot. Add the water and soy milk, and bring to a low simmer. Cover the pot and allow the soup to simmer for 15-20 minutes or until the potatoes and yams have softened. Remove from heat. Blend half of the soup in a blender and stir it back into the pot with the remaining unblended soup. Serve with slices of hearty multigrain bread. *Serves 6.*

INGREDIENTS:

2 tbsp olive oil (30 ml)
4 leeks, cleaned and thinly sliced (4)
6 potatoes, chopped into ½-inch cubes (6)
1 large yam, peeled and chopped into ½-inch cubes (1)
5 cloves garlic, peeled and diced (5)
2 tsp dried dill weed (10 ml)
1-2 tbsp coarse sea salt (15-30 ml)
6 cups water (1,500 ml)
2 cups soy milk (500 ml)
fresh ground black pepper, to taste (optional)

Curried Squash Pear Soup

A delightful, bright orange soup packed with flavor and beta-carotene, this is one of our household favorites on the farm. It is hard to grow enough winter squash to meet the consumption demands on our farm alone! I continue to allot more and more ground for growing these delectable staples. Our pear trees and fresh, crunchy carrots provide us with the sweet components of this enticing soup.

INGREDIENTS:

2 tbsp olive oil (30 ml)
1 onion, diced (1)
1 kabocha or buttercup squash peeled, seeded and chopped into 1-inch chunks (1)
5 carrots, thinly sliced (5)
2 pears, peeled, cored and sliced (2)
1 tsp cumin, ground (5 ml)
1 tsp turmeric (5 ml)
½ tsp cinnamon (2 ml)
1 tbsp fresh gingerroot, grated (15 ml)
2 tbsp coarse sea salt (30 ml)
8-10 cups water (2,000-2,500 ml)

DIRECTIONS:

In a large saucepan, sauté the onion in the oil on medium heat. As the onion becomes translucent, add the squash, carrots, pears, cumin, turmeric, cinnamon, gingerroot and salt, stirring to prevent any burning on the bottom of the pan. Add the water and bring to a simmer. Cover the soup, allowing it to simmer for about 15-20 minutes. The squash and carrots should be soft but not mushy. Remove from heat. Blend half of the soup in a blender and return it to the pot with the remaining unblended soup. Stir and enjoy. This makes a large pot of soup that can be kept in the refrigerator for several days or frozen for meals at a later time. *Serves 6-8.*

Tomato Garbanzo Spinach Soup

A zesty soup that demands a loaf of fresh bread for wiping your bowl clean.
This soup tastes best on the second day, so if you can prepare it ahead of time,
you'll be rewarded with a more flavorful soup. If you have fresh herbs in your
garden, such as basil, dill, tarragon or oregano, try adding them to this soup.

DIRECTIONS:

In a medium pan, sauté the onion and garlic in the olive oil on medium heat. Add the herbs, salt, pepper, celery, artichokes, garbanzo beans and mushrooms, stirring so that the vegetables do not stick to the bottom of the pan. Add the tomato paste and water. Bring to a low simmer and let it cook covered for 10-15 minutes. Add the spinach and olives and cover again, allowing the spinach to wilt in the steam from the soup. Serve warm with fresh focaccia bread or sliced baguette. *Serves 6.*

INGREDIENTS:

2-3 tbsp olive oil (30-45 ml)
1 medium onion (1)
5 garlic cloves (5)
½ tsp each dried oregano,
thyme, sage (2 ml)
3-4 tsp coarse sea salt (15-20 ml)
Several dashes ground black pepper
4 ribs celery, finely chopped (4)
14 oz can artichoke hearts (400 ml)
14 oz can garbanzo beans (400 ml)
10 button mushrooms, thinly sliced (10)
6 oz can tomato paste (156 ml)
6 cups water (1,500 ml)
⅔ cup black olives, sliced (150 ml)
1 bunch fresh spinach, cleaned,
stems removed and finely chopped (1)

Ginger Oyster Mushroom Soup

This is a wonderfully aromatic broth brimming with slivers of onions and oyster mushrooms, and spiced with a generous amount of fresh ginger. One of the simplest soups to make, and one of the quickest to disappear, this soup makes just enough for a couple of people, so double the recipe if you want more—you probably will.

Ingredients:

3 tbsp olive oil (45 ml)
1 medium onion, thinly sliced (1)
3 tbsp fresh gingerroot, grated (45 ml)
2 cups oyster mushrooms, thinly sliced (500 ml)
2 tbsp tamari (30 ml)
3 cups water (750 ml)

Directions:

In a medium pan, sauté the onion and ginger in the olive oil on medium-low heat. Stir in the mushrooms and tamari. Add the water and bring the soup to a gentle simmer, allowing it to cook covered for 10-15 minutes. Enjoy!
Serves 2.

Sesame Shiitake Noodle Soup

*This is a delicious soup that is hearty enough to be served as a meal.
The flavors of ginger, sesame and shiitake mushrooms combine
wonderfully to create a tantalizing broth loaded with nutritious vegetables
and delightful noodles. This is a pleasant combination of Asian
flavors and our own country farm vegetables.*

DIRECTIONS:

Pour the olive oil into a large pot on medium-low heat. Add the green onions, ginger and garlic, stirring gently as the shallots soften. Add the carrots, cabbage and mushrooms, stirring regularly. Stir in the salt, sesame oil, kale, tamari, sake and water. Increase the heat and bring the water to the simmering point. Reduce heat to medium-low, add the noodles and stir the mixture thoroughly. Cover to allow the noodles to absorb some of the flavor of the broth. Leave covered for 5-10 minutes. Serve hot.

Serves 6.

INGREDIENTS:

3-4 tbsp olive oil (45-60 ml)

10 green onions, finely chopped (10)

2 tbsp fresh gingerroot, grated (30 ml)

3 cloves garlic (3)

5 carrots, cut into long, thin slices (5)

½ head of red cabbage, cut into long, thin slices (½)

10 fresh shiitake mushrooms, stems removed, thinly sliced (10)

1 tbsp coarse sea salt (15 ml)

1½ tbsp sesame oil (20 ml)

1 bunch kale or spinach, stems removed and finely chopped (1)

3 tbsp tamari (45 ml)

1 cup sake (250 ml)

6-7 cups water (1,500-1,750 ml)

4 7-oz packages udon noodles (4 200-g)

VARIATION: use ½ lb vermicelli rice noodles cooked, strained and added to soup

Mint Pea Lime Soup

This elegant, zesty green soup has a stunningly bright color and a unique minty flavor that intrigues most every palate. It is also packed with vitamins, minerals, calcium, iron and protein. Using fresh peas and mint from the garden makes for an unrivalled fresh and flavorful soup.

INGREDIENTS:

3 tbsp olive oil (45 ml)
3 cups yellow onion, diced (750 ml)
3 cloves garlic, diced (3)
3 cups peas, fresh or frozen (750 ml)
1 bunch fresh spinach, stems removed (1)
1 tbsp coarse sea salt (15 ml)
4 cups water (1,000 ml)
10 sprigs fresh mint (10)
juice of 1 lime

DIRECTIONS:

In a medium saucepan, sauté the onion and garlic in the oil on medium heat. Stir in the peas, spinach and salt, and continue stirring for another minute. Add the water and simmer for several minutes, until the peas turn a bright green. Be careful not to overcook! Remove from heat and place half of the soup in a blender with 5 sprigs of mint. Blend until a creamy consistency is achieved. Blend the remaining half of the soup with the remaining mint until creamy. Combine the two batches then stir in the fresh lime juice and serve hot. Garnish with sprigs of fresh mint. *Serves 4.*

Parsnip Potato Soup

This creamy, thick soup has a lovely, delicate flavor, somewhat sweet from the apple and sharp from the wine, and is a beautiful yellow color. It is a fabulous winter soup to eat by the fire with fresh bread and biscuits. We love to make this soup on a grey day with our sweet garden parsnips and potatoes.

DIRECTIONS:

In a large pot, allow the olive oil to warm on medium heat. Add the onions, spices, herbs and potatoes, stirring regularly for about 10 minutes, ensuring they do not stick to the bottom of the pot. As the potatoes begin to soften, add the parsnips, celery, apple, salt, pepper and wine. Allow the vegetables to simmer in the wine for 5-10 minutes then add the water. Cover and simmer for another 15-20 minutes. Blend the soup (half at a time) in a blender until a creamy consistency is reached. Serve hot bowls of soup with a garnish of cilantro, parsley or green onions alongside fresh bread or biscuits.

Serves 6-8.

INGREDIENTS:

3 tbsp olive oil (45 ml)
2 onions, diced (2)
½ tsp nutmeg (2 ml)
1 tsp turmeric (5 ml)
½ tsp dried thyme (2 ml)
5½ cups unpeeled potatoes, cubed (1,375 ml)
2 cups unpeeled parsnips, cubed (500 ml)
4 ribs celery, thinly sliced (4)
1 apple, cored and cubed (1)
1½ tbsp coarse sea salt (20 ml)
Several dashes ground black pepper
1 cup white wine (250 ml)
4 cups water (1,000 ml)

GARNISH: cilantro, parsley, green onions

Creamy Onion Soup

*Caramelized onions simmered in sherry and herbs offer a
fabulous flavor and aroma to this lovely, smooth soup. Try serving
this soup with warm, fresh bread or hot garlic bread (page 134).*

INGREDIENTS:

3 tbsp olive oil (45 ml)
8 cups yellow onions, diced (2,000 ml)
5 cloves garlic, minced (5)
1 tsp thyme (5 ml)
1 tbsp coarse sea salt (15 ml)
Several dashes ground black pepper
1 cup sherry (250 ml)
2 tbsp tamari (30 ml)
*⅔ cup light spelt or wheat pastry flour
(most any flour will work) (160 ml)*
1 tbsp nutritional yeast (15 ml)
4 cups water (1,000 ml)

DIRECTIONS:

In a large pot, sauté the onions and garlic in the olive oil on medium heat for about 10 minutes. Stir in the thyme, salt, pepper, sherry and tamari, and allow the onions to simmer in the sherry mixture for another 10 minutes. Add the flour and yeast, then gently whisk to ensure that the flour dissolves in the liquid. Stir in the water and bring to a simmer for another 5 minutes. Remove from heat. Blend half of the soup in a blender on high for several minutes until a smooth and creamy consistency is reached. Blend the remaining half of the soup and combine the two batches.

As a garnish, sauté some onions, sliced in rings, until they reach a golden brown color. Serve the soup in bowls and place a few onions in the centre of each bowl of soup.
Serves 4-6.

Carrot Red Pepper Mint Soup

Crunchy carrots and crisp red peppers make a beautiful, bright orange soup.
Fresh mint adds a unique flavor to this creamy soup.

DIRECTIONS:

In a large pot, heat the olive oil on medium heat. Sauté the onions, carrots, garlic, ginger, salt, cashews, nutmeg and black pepper for 5-10 minutes, stirring regularly. Add the red pepper and sauté for another 5 minutes. Stir in the mint, water and soy milk, and bring to a boil. Reduce heat and simmer on low for 10 more minutes. Remove from heat and blend all ingredients in a blender until a smooth and creamy consistency is reached. Serve warm with sprigs of fresh mint and nasturtiums for garnish.

Serves 4-6.

INGREDIENTS:

3 tbsp olive oil (45 ml)

1 medium onion, chopped

10 medium carrots, sliced (10)

3 cloves garlic, chopped (3)

2 tbsp fresh gingerroot, grated (30 ml)

1 ½ tbsp coarse sea salt (20 ml)

1 cup raw cashews, whole or pieces (250 ml)

½ tsp nutmeg (2 ml)

Several dashes ground black pepper

1 medium red pepper, seeds and stems removed and sliced (1)

10 sprigs fresh mint, chopped (10)

4 cups water (1,000 ml)

1 cup soy milk (250 ml)

GARNISH: *sprigs of fresh mint, nasturtium flowers*

SALADS

Orange Walnut Fig Salad

Paul's Thai Noodle Salad

Fresh Greens and Arugula with Coconut Cilantro Lime Dressing

Sesame Spinach Salad

Faux Feta Greek Salad

Quinoa Three Bean Salad with Toasted Almonds

Zesty Green Bean and Potato Salad

Mint Beet Salad

Fern's Carrot Cabbage Kale Salad

Waldorf Salad with Soy Mayonnaise and Edible Flowers

Snow Pea Salad with Toasted Walnuts and Nasturtiums

Tuscan Bean Salad

Almond Strawberry Spinach Salad

Orange Walnut Fig Salad

Arugula is a year-round staple at our farm. It is incredibly hearty and prolific, not to mention deliciously spicy and a great way to get a source of greens in one's diet. We've planted fig trees in order to harvest our own fresh figs, as they are a marvel unto themselves. When you can't find fresh figs, try using dried ones, as they are delicious in their own right. Fresh toasted walnuts from our tree and zesty fresh onions create an incredible flavor combination when mixed with the citrus essence of mandarin oranges.

INGREDIENTS:

1 recipe Orange Vinaigrette (p. 52) (1)
3 mandarin oranges
(or 2 regular oranges) (3)
1 cup walnuts, toasted (250 ml)
1 cup fresh figs, sliced into thin wedges
(or calimyrna figs, dried) (250 ml)
¼ cup red onion, finely sliced (60 ml)
arugula (enough for 4 servings)

DIRECTIONS:

Separate the oranges in wedges and set aside. If you are using regular oranges, slice each wedge in half so the pieces are bite size.

Place the walnuts in a frying pan on medium heat and stir frequently until they begin to lightly brown (5-10 minutes). Remove from heat and set aside.

Chop each fig into 6 or 8 pieces and set aside.

Finely slice the red onion.

Clean the arugula and pat dry. Divide the arugula into four bunches and place each bunch onto a salad plate. Evenly distribute the orange wedges, walnuts, figs, and onions. When ready to serve, pour equal portions of Orange Vinaigrette (page 52) on each of the four plates and serve. *Serves 4.*

Paul's Thai Noodle Salad

My brother Paul is known for his zesty Thai noodle salad. Made in the height of summer with crisp red peppers, spinach, green onions and cilantro from the garden, it is a staple at our farm gatherings.

DIRECTIONS:

In a large frying pan, sauté the tofu strips in oil until they begin to brown. Stir them occasionally to brown them on each side. Stir in the tamari and yeast. Remove from heat and set aside.

Boil a medium sized pot of water with ½ tsp sea salt, Add the vermicelli, stirring to separate the noodles. These noodles cook quickly. Remove them from heat and strain the noodles, discarding the water. Place the noodles in a large mixing bowl. Add the remaining ingredients including the fried tofu, and gently mix together (tongs work well for this). Scoop the noodle salad into a large serving bowl and place in the refrigerator until chilled. Sprinkle the roasted peanuts on top and serve.

Serves 6-8.

INGREDIENTS:

½ pound dried rice vermicelli (250 g)

1 bunch spinach, cleaned, stems removed and finely chopped (1)

1 red pepper, seeds and stem removed, thinly sliced (1)

4 green onions, finely chopped (4)

1 cup fresh cilantro, finely chopped (250 ml)

2 tbsp lime juice, freshly squeezed (30 ml)

2 tbsp tamari (30 ml)

1 tbsp sesame oil (15 ml)

2 tbsp olive oil (30 ml)

a few dashes of hot pepper sauce (to taste)

1 lb medium or firm tofu, sliced into thin strips (500 g)

1-2 tbsp olive oil (15-30 ml)

2 tbsp tamari (30 ml)

1 tbsp nutritional yeast (15 ml)

⅓ cup peanuts, roasted and chopped (optional) (75 ml)

Fresh Greens and Arugula with Coconut Cilantro Lime Dressing

Arugula is a spicy Italian green that adds a wonderful punch to a salad. Topped with this creamy dressing and toasted cashews, it makes a refreshing summer salad.

INGREDIENTS:

1 recipe Coconut Cilantro Lime Dressing (p. 55)
⅓ lb fresh salad greens (150 g)
2 cups arugula leaves (500 ml)
½ cup cashews, toasted (125 ml)
¼ cup fresh cilantro (60 ml)
2 tbsp dried coconut (30 ml)

DIRECTIONS:

Prepare the Coconut Cilantro Lime Dressing (page 55) and set aside.

Place the cashews in a small frying pan and toast them on medium-low heat for about 5 minutes, stirring them until they turn a golden brown. Remove from heat and set aside.

Arrange the salad greens and arugula in a serving bowl. Sprinkle the toasted cashews, cilantro and coconut over top. Pour on the dressing and gently toss the salad before serving. *Serves 4-6.*

Sesame Spinach Salad

This quick and easy spinach dish can be served hot or cold as a spinach salad. Loaded with calcium and vitamins from the greens and sesame seeds, it is as delicious as it is nutritious. It is one of my son's favorites.

INGREDIENTS:

2 bunches spinach, washed, stems removed and chopped (2)
1 tbsp olive oil (15 ml)
½ tsp sesame oil (2 ml)
2 tbsp tamari (30 ml)
4 tbsp gomashio (p. 56) (60 ml)

DIRECTIONS:

In a large skillet, warm the olive and sesame oils on medium heat. Stir in the spinach until it starts to wilt. Pour the tamari over the spinach and sprinkle the gomashio over top. Pour into a serving bowl and serve hot, or allow the spinach to cool then chill it and serve as a cold spinach salad. *Serves 2-4.*

Faux Feta Greek Salad

This vegan version of Greek salad is a flavorful addition to any summer meal when fresh tomatoes and peppers are at the peak of sweetness!

DIRECTIONS:

Crumble the tofu into a large bowl. Add the vinegar, oil, tamari, pepper, oregano, garlic, and salt. Stir together with the tofu and refrigerate, allowing the tofu to absorb the sauce.

Prepare the remaining vegetables and add them to the tofu mixture and gently stir all ingredients together. Keep chilled in the refrigerator until ready to serve.
Serves 6-8.

INGREDIENTS:

16 oz package medium tofu (450-500 ml)
2 tbsp balsamic vinegar (30 ml)
4 tbsp olive oil (60 ml)
2 tbsp tamari (30 ml)
Several dashes ground black pepper
1 tsp oregano (5 ml)
1 clove garlic (1)
½ tsp fine sea salt (2 ml)
1 each red, orange, green and yellow peppers, seeds and stems removed, chopped into 1-inch cubes (1 each)
2 cups cherry tomatoes, sliced in halves (500 ml)
1 small cucumber, cubed (1)
¼ cup red onion, diced (60 ml)
1 cup Kalamata olives (250 ml)

Quinoa Three Bean Salad with Toasted Almonds

Quinoa is an incredible grain that is loaded with protein and is also quick to prepare. The almonds and beans in this dish add even more protein, and the fresh herbs and tangy dressing inspire a wonderful summer salad.

INGREDIENTS:

1 cup dry quinoa (250 ml)

2 cups water (500 ml)

1 tsp salt (5 ml)

½ cup toasted almonds, chopped (125 ml)

14 oz can each garbanzo beans and kidney beans (400 ml)

¾ cup edamame beans, shelled and thawed (175 ml)

2 tbsp fresh parsley, chopped (30 ml)

2 tbsp fresh mint, chopped (30 ml)

2 green onions, sliced (2)

½ cup red onion, diced (125 ml)

2 cloves garlic, finely chopped (2)

Several dashes ground black pepper

1½ tbsp balsamic vinegar (20 ml)

3 tbsp tamari (45 ml)

8 tbsp olive oil (120 ml)

5 tbsp lemon juice, freshly squeezed (75 ml)

DIRECTIONS:

In a medium pot, combine the quinoa, water and salt and bring to a boil. Reduce to a simmer and cook covered for 15 minutes on low heat. Remove from heat, remove lid and allow the quinoa to cool.

In a small frying pan, dry toast the almonds on medium-low heat for about 5 minutes until they start to lightly brown. Remove from heat and set aside to cool. Coarsely chop the almonds when they have cooled.

In a large bowl, combine the garbanzo, kidney and edamame beans. Stir in the parsley, mint, onions, garlic, pepper, vinegar, tamari, oil and lemon. Fold in the cooled quinoa and toasted almonds. *Serves 6-8.*

Zesty Green Bean and Potato Salad

We grow a variety of potatoes and beans at our farm each year and this lovely summer salad provides a zesty companionship. This salad is perfect for picnics or as an addition to a cool summer meal after a day of work in the hot sun.

DIRECTIONS:

In a large pot, bring salted water to a boil and add the potatoes. Cook the potatoes until they are soft—approximately 10 minutes. Drain and rinse the potatoes in cold water, and set aside.

Prepare the beans by removing stems and cutting them into 1-inch-long pieces. Place the beans in a steamer and steam them until they turn a bright green color—approximately 2 minutes. Remove the beans from the steamer immediately and run under cold water. Drain and set aside.

Prepare the dressing by combining the garlic, olive oil, mustard, dill, vinegar, salt and pepper in a large bowl and stirring together. Fold in the red onions, potatoes and green beans. Chill the salad for one hour or more before serving.

Serves 8-10.

INGREDIENTS:

10 cups water (2,500ml)

1 tbsp coarse sea salt (15 ml)

6 cups potatoes, peeled and cubed (1,500 ml)

3 cups green beans, stems removed and cut into 1-inch pieces (750 ml)

1 cup red onion, thinly sliced (250 ml)

3 cloves garlic (3)

4 tbsp olive oil (60 ml)

2 tsp Dijon mustard (10 ml)

½ tbsp dill leaf (7 ml)

3 tbsp balsamic vinegar (45 ml)

1 tsp fine sea salt (5 ml)

Several dashes ground black pepper

Mint Beet Salad

Beets, like most root vegetables, are a great source of vitamins and minerals.
Their sweet flavor and brilliant color make them a delight to eat.
We grow several varieties of beets, and any one of them works well in this recipe.
We like to eat this refreshing salad on a hot afternoon in the summer.

INGREDIENTS:

5 cups beets, sliced into thin rounds (1,250 ml)
2 cups water (500 ml)
1 tsp sea salt (5 ml)
2-3 tbsp fresh mint, chopped (30-45 ml)
¼ cup red onion, finely chopped (60 ml)
1 tsp fine sea salt (5 ml)
2 tbsp balsamic vinegar (30 ml)
2 tbsp olive oil (30 ml)
1 clove garlic (1)
Several dashes ground black pepper
GARNISH: *several sprigs of fresh mint*

DIRECTIONS:

In a medium-sized pot, place the beets, water and salt, and bring to a boil. Reduce heat to a low simmer, cover and allow the beets to simmer for about 10 minutes until they are soft. Remove from heat, drain and set aside.

In a mixing bowl, combine the remaining ingredients. I usually prepare these ingredients while the beets are cooking. Scoop the beets into the mixing bowl with the sauce and stir together. Chill the salad for 1-2 hours to allow the beets to absorb the flavors in the sauce. Scoop into a serving bowl and serve chilled. Garnish with a few sprigs of mint.
Serves 4-6.

Fern's Carrot Cabbage Kale Salad

My friend Fern makes a delicious salad similar to this, which was the inspiration for this recipe. It is a wonderful way to eat raw vegetables in a sweet and zesty salad.

DIRECTIONS:

Combine all ingredients in a large bowl and mix together thoroughly. Chill and serve.
Serves 6-8.

INGREDIENTS:

2 cups carrot, grated (500 ml)

2 cups green cabbage, grated (500 ml)

1 cup kale, finely chopped (250 ml)

5 tbsp olive oil (75 ml)

5 tbsp lemon juice, freshly squeezed (75 ml)

5 tbsp tamari (75 ml)

4 cloves garlic (4)

½ cup fresh parsley, finely chopped (125 ml)

1 cup raisins (250 ml)

½ cup walnuts, coarsely chopped (125 ml)

2 tbsp dulse flakes (30 ml)

Waldorf Salad with Soy Mayonnaise and Edible Flowers

Waldorf salad usually calls for regular mayonnaise, but this recipe uses soy mayonnaise and adds grape halves, dried apricots and edible flowers to brighten it up. This is a refreshing salad for a summer's day or as an addition to a picnic.

DIRECTIONS:

Place all of the ingredients, except for the edible flowers, in a large bowl and stir together. Chill for at least half an hour before serving. Just before serving sprinkle the edible flowers on top.
Serves 6-8.

INGREDIENTS:

3 ribs celery (3)

3 red apples, sliced into small chunks (3)

½ cup raisins (125 ml)

½ cup dried apricots, cut into thin slivers (125 ml)

1 cup red or green seedless grapes, cut into halves (250 ml)

1 cup toasted walnuts, coarsely chopped (250 ml)

2 tbsp lemon juice, freshly squeezed (30 ml)

¼ tsp fine sea salt (1 ml)

1 cup soy mayonnaise (250 ml)

½ cup edible flowers (125 ml)

Snow Pea Salad with Toasted Walnuts and Nasturtiums

Fresh, snappy peas are so sweet and tasty that they deserve a glorious presentation. This zesty pea salad provides just that, combining taste, texture and color to tantalize your senses. The nasturtium flowers add incredible appeal to the salad with their vibrant burst of color alongside the brilliant green of the steamed peas.

INGREDIENTS:

1 cup walnuts (250 ml)
5 cups snow peas, stems removed (1,250 ml)
⅓ cup orange juice, freshly squeezed (80 ml)
1 tbsp maple syrup (15 ml)
2 tbsp olive oil (30 ml)
2 tbsp tamari (30 ml)
3 cloves garlic (3)
1 tsp Dijon mustard (5 ml)
2 tbsp fresh mint, chopped (30 ml)
½ cup red onion, diced (125 ml)
10-20 nasturtium flowers (10-20)

DIRECTIONS:

Place the walnuts in a small skillet and dry toast them on medium heat for 5-8 minutes until they begin to lightly brown. Remove from heat and set aside.

Remove the stems from the snow peas. Bring 2 cups of water to boil in a steamer, and place the peas in the top of the steamer and steam for about 5 minutes, or until they turn bright green. Immediately remove them from the steamer and run them under cold water to halt cooking. Set aside.

In a large bowl, combine the orange juice, maple syrup, oil, tamari, garlic, mustard, mint and red onions, stirring all ingredients together thoroughly. Stir in the peas and walnuts until they are thoroughly coated with the dressing. Pour the salad into a serving bowl, sprinkle the nasturtium flowers on top and serve.

Serves 6-8.

Tuscan Bean Salad

This bean salad calls for cannelloni beans; you can use either dried beans or canned beans. You can sometimes find dried beans at your local farmers market and often canned cannelloni beans are available in Italian and Mediterranean specialty stores. If you are unable to find this variety then any good quality white bean will work, such as white navy beans. My friend Rebecca Jehn inspired this delicious recipe.

DIRECTIONS:

If using dried beans, wash and check them for dirt or stones. Cover the beans with 3 or 4 cups of water and bring to a boil. Remove from heat and soak the beans for at least one hour. Drain and rinse the beans and cover completely with fresh water and simmer until tender, about 1 hour, adding fresh water as needed to keep them covered. (Cooking time will depend on the freshness of the beans; if older they could take longer.) Drain and cool the beans. The strained juice may be stored and used in soups, stews, etc.

If using canned beans, rinse and drain the beans, and set aside. In a large bowl, combine the oil, red onion, garlic, sage, lemon, salt, pepper and sweet peppers. Stir together, then fold in the cannelloni beans. Chill and serve.

Serves 6-8.

INGREDIENTS:

3-4 cups water (750-1,000 ml)

1 cup dried cannelloni beans (250 ml) OR

2-14 oz cans cannelloni beans (2-400 ml)

¼ cup olive oil (60 ml)

½ cup medium red onion, thinly sliced (125 ml)

2-3 cloves garlic, pressed (2-3)

2 tsp dry sage leaves, minced (10 ml)

4 tbsp lemon juice, freshly squeezed (60 ml)

1 tsp fine sea salt (5 ml)

Several dashes ground black pepper

½ each medium red, green, yellow peppers, stems and seeds removed and chopped (½ each)

Almond Strawberry Spinach Salad

This is a lovely summer-time salad that is crisp and refreshing with fresh spinach, juicy strawberries, toasted almonds and a delicious maple poppy seed dressing.

INGREDIENTS:

1 bunch fresh spinach, cleaned
and stems removed (1)

2 cups strawberries, stems removed
and thinly sliced (500 ml)

⅔ cup whole almonds, toasted
and coarsely chopped (160 ml)

1 pear, peeled and thinly sliced (1)

¼ cup red onion, thinly sliced (60 ml)

DRESSING:

3 tbsp red wine vinegar (45 ml)

3 tbsp olive oil (45 ml)

2 tbsp maple syrup (30 ml)

½ tsp sea salt (2 ml)

2 tbsp poppy seeds (30 ml)

2 tsp Dijon mustard (10 ml)

DIRECTIONS:

In a large bowl place the spinach, sliced strawberries, toasted almonds, sliced pear and red onion. Set aside.

For the dressing, place all ingredients in a jar and shake well. Pour over the assembled salad and gently toss just before serving.

Serves 6.

DRESSINGS, TOPPINGS AND SAUCES

Orange Vinaigrette

Strawberry Jalapeno Dressing

Caesar-style Dressing

Everyday Dressing

Sesame Maple Ginger Lime Dressing

Dijon Maple Balsamic Dressing

Coconut Cilantro Lime Dressing

Jessica's Red Pepper Lemon Sauce

Gomashio

Miso Lemon Tahini Sauce

Peanut Sauce

Spicy Peanut Coconut Sauce

Paul's Spinach Parsley Sauce

Spinach Cilantro Pesto

Pumpkin Seed Arugula Pesto

Orange Vinaigrette

This tasty vinaigrette is scrumptious poured over
Orange Walnut Fig Salad (page 40).

INGREDIENTS:

Juice of 1 orange
1 tbsp mirin (15 ml)
3 tbsp red wine vinegar (45 ml)
3 tbsp nutritional yeast flakes (45 ml)
½ tsp sea salt (2 ml)
1 tbsp tamari or soy sauce (15 ml)
2 tbsp olive oil (30 ml)

DIRECTIONS:

Combine all ingredients in a jar and shake well. Pour over green salad.

Serves 4-6.

Strawberry Jalapeno Dressing

Serve this bright and refreshing salad dressing over fresh mixed salad
greens on a warm summer evening. Jalapenos can vary in their
intensity, so you may want to add half of the pepper first and taste the
dressing to see if you want it spicier before adding the remaining half.

INGREDIENTS:

1 cup strawberries (250 ml)
2 tbsp olive oil (30 ml)
2½ tbsp lime juice, freshly squeezed (40 ml)
½ tsp sea salt (2 ml)
1 jalapeno pepper (1)
1 tbsp red onion, diced (15 ml)

DIRECTIONS:

Remove and discard the stem and seeds from the jalapeno pepper. Place all ingredients in a blender and blend thoroughly until smooth. Serve over fresh salad greens.

Serves 4-6.

Caesar-style Dressing

*This is a delicious egg-free version of
the traditional Caesar dressing.*

DIRECTIONS:

Place all ingredients in a small jar and shake vigorously until mixture is thoroughly combined and smooth. Serve over romaine lettuce and top with croutons.
Serves 4-6.

INGREDIENTS:

½ cup rice milk (125 ml)
Juice of 1 lemon
2 tbsp tahini (30 ml)
½ tsp fine sea salt (2 ml)
1½ tbsp nutritional yeast (20 ml)
4 cloves garlic, chopped fine (4)
1 tsp Dijon mustard (5 ml)
1½ tbsp poppy seeds (20 ml)

Everyday Dressing

*The flax oil in this dressing adds a unique flavor, and provides
a great source of Omega 3 and 6 essential fatty acids.
If you do not have flax oil, olive oil is a good substitute.*

DIRECTIONS:

Place all ingredients in a jar and shake vigorously until the ingredients are emulsified. Serve with a salad of your choice or as a topping for steamed vegetables or rice.
Serves 4-6.

INGREDIENTS:

⅓ cup olive or flax oil (80 ml)
3 cloves garlic, finely diced (3)
1 tbsp fresh gingerroot, grated (15 ml)
2 tbsp tamari (30 ml)
2 tbsp nutritional yeast (30 ml)
2 tbsp lemon juice, freshly squeezed (30 ml)
1 tsp Dijon mustard (5 ml)

53

Sesame Maple Ginger Lime Dressing

*This sweet sesame dressing is one of my
favorites poured over fresh salad greens.*

INGREDIENTS:

¼ cup olive oil (60 ml)
½ tbsp sesame oil (7 ml)
1 tbsp maple syrup (15 ml)
2 tbsp lime juice, freshly squeezed (30 ml)
2 tbsp fresh gingerroot, grated (30 ml)
2 tbsp tamari (30 ml)
1 tbsp tahini (15 ml)

DIRECTIONS:

Place all ingredients in a jar and shake vigorously until the ingredients are emulsified. Serve with a salad of your choice or as a topping for steamed vegetables or rice.
Serves 4-6.

Dijon Maple Balsamic Dressing

*Dijon mustard and balsamic vinegar give
this tasty dressing a bit of a kick.*

INGREDIENTS:

⅓ cup olive oil (80 ml)
1 tbsp maple syrup (15 ml)
1 tbsp balsamic vinegar (15 ml)
2 tbsp nutritional yeast (30 ml)
2 tbsp tamari (30 ml)
1 tsp Dijon mustard (5 ml)

DIRECTIONS:

Place all ingredients in a jar and shake vigorously until the ingredients are emulsified. Serve with a salad of your choice or as a topping for steamed vegetables or rice.
Serves 4-6.

Coconut Cilantro Lime Dressing

This creamy dressing is wonderful over a bed of fresh salad greens and arugula with toasted cashews and cilantro for garnish.

DIRECTIONS:

Place all ingredients in a jar and shake vigorously until the ingredients are emulsified. Serve with a salad of your choice or as a topping for steamed vegetables or rice.
Serves 4-6.

INGREDIENTS:

⅔ cup coconut milk (160 ml)

3 tbsp tamari (45 ml)

3 tbsp lime juice, freshly squeezed (45 ml)

¼ cup fresh cilantro, finely chopped (60 ml)

2 tbsp cashew butter (30 ml)

Dash chili powder or cayenne powder, to taste

Jessica's Red Pepper Lemon Sauce

My friend Jessica first developed this fabulous red pepper sauce. It has since had many incarnations but this is my favorite.

DIRECTIONS:

Grill the sweet red peppers over a gas flame or hot grill until the skin is blistered and blackened. The flesh will soften but should still be slightly firm. Scrape off the blistered skin, and remove the stem and seeds.

Place the peppers, lemon juice, oil, salt, tahini, tamari and garlic in a food processor. Process on high until a creamy consistency is achieved. Serve over steamed vegetables, rice, as a dip for raw vegetables or as a sauce on pizza.
Serves 4.

INGREDIENTS:

2 red peppers, roasted (2)

2½ tbsp lemon juice, freshly squeezed (40 ml)

1 tbsp olive oil (15 ml)

½ tsp fine sea salt (2 ml)

6 tbsp tahini (90 ml)

1 tsp tamari (5 ml)

1 clove garlic (1)

55

Gomashio

*This traditional Japanese topping is a wonderful condiment on steamed
vegetables, grains, toast, sushi and many other foods. Sesame seeds
are full of calcium and the addition of dulse adds valuable minerals.*

INGREDIENTS:

*2 cups brown sesame seeds,
unhulled (500 ml)*
2 tbsp coarse sea salt (30 ml)
3 tbsp dulse flakes (45 ml)

DIRECTIONS:

In a frying pan on medium heat, toast the sesame seeds for several minutes, stirring constantly to ensure even toasting. The seeds should begin to pop in the pan and turn a golden brown. Remove from heat and place the seeds in a bowl to cool.

Once the seeds have cooled, place one cup at a time in a blender with half of the dulse and salt. Blend until a coarse texture is achieved . Blending helps to break down the sesame seeds which will allow for greater digestion and absorption of nutrients. Blend the remaining half of the sesame seeds, dulse and salt. Store the gomashio in a sealed glass jar for up to one week in the refrigerator.

Miso Lemon Tahini Sauce

*This sauce adds a nice touch to spring rolls and
is delicious on steamed vegetables.*

INGREDIENTS:

⅓ cup tahini (80 ml)
1 tbsp light miso (15 ml)
1 tbsp lemon juice (15 ml)
½ tbsp tamari (7 ml)
¼ tsp Dijon mustard (1 ml)
¼ cup water (60 ml)

DIRECTIONS:

Place all ingredients in a small bowl and mix together thoroughly until smooth and creamy.
Serves 4.

Peanut Sauce

*This tangy peanut sauce can be served chilled. It tastes lovely
with spring rolls or even as a vegetable dip or spread. It is quick
to make and a great way to add some protein to a meal.*

DIRECTIONS:

Place all ingredients in a small bowl and mix together well with a fork until a creamy consistency is achieved. Chill. *Serves 4.*

INGREDIENTS:

½ cup crunchy peanut butter (125 ml)

1 tbsp lemon juice, freshly squeezed (15 ml)

*1-2 cloves garlic, peeled
and finely chopped (1-2)*

1 tsp tamari (5 ml)

Dash fine sea salt, to taste

Spicy Peanut Coconut Sauce

*This peanut sauce is best served warm and is delicious poured over fried tofu,
vegetables and rice. We grow wonderfully aromatic cilantro at our farm and it
is always fun to come up with interesting recipes using this lovely herb.*

DIRECTIONS:

In a small cooking pot, fry the onion, garlic and chilis in olive oil on medium heat until the onions become translucent and start to gently brown on the edges. Whisk the peanut butter and water into the onion mixture. Stir in the coconut milk, lime and tamari, and continue to whisk all ingredients together. Stir in the cilantro just before serving. If the sauce is too thick, add more water as necessary to reach the desired consistency. Serve hot over cooked vegetables, grains, fried tofu or tempeh. *Serves 6-8.*

INGREDIENTS:

½ medium onion, very finely chopped (½)

1 tbsp olive oil (15 ml)

3 cloves garlic, peeled and finely chopped (3)

*½-1 tsp chili flakes (depending on how
spicy you like your food!) (2-5 ml)*

*⅔ cup crunchy or smooth peanut
butter (160 ml)*

¾ cup water (175 ml)

14 oz can coconut milk (400 ml)

1 tbsp lime juice, freshly squeezed (15 ml)

2 tbsp tamari (30 ml)

¼ cup fresh cilantro, finely chopped (60 ml)

Paul's Spinach Parsley Sauce

INGREDIENTS:

1 cup sunflower seeds (250 ml)

3-4 cloves garlic (3-4)

juice of 1 lemon

⅓ cup olive oil (80 ml)

1 bunch fresh spinach,
washed and stems removed

½-1 tsp sea salt (2-5 ml)

1 tbsp fresh chives, chopped (15 ml)

½ cup fresh parsley, chopped (125 ml)

My brother Paul sometimes finds a perfect combination of flavors in his experimental culinary moments, and this sauce is an example. This is a wonderful base for a pizza, as a substitute for tomato sauce or poured over steamed vegetables, pasta, grains or even on a salad. Delightfully versatile!

DIRECTIONS:

In a food processor, blend the sunflower seeds and garlic until fine. Add the lemon and oil, blending again. Add remaining ingredients and process together on high until a smooth consistency is achieved.
Serves 4-6.

Spinach Cilantro Pesto

INGREDIENTS:

5 cloves garlic (5)

3 green onions (3)

4 tbsp lemon juice, freshly squeezed (60 ml)

3 cups fresh spinach,
stems removed (750 ml)

1½ cups fresh cilantro (375 ml)

1 tsp fine sea salt (5 ml)

4 tbsp olive oil (60 ml)

1½ cups cashews (375 ml)

Fresh spinach and cilantro from the garden in the spring make a wonderful fragrant pesto, and the cashews make it extra creamy. Try spreading this one over pastas or on bread, or use it as a pizza sauce.

DIRECTIONS:

Combine all ingredients in a food processor and blend until creamy. You may have to push down the sides of the food processor occasionally with a spatula to ensure that all of the ingredients are thoroughly combined.
Serves 6-8.

Pumpkin Seed Arugula Pesto

*This twist on pesto has a wonderful spice from the garlic and arugula,
and can be used in the same manner as traditional pesto. Spread it over bread,
pasta or crackers, or try a dollop on top of steamed vegetables. It is
unbeatable as a topping on fresh pizza—absolutely delightful! It's easy to
make, and arugula and parsley can be grown virtually year round in
our coastal garden, providing ingredients for pesto for every season.*

DIRECTIONS:

You can use raw pumpkin seeds for this recipe but some prefer to toast the seeds first. For toasting them, simply place the pumpkin seeds in a cast-iron frying pan on medium heat and continue to stir until they begin to brown slightly. Remove from the pan and cool before continuing.

Place the pumpkin seeds in a food processor and blend them until fine. Add the garlic and salt and blend again. While the food processor is running, add handfuls of arugula and parsley through the top opening of the machine. Keep adding as these get blended in until all of the greens are incorporated. Pour the oil through the top opening and continue blending. You may have to stop occasionally to scrape down the sides of the food processor. When the ingredients have been thoroughly combined, add a bit more salt or oil to reach your desired flavor. Scoop the pesto into a jar, cover with a thin layer of oil and keep refrigerated until use. Enjoy!
Serves 6-8.

INGREDIENTS:

1 ½ cups pumpkin seeds, shelled (375 ml)

3 ½ cups arugula, chopped (875 ml)

½ cup fresh parsley, chopped (125 ml)

4 cloves garlic (4)

½ tsp sea salt (2 ml)

½ cup olive oil (125 ml)

Coconut Cilantro Rice Pilaf

Ginger Sesame Tofu

Paul's Ginger Fried Rice with Vegetables

Curried Rice Pilaf with Apricots

Coconut Lime Cashew Red Lentils

Smoky Baked Beans

Lemon Curried Lentils and Potatoes

Wild Rice Almond Cherry Pilaf

Tofu Baked in Almond Mint Cilantro Sauce

Garbanzo and Edamame Beans with Spinach and Shiitake Mushrooms

Lemon Cardamom Rice with Green Peas

Black Bean Sweet Potato Almond Burgers

Coconut Cilantro Rice Pilaf

*This exotic and tantalizing rice dish is absolutely wonderful as a side
dish but can hold its own as a meal's centerpiece. The combination
of flavors from the cilantro, lime, coconut and cashews is perfected by
the hint of spice from the jalapenos. Definitely a crowd pleaser!*

INGREDIENTS:

3 cups brown basmati rice, cooked
and cooled (750 ml)

2-3 tbsp olive oil (30-45 ml)

1 onion (1)

1 tbsp fresh gingerroot, grated (15 ml)

2 jalapenos, seeds and stems
removed and diced (2)

¾ cup dried medium coconut (175 ml)

2 tbsp tamari (30 ml)

¾ cup cashews, raw (175 ml)

½ cup fresh cilantro,
finely chopped (125 ml)

2½ tbsp lime juice, freshly squeezed (35 ml)

DIRECTIONS:

Prepare basmati rice and let cool. Leftover rice is perfect for use in this recipe.

In a large pan or wok, fry the onion, ginger and jalapenos in the olive oil on medium-low heat. Be careful not to brown them too quickly. As the onions become translucent, add the coconut and tamari and stir together thoroughly. Mix in the pre-cooked rice, then stir in the cashews until the mixture has reached a hot serving temperature. Remove from heat and stir in the cilantro and lime juice. Serve.

Serves 6-8.

Ginger Sesame Tofu

*This is a quick and easy way to prepare a delicious tofu snack or side dish.
It's a great recipe when you need to add a bit of protein to a meal.*

INGREDIENTS:

1 lb tofu, medium or firm,
cut into long strips (500 g)

½ tbsp sesame oil (7 ml)

1 tbsp olive oil (15 ml)

1 tbsp fresh gingerroot, grated (15 ml)

3 cloves garlic (3)

1½ tbsp tamari (20 ml)

1½ tbsp sesame seeds (20 ml)

DIRECTIONS:

In a large frying pan, heat the olive and sesame oils on medium. Stir in the ginger and garlic, then add the tofu slices. Allow the tofu to brown slightly on one side before stirring again. After 10-15 minutes, all of the tofu should be browned. Stir in the tamari and sesame seeds and fry for 5 more minutes. Remove from heat and serve.

Serves 4-6.

Paul's Ginger Fried Rice with Vegetables

My brother Paul created this delightfully zingy fried rice. It is simple to make and is a great way to use up leftover rice. I like to raid the garden in the summer, collecting fresh onions, carrots, zucchini, broccoli heads and crisp bok choy to add to this tantalizing dish. This recipe works best with rice that has been thoroughly cooled—even better if the rice is prepared the day before.

DIRECTIONS:

In a large pan or wok, heat the oil on medium-low. Add the onion, ginger and cayenne, stirring to make sure they do not stick to the pan. As the onions become translucent, stir in the carrots and broccoli. Cover for 5-10 minutes, allowing the vegetables to cook more thoroughly. Stir occasionally. When the carrots and broccoli begin to soften, add the zucchini, mushrooms and bok choy. Replace the cover for several more minutes, stirring occasionally. Add the precooked rice, walnuts and tamari and allow the mixture to cook a few more minutes uncovered. Serve.
Serves 6-8.

INGREDIENTS:

4 cups precooked brown rice (short grain, long grain or basmati) (1,000 ml)
1 medium onion, diced (1)
2-3 tbsp oil (30-45 ml)
3-4 tbsp fresh gingerroot, grated (45-60 ml)
2-4 tbsp tamari (to taste) (30-60 ml)
Dash cayenne (optional)
3 carrots, chopped (3)
1 medium zucchini, sliced (1)
1 large head of broccoli, chopped (1)
2 cups button mushrooms, sliced (500 ml)
2 cups bok choy, chopped (500 ml)
½ cup walnuts, coarsely chopped (125 ml)

Curried Rice Pilaf with Apricots

Basmati rice has an incredible flavor and aroma that lends itself well to curry spices. Slivers of sweet diced apricots and raisins mixed with the crunch of cashews create a satisfying texture. This colorful pilaf can be served cold or warm.

INGREDIENTS:

2 tbsp olive oil (30 ml)
1 medium onion, diced (1)
1 tsp each turmeric, garam marsala, mustard seeds (5 ml)
2 tsp coarse sea salt (10 ml)
1 tbsp fresh gingerroot, grated (15 ml)
3 cloves garlic (3)
1½ cups brown basmati rice (375 ml)
3 cups water (750 ml)
⅔ cups each toasted cashews, dried apricots, raisins (160 ml)

DIRECTIONS:

In a medium pan, heat the oil on medium and sauté the onion, spices, salt, ginger and garlic, until the onions become translucent and start to caramelize. Stir in the rice. Add the water and bring to a boil. Reduce to a simmer and cover, allowing the rice to cook for 45-50 minutes. When the rice is done and there is no water at the bottom of the pan, remove from heat and uncover, allowing the rice to cool slightly.

Meanwhile, prepare the cashews by gently toasting them in a frying pan on medium heat, stirring constantly, until they begin to turn a golden brown. Remove from heat, chop into small pieces and set aside. Prepare the dried apricots by cutting them into long, thin slivers.

Stir the cashews, apricot slivers and raisins into the rice dish. You can reheat the dish by adding a splash of water and stirring it on medium-low heat, or chill it until you are ready to serve again.

Serves 4-6.

Coconut Lime Cashew Red Lentils

This is a somewhat exotic meal at our farm. Occasionally we like to taste
something completely different and appreciate the flavors from other cultures.
This red lentil dish is full of protein and rich flavors.

DIRECTIONS:

In a large pot, fry the green onions, curry powder, mustard, turmeric and red lentils in the olive oil on medium-high heat for 5-10 minutes. Stir frequently to prevent the lentils from sticking to the bottom of the pot. If all of the oil is absorbed, add a bit more. Add the coconut milk, salt, cilantro, lime juice and water and stir all the ingredients together. Bring to a boil then reduce to a low simmer. Cover the pot with a lid and let it simmer for about 30 minutes, stirring occasionally to prevent sticking. If you find the lentils are not quite done but the liquid has all evaporated, add more water as necessary. Stir in the cashews. Serve warm over a bed of fresh basmati rice and garnish with additional cilantro, lime wedges and cashews. *Serves 6-8.*

INGREDIENTS:

6 green onions (6)
4 tbsp olive oil (60 ml)
2 tsp madras curry powder (10 ml)
1 tsp mustard seeds (5 ml)
½ tsp turmeric (2 ml)
2½ cups red lentils (625 ml)
½ tbsp coarse sea salt, to taste (7 ml)
2 14 oz cans coconut milk (2 400 ml)
½ cup cilantro, finely chopped (125 ml)
3 tbsp lime juice, freshly squeezed (45 ml)
4 cups water (1,000 ml)
¾ cup whole cashews (175 ml)

GARNISH: chopped cilantro leaves, lime wedges, cashews

Smoky Baked Beans

Baked beans are a delicious winter staple at our farm.
Full of protein, they provide a hearty addition to
our meals. Smoked tofu adds a wonderful flavor to this dish.

INGREDIENTS:

2½ cups pinto beans, soaked in 6 cups
of water overnight (625 ml)
5-6 cups water (1,250-1500 ml)
1 tsp sea salt (5 ml)
5 cloves garlic (5)
3 tbsp fresh gingerroot, grated (45 ml)
2 tbsp olive oil (30 ml)
2 tbsp tamari (30 ml)
2 tsp Dijon mustard (10 ml)
2 tbsp maple syrup (30 ml)
1 cup packaged smoked tofu,
chopped into small cubes (225 g)

DIRECTIONS: 350°F (175°C); 30-40 MINUTES

Soak pinto beans in a pot of water (about 6 cups) overnight. Drain the water in the morning, and refill with about 5 cups of clean water. Bring the beans to a boil, reduce to a low simmer covered, allowing them to cook on low heat for 2-3 hours until the beans are soft. Check the water level throughout the cooking time to be sure that you do not run out of water. Add more if necessary.

When the beans are soft and there is still a bit of liquid in the pot, stir in the remaining ingredients and combine thoroughly. Pour the contents into a deep casserole dish and bake in a preheated oven for 30-40 minutes. Serve hot.

Serves 8-10.

Lemon Curried Lentils and Potatoes

This delicious and hearty dish is a wonderful complement to a medley
of vegetables and greens, such as Steamed Red Cabbage with Cilantro and
Balsamic Vinegar (page 87) and Lemon Sesame Kale (page 91).

DIRECTIONS:

This recipe has several steps, but is very simple to make.

First, boil the water in a medium pot and add the salt and lentils. Cover, reduce to simmer, and allow the lentils to cook for about 45 minutes or until the water is absorbed.

While the lentils are cooking, bring a large pot of salted water to boil. Add the potatoes and allow them to boil until soft, about 15-20 minutes. Strain the potatoes and set aside.

In a frying pan, heat the olive oil on medium then sauté the onions with the garlic and ginger. Add the garam marsala, curry, turmeric and pepper. Continue stirring occasionally until the onions begin to turn translucent. Remove from heat and set aside.

For the finale, combine the lentils, potatoes and onion mixture in the large pot. Stir in the tamari, lemon and parsley or cilantro. Serve warm. *Serves 6-8.*

INGREDIENTS:

2 cups water (500 ml)

1 tsp sea salt (5 ml)

1 cup green, brown or French lentils (250 ml)

4 cups medium potatoes, peeled and cubed (1,000 ml)

3 tbsp olive oil (45 ml)

1 large onion, diced (1)

2 cloves garlic (2)

1 tbsp fresh gingerroot, grated (15 ml each)

1 tsp each garam marsala, curry powder, turmeric (5 ml each)

Several dashes ground black pepper

2 tbsp tamari (30 ml)

2 tbsp lemon juice, freshly squeezed (30 ml)

1 tsp fresh parsley or cilantro, finely chopped (5 ml)

Wild Rice Almond Cherry Pilaf

*The rich flavor of wild rice combined with aromatic basmati rice creates
the perfect base for this savory pilaf. Dried cherries, toasted
almonds and a hint of sherry create an alluring combination of flavors.*

INGREDIENTS:

3 tbsp olive oil (45 ml)

1½ cups onion, diced (375 ml)

1½ cups celery (2 ribs),
thinly sliced (375 ml)

4 cloves garlic, diced (4)

1 cup brown basmati rice (250 ml)

1 cup wild rice (250 ml)

1 tbsp coarse sea salt (15 ml)

2 tsp dried summer savory (10 ml)

½ cup dry sherry (125 ml)

1 cup dried cherries, finely chopped (250 ml)

4 cups water (1,000 ml)

¾ cups almonds, toasted
and coarsely chopped (175 ml)

½ cup fresh parsley, chopped (125 ml)

1 tbsp tamari (15 ml)

DIRECTIONS:

Toast the almonds in a small frying pan for 5-10 minutes on medium heat, until they begin to lightly brown. Remove from heat and allow the nuts to cool. When cool, chop into coarse chunks and set aside.

In a large cooking pot, sauté the onion, celery and garlic in the olive oil on medium heat. When the onions become translucent, stir in the basmati and wild rice. Add the salt, savory and sherry and allow the rice to simmer in the sherry for 5-10 minutes. Stir in the cherries and water and bring to a boil. Cover and reduce heat to low and allow the rice to simmer for about 45 minutes. Check to make sure that all of the water is evaporated. You may need to cook the rice a few minutes longer to ensure that it is thoroughly done. When all of the water has evaporated, remove from heat and allow the rice to cool for 5-10 minutes. Stir in the toasted almonds, parsley and tamari. Transfer the rice to a serving dish and enjoy.

Serves 6-8.

Tofu Baked in Almond Mint Cilantro Sauce

This absolutely scrumptious dish is wonderful when served on a bed of fresh basmati rice. Almond butter creates a rich, protein-packed sauce that is heightened by the combination of mint, chilies and cilantro. The smoked tofu adds more complexity to the dish.

DIRECTIONS: 350°F (175°C); 40 MINUTES

Cube the tofu and place it in a large bowl with the green peas. Stir together and set aside.

To prepare the sauce, place a medium saucepan on medium heat. Place the almond butter, tamari, mirin, garlic, ginger, sesame oil, mint and cilantro in the pot and stir together. Add ½ cup of water and thoroughly mix it into the almond butter mixture. Add another ½ cup of water and continue stirring until the mixture thickens. Add the remaining ½ cup water and stir again until the sauce has thickened and all the water is thoroughly incorporated into the other ingredients. Remove from heat. Pour the sauce over the tofu and peas and gently stir. Pour the ingredients into a medium casserole dish and place in a preheated oven. Bake for about 40 minutes. Remove from oven and serve over a bed of warm basmati rice, or use as a side dish on its own. *Serves 6-8.*

INGREDIENTS:

1½ cups smoked tofu, chopped into cubes (375 ml)

2 cups firm tofu, chopped into cubes (500 mg)

1½ cups shelled green peas, fresh or frozen (375 ml)

SAUCE:

½ cup almond butter (125 ml)

2 tbsp tamari (30 ml)

1 tbsp mirin (15 ml)

3 cloves garlic (3)

1 tbsp fresh gingerroot, grated (15 ml)

1 tbsp sesame oil (15 ml)

5 sprigs fresh mint, diced (5)

⅔ cup fresh cilantro, diced (160 ml)

1½ cups water (375 ml)

Garbanzo and Edamame Beans with Spinach and Shiitake Mushrooms

This is a quick recipe to create and offers a tasty combination of proteins, vitamins and minerals. Edamame beans (soybeans) have grown increasingly popular and can be found in most supermarkets and health food stores in the freezer section.

INGREDIENTS:

3 tbsp olive oil (45 ml)

1 onion, diced (1)

1 tsp fine sea salt (5 ml)

1 cup shiitake mushrooms, stems removed and thinly sliced (250 ml)

1 tbsp fresh gingerroot, grated (15 ml)

1 cup edamame beans, frozen or fresh and shelled (250 ml)

1 tbsp dulse flakes (15 ml)

1 tbsp tamari (15 ml)

14 oz can garbanzo beans, drained and rinsed (400 ml)

¾ cup water (175 ml)

1 tbsp arrowroot powder (15 ml)

1 bunch fresh spinach, stems removed, washed and chopped (1)

juice of 1 lime

DIRECTIONS:

In a large frying pan, sauté the onion in the oil on medium heat. As the onions become translucent, add the salt, mushrooms and ginger. Continue sautéing for 5 minutes. Stir in the edamame, dulse, tamari and garbanzos. Continue sautéing. In a separate bowl, dissolve the arrowroot powder in water, then pour the mixture into the frying pan with the beans. Stir in the spinach and sauté until the spinach has wilted. Remove from heat and stir in the lime juice. Serve warm over a bed of fresh basmati rice or alongside steamed vegetables.

Serves 4-6.

Lemon Cardamom Rice with Green Peas

This aromatic rice gets its lovely shade of yellow from the turmeric powder.
The peas add a splash of green to this simple yet delicious rice dish.

DIRECTIONS:

Place the rice, water, salt, lemon rind, turmeric and cardamom in a large pot. Cover and bring to a boil, then reduce to a low simmer and cook for about 45-50 minutes. Check to make sure that there is no water left in the bottom of the pot. Remove from heat and pour the peas on top of the rice. Cover and allow the peas to cook in the steam for about 5 minutes. Stir the peas into the rice and serve.

Serves 6-8.

INGREDIENTS:

2 cups brown basmati rice (500 ml)
4 cups water (1,000 ml)
1 tbsp coarse sea salt (15 ml)
3 tbsp lemon rind, grated (45 ml)
1 tsp turmeric (5 ml)
½ tsp black cardamom seeds, ground (2 ml)
1 cup green peas, fresh or frozen (250 ml)

Black Bean Sweet Potato Almond Burgers

*These delicious burgers are a great source of
protein and are simple to prepare.*

INGREDIENTS:

*14 oz can black beans (2 cups/500 ml)
cooked black beans (400 ml)*

1 cup sweet potato, grated (250 ml)

½ cup almond butter (125 ml)

½ cup red onion, diced (125 ml)

¼ cup Sicilian olives, diced (60 ml)

*¼ cup whole spelt flour or
other flour (60 ml)*

2 tbsp tamari (30 ml)

3 cloves garlic, diced (3)

1 tbsp fresh gingerroot, grated (15 ml)

DIRECTIONS:

Drain and rinse one can of black beans. Place them in a medium bowl and mash. Stir in the remaining ingredients. Scoop ⅓ cup of batter at a time to form individual burger patties. Place a cast-iron frying pan on the stove on medium heat. Add a bit of oil to the pan and place a few burger patties in the oil. Fry each burger for 7-10 minutes on one side, then flip them over and fry an additional 5-7 minutes on the other side, or until the centers of the burgers are cooked through. If they brown too quickly, just turn the heat down a bit to allow them to cook more slowly. Serve hot on burger buns with condiments of your choice.
Makes 10-12 burgers.

Pastas

Creamy Basil Oyster Mushroom Pasta

Roasted Vegetable Tomato Sauce on Spaghetti

Vegan Pad Thai

Quick Noodles with Miso Lemon Tahini Sauce

Fresh Avocado, Tomato and Artichoke Sauce on Garlic Rotini Noodles

Penne with Spinach Cilantro Pesto and Arugula

Tahini Ginger Seitan and Vegetables with Udon Noodles

Spinach Tempeh Mushroom Stroganoff on Semolina Linguine

Coconut Ginger Vegetables with Udon Noodles

Soba Noodles with Vegetables in Sesame Peanut Sauce

Creamy Basil Oyster Mushroom Pasta

Fresh basil from the greenhouse is unbeatable in this tasty pasta dish. I love to walk into the greenhouse on a hot summer's day, where the scent of fresh basil is overwhelmingly lovely.

INGREDIENTS:

1 medium onion, finely diced (1)

4 cups oyster mushrooms, chopped (1,000 ml)

3 tbsp olive oil (45 ml)

¼ cup brown rice flour (or other flour) (60 ml)

2 tbsp tamari (30 ml)

1 cup fresh basil, finely chopped (250 ml)

2 cups water (500 ml)

2 tbsp nutritional yeast flakes (30 ml)

4 cups rotini noodles (1,000 ml)

DIRECTIONS:

Bring a large pot of salted water to a boil. Cook the pasta according to package instructions. Drain and season with olive oil and salt. As the water is boiling and the pasta cooks, begin preparing the sauce.

In a large frying pan or saucepan, sauté the onion in the oil on medium heat for about 5 minutes. Add the oyster mushrooms and sauté for an additional 5 minutes. Stir in the flour, basil and tamari, and sauté 5 more minutes. Pour in the water one cup at a time, stirring until the sauce thickens. Bring to a low simmer and cook for 5-10 minutes, stirring occasionally. Stir in the nutritional yeast and simmer for 5 more minutes. Remove from heat and pour over cooked pasta. *Serves 6.*

Roasted Vegetable Tomato Sauce on Spaghetti

My brother Paul, who truly makes the most delicious spaghetti sauce I've ever eaten, inspired this recipe. Roasting the vegetables beforehand helps to bring out their distinct flavors, and roasted garlic will make anyone smile with satisfaction. The red wine and herbs in this recipe add an extra depth to the tomato flavor.

DIRECTIONS: 350°F (175°C); 20 MINUTES

Slice the eggplant, peppers and zucchini into bite-size pieces and place them into a large bowl. Peel the bulbs of garlic and place the separated cloves into the bowl as well. Add the oil and salt and stir together. Place the vegetables on a baking sheet and roast in a preheated oven for about 20 minutes. You may need to stir the vegetables on the tray to ensure that they do not stick to the pan. Remove from oven and set aside.

In a large sauce pan, add the olive oil and begin sautéing the onions on medium heat. After a few minutes, add the herbs, pepper, mushrooms, artichoke hearts, olives and roasted vegetables. Stir in the wine and salt. Add the tomato sauce. Bring the sauce to a simmer, cover and allow to simmer for 20-25 minutes, stirring occasionally.

Prepare spaghetti noodles as directed on package. After straining the noodles, stir in 2 tbsp olive oil and ½ tsp sea salt. Serve the sauce on top of the hot noodles with a piping-hot loaf of garlic bread and some red wine. Fabulous!
Serves 6-8.

INGREDIENTS:

1 eggplant (1)
1 each red, yellow and orange peppers (1 each)
1 small zucchini (1)
2 bulbs garlic (2)
2 tbsp olive oil (30 ml)
1 tbsp sea salt (15 ml)
2 tbsp olive oil (30 ml)
1 medium onion, diced (1)
1 tsp each dried oregano, rosemary and basil (5 ml)
Several dashes ground black pepper
10 button mushrooms, thinly sliced (10)
14 oz can artichoke hearts (400 ml)
14 oz can black olives, sliced (400 ml)
1 cup red wine (250 ml)
1 tbsp sea salt (15 ml)
56 oz tomato sauce (1,600 ml)

INGREDIENTS:

2 tbsp brown rice vinegar (30 ml)

5 tbsp tamari (75 ml)

4 tbsp brown rice syrup (60 ml)

1 ½ tbsp peanut butter or peanut oil (20 ml)

3 tbsp olive oil (45 ml)

1 lb firm tofu, cut into small cubes (450 g)

2-3 cloves garlic (2-3)

2 tbsp gingerroot, fresh grated (30 ml)

10 scallions, chopped (10)

½ tsp chili flakes (2 ml)

1 tsp sea salt (5 ml)

*2 cups yams, cut into long,
thin slices (500 ml)*

1 red pepper, cut into long, thin slices (1)

1 bok choy, chopped (1)

2 cups mung bean sprouts (500 ml)

½ cup water chestnuts, sliced (125 ml)

2 tbsp lime juice, freshly squeezed (30 ml)

½ lb rice noodles, cooked and drained (225 g)

GARNISH:

*⅔ cup peanuts, toasted and
chopped (160 ml)*

¼ cup scallions, finely chopped (60 ml)

Vegan Pad Thai

*Traditional Pad Thai is served with eggs and often has
fish sauce mixed into it. This vegan version is scrumptious
and adds extra vegetables and tofu.*

DIRECTIONS:

In a small bowl, combine the rice vinegar, tamari, rice syrup, peant butter and olive oil. Stir together thoroughly and set the sauce aside.

In a wok, sauté the tofu, garlic, ginger, scallions, chili, salt and yams in olive oil for several minutes, stirring frequently to prevent them from sticking to the pan. When the yams begin to soften, stir in the red pepper, sprouts, bok choy and water chestnuts. Continue sautéing for several minutes, then pour in the prepared sauce and cooked noodles. Gently stir the noodles into the vegetables and sauce. Remove from heat and add the lime juice. Garnish with toasted peanuts and scallions. Serve hot.

Serves 6-8.

Quick Noodles with Miso Lemon Tahini Sauce

Everybody goes through periods when they feel they barely have time to eat, let alone prepare a hearty healthy meal. These tasty noodles are quick to prepare and just as quick to disappear. They are a swift and delicious snack for kids (or adults) who need food—right away! They are also a tasty side dish served with a variety of other items such as Lemon Sesame Kale (page 91), or Steamed Red Cabbage with Cilantro and Balsamic Vinegar (page 87).

DIRECTIONS:

Prepare the pasta according to package directions. Strain the noodles and return to the pot. Stir in the remaining ingredients and mix together thoroughly. Serve immediately.
Serves 4.

INGREDIENTS:

½ lb rotini (225 g)
2 tbsp light miso (30 ml)
2 tbsp tahini (30 ml)
2 tbsp tamari (30 ml)
2 tbsp nutritional yeast (30 ml)
2 tbsp lemon juice, lightly squeezed (30 ml)
2 tbsp olive oil (30 ml)
2 cloves garlic, minced (2)

Fresh Avocado, Tomato and Artichoke Sauce on Garlic Rotini Noodles

INGREDIENTS:

4 cups dry rotini noodles (1,000 ml)

2 tbsp olive oil (30 ml)

2 tbsp tamari (30 ml)

3 cloves garlic, finely chopped (3)

1 tbsp nutritional yeast (15 ml)

3 tbsp olive oil (45 ml)

1½ cups red onion, chopped (375 ml)

1 pint cherry tomatoes, sliced in halves (500 ml)

1 tsp fine sea salt (5 ml)

Several dashes ground black pepper

¼ cup fresh basil leaves, chopped (60 ml)

14 oz can artichoke hearts (in water), chopped (400 ml)

2 ripe avocados, flesh scooped out and sliced (2)

2 cups fresh arugula, chopped (500 ml)

3½ tbsp lime juice, freshly squeezed (50 ml)

We grow some wonderful heirloom tomatoes at Phoenix Farm in the summers. Sweet, juicy tomatoes right out of the field or greenhouse have an unbeatable flavor. Combining red, green and yellow cherry tomatoes for this dish adds a pleasant splash of color. Fresh parsley and arugula give the dish a tangy, unforgettable bite.

DIRECTIONS:

Cook the pasta according to package directions. Make sure to add some salt to the boiling water. While the noodles are boiling, prepare the sauce for the pasta.

In a large frying pan, heat 3 tbsp of olive oil on medium-low and sauté the onions until lightly brown around the edges. Stir in the cherry tomatoes, salt, pepper and basil leaves. Add the artichokes, avocado slices and arugula. Stir gently until the arugula begins to wilt. Remove from heat and set aside.

When the noodles are done cooking, drain thoroughly and return them to the pot. Stir in 2 tbsp olive oil, along with the tamari, garlic and yeast. Gently fold the tomato mixture into the pasta, and add the parsley and lime juice. Serve at once as a warm pasta dish.

Serves 6-8.

Penne with Spinach Cilantro Pesto and Arugula

The creamy consistency of the Spinach Cilantro Pesto combined with the spicy bite of fresh arugula makes a wonderful collage of flavors in this pasta dish. Spinach, cilantro and arugula can be grown on the West Coast most of the year and provide an assortment of calcium, iron and other vitamins and minerals.

DIRECTIONS:

Prepare one recipe of Spinach Cilantro Pesto (page 58) and set aside.

Cook the noodles according to directions on the package, being sure to add 1 tsp of salt to the boiling water. When the noodles are done, drain them thoroughly and return them to the pot. Splash with a bit of olive oil and set aside.

While the noodles are cooking, begin preparing the arugula mixture. In a skillet, sauté the onion in the olive oil on medium heat. When the onion becomes translucent and starts to lightly brown, stir in the arugula and tamari and cook for a couple of minutes until the arugula has wilted. Stir the arugula mixture and pesto into the noodles and serve warm.

Serves 6-8.

INGREDIENTS:

1 recipe Spinach Cilantro Pesto (page 58) (1)

5 cups dry penne pasta (1,250 ml)

2 tbsp olive oil (30 ml)

1 onion, diced (1)

2-3 cups fresh arugula, chopped (500-750 ml)

1 tbsp tamari (15 ml)

Tahini Ginger Seitan and Vegetables with Udon Noodles

Seitan is a chewy, wheat-gluten product and a source of protein. You can usually find it in health food and grocery stores. We use freshly picked, seasonal vegetables for this dish when possible. The tahini ginger sauce combined with the udon noodles lends an Asian flair to this dish. It's wonderful as a hearty lunch or dinner.

Ingredients:

2 tbsp olive oil (30 ml)

1 small onion, diced (1)

3 green onions, chopped (3)

1 tbsp fresh gingerroot, grated (15 ml)

2 cloves garlic, diced (2)

1 jalapeno, seeds and stem removed and diced (1)

3 carrots, chopped (3)

2 cups broccoli florets (500 ml)

1 cup red cabbage, chopped (250 ml)

2 ribs celery, sliced (2)

2 cups field mushrooms, sliced (500 ml)

½ red pepper, seeds removed and chopped (½)

14 oz fresh udon noodles (400 g)

8-oz seitan or wheat cutlets (marinated varieties are best), chopped (225 g)

3 tbsp soy sauce (45 ml)

2 tbsp tahini (30 ml)

Directions:

In a large saucepan, sauté the onions, ginger, jalapeno and garlic in the olive oil on medium-low heat, stirring occasionally. When the onions begin to turn translucent, stir in the carrots and broccoli and sauté for 5 minutes. Add the cabbage and celery and sauté for 5 more minutes. Stir in the mushrooms, peppers, udon noodles (they do not need to be precooked), seitan, soy sauce and tahini. Allow the vegetables to cook until they begin to soften but still have some crunch to them. Continue stirring to keep the vegetables from sticking to the bottom of the pan. Remove from heat and serve.

Serves 6-8.

Spinach Tempeh Mushroom Stroganoff on Semolina Linguine

This dish is excellent served with steamed vegetables or Lemon Sesame Kale (page 91). Full of protein from the tempeh and cashew butter, this creamy, warming sauce is part of a delicious and hearty winter meal.

DIRECTIONS:

In a large skillet or saucepan, heat the oil on medium heat. Stir in the onion, garlic and basil, sautéing for 5-10 minutes. Add the tempeh and mushrooms, cooking for another 5-10 minutes until the tempeh begins to brown. While the tempeh is sautéing, combine the cashew butter, rice milk, lemon, tamari, yeast, water and pepper in a blender. Blend the ingredients on high for several minutes until creamy. Pour this mixture into the sautéing tempeh and stir together. Gently stir in the spinach and reduce heat to low, allowing the spinach to wilt in the sauce.

Bring a pot of salted water to a boil for the linguine in. Coordinate cooking time so that your linguine will be done at about the same time your sauce is finished. Add the noodles to the boiling water and cook according to instructions on the package. When the noodles are ready, drain thoroughly, then return back to the pot. Stir in 2 tbsp olive oil and a few dashes of fine sea salt. Serve onto plates and scoop a generous ladle of sauce into the center of the noodles. *Serves 6-8.*

INGREDIENTS:

2-3 tbsp olive oil (30-45 ml)

½ cup red onion, diced (125 ml)

3 cloves garlic, diced (3)

1 tbsp fresh basil, chopped (15 ml)

4 cups tempeh, cubed (900 g)

3 cups field mushrooms, sliced (750 ml)

1 cup cashew butter (250 ml)

1 cup rice milk (250 ml)

2 tbsp each lemon juice, tamari and nutritional yeast (30 ml)

1 cup water (250 ml)

Several dashes ground black pepper

2 cups fresh spinach, stems removed, then chopped (500 ml)

24 oz semolina or spinach linguine (680 g)

2 tsp fine sea salt (10 ml)

2 tbsp olive oil (30 ml)

81

Coconut Ginger Vegetables with Udon Noodles

This quick noodle dish is delicious and easy to prepare. Try adding other vegetables that are in season, such as sweet peppers, snow peas, broccoli or green beans.

INGREDIENTS:

3-4 tbsp olive oil (45-60 ml)

1 yellow onion, diced (1)

2-3 tbsp fresh gingerroot, grated (30-45 ml)

1 tsp ground cumin (5 ml)

1 tbsp coarse sea salt (15 ml)

4 medium carrots, cut into thin slices (4)

½ head red cabbage, cut into thin slices (½)

1 cup green peas, fresh or frozen (250 ml)

2 cups kale, spinach or chard, chopped (500 ml)

3 7-oz packages udon noodles (3-200 gm)

14 oz can coconut milk (400 ml)

3 tbsp tamari (45 ml)

1 cup fresh cilantro, chopped (250 ml)

2 tbsp lime juice, freshly squeezed (30 ml)

1 cup cashews (250 ml)

DIRECTIONS:

In a large pot or wok, sauté the onion in the olive oil on medium heat for 3-5 minutes. Add the ginger, cumin and salt, and stir so that the onions cook evenly. Stir in the carrots, cabbage, peas, greens and noodles. Sauté for an additional 5 minutes, stirring occasionally. Pour in the coconut milk and tamari and sauté for 5-10 more minutes, until the vegetables are tender yet still slightly crunchy. Stir in the cilantro, lime juice and cashews, and cook for 2 more minutes. Remove from heat and serve. *Serves 6.*

Soba Noodles with Vegetables in Sesame Peanut Sauce

Soba noodles are typically made from a mix of wheat and buckwheat flours, though there are some available on the market now that are made solely from buckwheat. Crisp summer vegetables sautéed in a sesame peanut sauce make a fabulous topping for these noodles.

DIRECTIONS:

In a large wok, sauté the carrots and ginger in the olive and sesame oils on medium-low heat for 5-10 minutes. Stir in the red pepper, peas, cabbage and bean sprouts, and sauté an additional 5-10 minutes. In a small bowl, combine the tamari, peanut butter, syrup, arrowroot powder and water, stirring together thoroughly so that the peanut butter and syrup dissolve. Pour this sauce onto the vegetables and cook for 5 more minutes.

While preparing the vegetables, bring a large pot of salted water to a boil. Follow the instructions on the noodle package to determine cooking time. Drop the noodles into the water just before the vegetables are done so that you can serve everything together. When the noodles are done, drain them and drizzle on a bit of olive oil and a few dashes of salt, and pour vegetables over top.

Serves 6-8.

INGREDIENTS:

3 tbsp olive oil (45 ml)

1 tbsp sesame oil (15 ml)

3 tbsp fresh gingerroot, grated (45 ml)

3 carrots, cut into long, thin strips (3)

2 red peppers, cut into long, thin slivers (2)

4 cups snow peas or snap peas, stems removed (1,000 ml)

2 cups red cabbage, finely sliced (500 ml)

2 cups bean sprouts (500 ml)

3 tbsp tamari (45 ml)

¼ cup peanut butter (60 ml)

1½ tbsp brown rice syrup (20 ml)

1 tbsp arrowroot powder (15 ml)

½ cup water (125 ml)

3 7-oz packages soba noodles (3-200 g)

83

Vegetable Matters: Side Dishes

Baked Paprika Yam Sticks

Steamed Red Cabbage with Cilantro and Balsamic Vinegar

Mashed Rutabagas and Yams

Basil Scalloped Potatoes with Oyster Mushrooms

Beets with Sherry Horseradish Sauce

Lemon Sesame Kale

Simple Ginger Carrots

Red and Green Sesame Cabbage

Roasted Root Vegetables and Squash

Roasted Vegetables Wrapped in Steamed Chard

Potato Yam Pancakes

Citrus Beets

Steamed Broccoli in Lemon Sherry Sauce

Spiced Cabbage and Apple with Apricots

Fresh Basil and Mint Green Beans

Sesame Glazed Carrots

Mixed Heirloom Potato Hashbrowns

Baked Beets, Parsnips and Carrots with Orange Spice Sauce

Baked Paprika Yam Sticks

*A simple, yet satisfying standby for many of our dinners, these baked sticks of
yam are delicious and add a wonderful burst of color to a meal. Our two resident
pigs happen to be named Paprika and Nutmeg, so when those spices
are used in our kitchen—which is often—it is always with a bit of a smile.*

INGREDIENTS:

3-5 medium yams (3-5)
2-3 tbsp olive oil (30-45 ml)
1 tsp sea salt (5 ml)
*Several dashes paprika (smoked
or Spanish) and nutmeg*

DIRECTIONS: 350°F (175°C); 30 MINUTES

Slice the yams lengthwise into wedges of similar thickness (no more than one-inch thick). Place the yams in a large bowl and coat with oil. Sprinkle on the salt and several dashes of paprika and nutmeg. Stir the yams in the bowl so that they are entirely coated with the oil, salt and spices. Spread out the yams on a cookie sheet. Bake in a pre-heated oven for about 30 minutes. Test to make sure the yams are done by poking a few with a fork; they should be soft all the way through the wedges. Bake a little longer if you like the edges to be crispier. Remove from the oven and serve as a side dish.
Serves 6-8 as a side dish.

Steamed Red Cabbage with Cilantro and Balsamic Vinegar

I could eat red cabbage every day of the year! I just love this dish, and many of the folks who have worked on our farm have told me how much they enjoy this dish and how happy they were to hear it was on the evening's menu. We can never seem to grow enough red cabbage to meet the demand! Fresh cilantro is an unbeatable topping.

DIRECTIONS:

Place the sliced cabbage in a medium pot and add 2 cups of water and a dash of sea salt. Bring the water to a boil, then reduce to a simmer and cover for about 5-7 minutes. Do not overcook; the cabbage should be bright purple and still be somewhat firm. Drain the water and stir in the remaining ingredients. Serve immediately.

Serves 4-6 as a side dish.

INGREDIENTS:

½ head of red cabbage, sliced lengthwise, very thinly into long strips (½)

2 cups water, salted (500 ml)

2 tbsp balsamic vinegar (30 ml)

2 tbsp flax or olive oil (30 ml)

2 tbsp tamari (30 ml)

¼ cup fresh cilantro, finely chopped (60 ml)

Mashed Rutabagas and Yams

*Rutabagas are a wonderful winter crop to grow in our coastal climate.
Our very first WWOOFer, Daniel from Scotland, helped us to plant our first
crop of winter rutabagas. They were so prolific and grew throughout
the winter season, providing us with a hearty and highly nutritious
root vegetable packed with minerals. Combining them with the sweetness of
yams creates a unique twist on the traditional mashed potato recipe.*

INGREDIENTS:

6 cups water (1,500 ml)
2 large rutabagas, peeled and chopped (2)
4 yams, peeled and chopped (4)
½ tbsp sea salt (7 ml)
2 tbsp olive oil (30 ml)
4 tbsp soy milk (60 ml)
½ tsp onion powder (2 ml)
¼ cup pecans (60 ml)
¼ cup dried cranberries (60 ml)

DIRECTIONS: 350°F (175°C); 15-20 MINUTES

In a large pot, bring the salt and water to a boil. Add the rutabagas and yams. Cook until the vegetables are soft. Strain. Add the oil, soy-milk and onion powder and mash thoroughly in the pot until the vegetables are completely broken down and smooth. Add more salt to taste. Scoop the mixture into a small baking pan and top with chopped pecans and dried cranberries. Place in a preheated oven and bake for 15-20 minutes. Serve warm.
Serves 6-8 as a side dish.

Basil Scalloped Potatoes with Oyster Mushrooms

A creamy and rich version of scalloped potatoes, wonderfully complemented by hints of fresh basil in every mouthful. Our potatoes have been remarkably prolific on the farm and this is a fabulous dish to create in the summer when both potatoes and basil are at the height of production and freshness.

DIRECTIONS: 350°F (175°C); 35 MINUTES

Prepare the onion, potatoes and mushrooms and set aside.

In a medium saucepan, bring 1½ cups of the soy milk to a low simmer. In a small bowl, combine the remaining ½ cup soy milk with the arrowroot powder and stir until the powder is dissolved. Pour this into the simmering soy milk, whisking continuously. Add the basil, salt, tamari, cashew butter and nutritional yeast, whisking thoroughly to incorporate all ingredients. Remove from heat and set aside.

Lightly oil a large casserole dish or baking pan. Place a layer of red onions on the bottom, followed by a layer of potatoes spread evenly over top, followed by a layer of oyster mushrooms, using about ⅓ each of the onion, potatoes and mushrooms. Pour ⅓ of the cream sauce evenly over top and spread it around gently so that it reaches into the corners of the pan. Repeat the layering process twice more. Once you have layered all the ingredients, sprinkle paprika over the top, and place in a preheated oven to bake for about 35 minutes. Poke the potatoes with a fork to be sure that they are cooked through. Serve hot from the oven.

Serves 6-8 as a side dish.

INGREDIENTS:

1 medium red onion, thinly sliced (1)

6 medium potatoes, thinly sliced (6)

2 cups fresh oyster mushrooms, chopped (500 ml)

CREAM SAUCE:

2 cups rice milk or soy milk (500 ml)

1 tbsp arrowroot powder (15 ml)

2 tbsp fresh basil, finely chopped (30 ml)

¼ tsp sea salt (1 ml)

1 tsp tamari (5 ml)

1 tbsp cashew butter (15 ml)

1½ tbsp nutritional yeast (20 ml)

GARNISH: *paprika*

Beets with Sherry Horseradish Sauce

These beets are a tasty side dish for a hearty winter meal. We grow several varieties of beets on our farm and any one of them is suitable for this dish.

INGREDIENTS:

5-6 beets, sliced into long thin pieces (5-6)

2½ cups water (625 ml)

1 tsp fine sea salt (5 ml)

3 tbsp olive oil (45 ml)

2-3 tsp fresh horseradish (10-15 ml)

4 cloves garlic (4)

¼ cup spelt flour (60 ml)

¼ cup dry sherry (60 ml)

¾-1 cup rice milk or soy milk (175-250 ml)

Several dashes fresh ground pepper

1 tbsp tamari or soy sauce (15 ml)

DIRECTIONS:

Place the beets, water and salt in a medium saucepan. Bring to a boil, then cover and simmer for 5-10 minutes. Check to see that the beets have just begun to soften (be careful not to overcook), then drain the water and set aside.

In a saucepan on medium heat, combine the oil, horseradish, garlic and flour, stirring together to make a paste. Add the sherry, rice milk, ground pepper and tamari, stirring thoroughly to dissolve any lumps. A whisk works best for this. Fold in the prepared beets and serve immediately *Serves 4-6 as a side dish.*

Lemon Sesame Kale

*Kale, loaded with calcium and delicious, is an extraordinarily
beneficial vegetable to include in one's diet. This is a
quick, zesty way to serve it up, and it's a standby in our household.*

DIRECTIONS:

On low heat, gently toast the sesame seeds, stirring constantly, until they begin to brown slightly and pop in the pan. This should take 5-10 minutes. Remove from heat and set aside.

Prepare the kale. I find removing the stems makes the kale more palatable, as the stems tend to be tough. Place the kale in a steamer and allow it to steam until it turns a bright green. Be careful not to overcook it! Remove the kale from the steamer and place on a serving dish.

In a separate bowl, combine the lemon, tamari and oil. Pour this mixture onto the kale and sprinkle the toasted sesame seeds on top. Enjoy!
Serves 4 as a side dish.

INGREDIENTS:

*1 bunch kale, stems removed
and chopped (1)*

2 tbsp lemon juice, freshly squeezed (30 ml)

2 tbsp tamari (30 ml)

2 tbsp olive, flax or hempseed oil (30 ml)

2 tbsp sesame seeds, toasted (30 ml)

Simple Ginger Carrots

*This easy-to-create recipe is a bright side dish, packed with
beta-carotene and vitamins. So often good food is simple food.*

INGREDIENTS:

10 carrots (10)

3 slices fresh gingerroot (3)

½ tsp sea salt (2 ml)

1 cup water (250 ml)

GARNISH:

*2 tbsp chopped parsley or
green onions (30 ml)*

2 tbsp flax oil (30 ml)

DIRECTIONS:

In a medium pot, bring water, salt and slices of gingerroot to a boil. Add the carrots and lower to a simmer. Cover and allow the carrots to simmer for about 5 minutes. Most of the water should be evaporated, and the carrots just softened, not mushy. Remove from heat, strain and remove ginger, then place in a serving bowl. Drizzle flax oil over top and sprinkle with parsley or green onions. Serve hot.
Serves 4-6 as a side dish.

Red and Green Sesame Cabbage

*This cabbage dish is very simple to make and delicious.
We make it often at our farm in the fall when cabbages
are large and crisp and ready to be eaten.*

INGREDIENTS:

1 onion, sliced into thin slivers (1)

2 tbsp olive oil (30 ml)

3 cloves garlic, diced (3)

1 tbsp fresh gingerroot, grated (15 ml)

¾ tbsp sesame oil (12 ml)

*½ each red and green cabbage sliced into
long, thin slices (½)*

2 tbsp tamari (30 ml)

1 tbsp brown rice syrup (15 ml)

3 tbsp sesame seeds, unhulled (45 ml)

DIRECTIONS:

In a large frying pan, sauté the onion, garlic, and ginger in the oils on medium heat. Stir in the sliced red and green cabbages, sautéing until they begin to soften. Stir in the tamari, brown rice syrup and sesame seeds and sauté for an additional 5 minutes. Remove from heat and serve hot.
Serves 6-8 as a side dish.

Roasted Root Vegetables and Squash

Root vegetables are loaded with minerals and nutrients. Slow roasting them with spices in the oven brings out their hearty, natural sweetness, making them delectable.

DIRECTIONS: 350°F (175°C); 60 MINUTES

Prepare all of the vegetables and place them in a large baking pan. Add the oil, spices, salt and tamari and stir all of the ingredients together. Place in a preheated oven and bake for about 1 hour, stirring the vegetables occasionally to ensure even cooking. Remove from heat and serve.

Serves 6-8 as a side dish.

INGREDIENTS:

3 red or white onions, cut into quarters or eighths (3)

10 carrots, sliced diagonally (10)

2 rutabagas, cubed (2)

2 turnips, cubed (2)

3 beets, cubed (3)

1 kabocha or buttercup squash, stem and seeds removed, cut into bite-size pieces (1)

3 medium potatoes, any variety, cubed (purple potatoes add color) (3)

1 medium sweet potato, cubed, skins on (1)

¼-⅓ cup olive oil (60-80 ml)

1 tsp each nutmeg, Spanish paprika and dried oregano (5 ml)

1 tbsp coarse sea salt (15 ml)

2 tbsp tamari (30 ml)

Roasted Vegetables Wrapped in Steamed Chard

This is an elegant presentation for a spin on Roasted Root Vegetables and Squash (page 93). Wrapping the vegetables in steamed chard leaves creates a charming side dish.

INGREDIENTS:

1-2 bunches of Swiss chard (1-2)

1 recipe Roasted Root Vegetables and Squash (page 93) (1)

DIRECTIONS: 300°F (150°C); 15-20 MINUTES

Prepare one recipe of Roasted Root Vegetable and Squash (page 93) and set aside.

Cut off the ends of the chard stems and discard. In a steamer with boiling water, place the whole leaves of chard and allow them to steam for a few minutes, until soft. Remove from the steamer and rinse the chard under cold water so that they are cool enough to handle.

Take one leaf of chard and place 2 scoops of prepared and cooked root vegetable mixture in the centre of the leaf. Fold over the sides, then fold over the ends to seal the root vegetables inside. Place on a platter seam-side down. Prepare the remaining leaves of chard in the same fashion. Serve while warm.

If you want to serve these hot at a later time, place the bundles in a baking pan and brush with a bit of oil, then place them in a 300°F (150°C) oven for 15-20 minutes before serving time. *Serves 8-10 as a side dish.*

Potato Yam Pancakes

*My parents used to make potato pancakes for us when we were kids,
and it was always one of my favorite things to have for breakfast.
Now my son eats these tasty renditions by the plateful. They are
also wonderful as a side dish with lunch or evening meals. You can
easily halve this recipe if you do not want as many pancakes.*

DIRECTIONS:

Grate the clean potatoes and yams and place them in a large mixing bowl. Stir in the remaining ingredients and mix together thoroughly.

Place a cast iron frying pan on the stove and heat on medium. Add some olive oil to the pan so that the bottom is thinly coated in oil. Immediately grab a handful of pancake mixture, shape it into a ball, flatten between your hands to about half an inch thick and place it at the edge of the pan. Add three more pancakes of the same size to the frying pan. With a metal pancake flipper, press down the top of each pancake to ensure that they are cooked evenly on the bottom. Allow the cakes to cook for several minutes until the edges begin to turn a golden brown. When the bottoms are golden, flip the cakes over and cook the other side. The heat should be low enough to allow the cakes to cook all the way through in the time that it takes them to become golden and crispy on the edges.

Remove the cakes from the pan and serve immediately, or place them in a baking dish and put them in the oven on low heat to keep warm until you have made all of the pancakes.
Makes about 20 pancakes.

INGREDIENTS:

*4½ cups potatoes, skins on
and grated (1,125 ml)*

*4½ cups yams, skins on
and grated (1,125 ml)*

1 medium white onion, finely sliced (1)

2½-3 tsp fine sea salt (12-15 ml)

Several dashes ground black pepper

1½ cups soy milk (375 ml)

1⅓ cups brown rice flour (330 ml)

⅓ cup olive oil (80 ml)

¾ tsp each dill and nutmeg (4 ml)

Citrus Beets

We grow many varieties of beets at our farm, from round or cylindrical red ones to golden yellow and striped chioggia ones. All are delicious and would work wonderfully in this dish in any combination.

INGREDIENTS:

5 cups beets, cleaned and sliced into thin rounds (1,250 ml)

2 cups water (500 ml)

1 tsp sea salt (5 ml)

2 tbsp brown rice syrup (30 ml)

½ cup orange juice, freshly squeezed (125 ml)

1 tbsp fresh gingerroot, grated (15 ml)

Dash nutmeg

1 tbsp olive oil (15 ml)

1½ tsp arrowroot powder (7 ml)

GARNISH: 1 tsp orange rind, grated (optional) (5 ml)

DIRECTIONS:

Place the beets, water and salt in a medium sauce pan. Bring to a boil, then cover and simmer for 5-10 minutes. Check to see that the beets have just begun to soften (be careful not to overcook), then drain the water and set the beets aside. In a small saucepan, combine the orange juice, rice syrup, ginger, nutmeg, oil and arrowroot powder.

Whisk the ingredients together to dissolve the arrowroot, then begin heating the mixture on medium heat. Continue to whisk as the mixture thickens and gently bubbles. Remove from heat and pour over the beets. Gently stir the beets and sauce together and serve warm. Garnish with grated orange rind. *Serves 4-6 as a side dish.*

Steamed Broccoli in Lemon Sherry Sauce

Fresh steamed broccoli is just wonderful and packed with calcium, vitamins and antioxidants. The zesty sauce adds a delightful kick to this versatile vegetable.

DIRECTIONS:

In a steamer pot, steam the broccoli until it turns a bright green color and still retains most of its crispness. Remove from heat and set aside, uncovered.

In a skillet, sauté the onion in the oil on medium heat until translucent. Stir in the flour, then add the sherry, salt and pepper. Add the water 1/4 cup at a time, slowly whisking or stirring it in so that the flour mixture thickens with each 1/4 cup. When all of the water is incorporated, remove from heat and stir in the lemon juice and broccoli florets. Pour into a serving dish and serve.

Serves 4-6 as a side dish.

INGREDIENTS:

5 cups broccoli florets (1,250 ml)

2 tbsp olive oil (30 ml)

1/2 cup onion, diced (125 ml)

1 tbsp light spelt or wheat flour (rice flour also works) (15 ml)

1/4 cup dry sherry (60 ml)

1/4 tsp fine sea salt (1 ml)

Several dashes ground black pepper, to taste

1 cup water (250 ml)

3 tbsp lemon juice, freshly squeezed (45 ml)

Spiced Cabbage and Apple with Apricots

The aroma of this dish alone draws people into the kitchen. This is a fabulous combination of sweet and sour flavors, fragrant spices and colorful vegetables.

INGREDIENTS:

2 tbsp olive oil (30 ml)
1 large onion, diced (1)
½ tsp cinnamon (2 ml)
¼ tsp nutmeg (1 ml)
⅛ tsp cloves (0.5 ml)
1 tbsp fresh gingerroot, grated (15 ml)
1 tsp fine sea salt (5 ml)
½ red cabbage, thinly sliced (½)
½ green cabbage, thinly sliced (½)
1 apple, grated (1)
¼ cup dried apricots, thinly sliced (60 ml)
2 tbsp each red wine vinegar and maple syrup (30 ml)

DIRECTIONS:

In a large pot, heat the oil on medium, then sauté the onion, cinnamon, nutmeg, cloves and ginger. When the onions become translucent, stir in the salt, cabbages and apple and cook for another 5 minutes. Stir in the apricots, vinegar and maple syrup, and cook for an additional 5 minutes. Serve hot. *Serves 6-8 as a side dish.*

Fresh Basil and Mint Green Beans

Fresh green beans abound in the summer and this is a delightful way to serve them up with fresh basil and mint from the garden. Using edible flowers as a garnish adds an incredible splash of color to the bright green beans.

DIRECTIONS:

Bring 2 cups water to a boil in a saucepan with a steamer basket. Place the beans in the steamer basket and steam for 5-7 minutes, until they turn a bright green. Immediately remove them from the steamer and rinse with cold water to stop the beans from cooking any longer. Set aside.

In a large skillet, warm the olive oil on medium heat. Stir in the garlic, almonds and salt, and sauté for 3-5 minutes. Add the green beans, mint and basil, and sauté for an additional 2-3 minutes. Remove from heat and stir in the lime juice. Scoop the beans and almonds onto a serving platter and serve at once. Garnish with fresh sprigs of mint and basil, as well as edible flowers such as purple Johnny Jump-ups, pansies, or nasturtiums for a brilliant splash of color.

Serves 4-6 as a side dish.

INGREDIENTS:

3 cups (about 12 oz) green beans, stems removed (750 ml)

2 tbsp olive oil (30 ml)

3 cloves garlic (3)

¼ cup almonds, slivered (60 ml)

½ tsp fine sea salt (2 ml)

1 tbsp fresh mint leaves, finely chopped (15 ml)

2 tbsp fresh basil leaves, finely chopped (30 ml)

½ tbsp lime juice, freshly squeezed (7 ml)

GARNISH: *sprigs of fresh mint and basil, edible flowers*

Sesame Glazed Carrots

Sometimes simplicity is the best philosophy with food preparation.
This recipe is a simple and elegant way to prepare a side dish
of carrots that adds a wonderful splash of color to a meal.
Fresh, sweet, crunchy carrots yield the most satisfying results.

INGREDIENTS:

10 carrots, peeled and sliced
into thin sticks (10)
2 tbsp olive oil (30 ml)
2 tbsp fresh gingerroot, grated (30 ml)
2 tsp fine sea salt (10 ml)
2 tbsp sesame seeds (30 ml)
3 tbsp brown rice syrup (45 ml)

DIRECTIONS:

In a large skillet, heat the oil on medium. Stir in the carrots, ginger, salt and sesame seeds, and sauté for 3-5 minutes. Stir in the brown rice syrup and sauté for 1-2 minutes more, until the syrup has dissolved. Remove from heat and serve immediately. Be sure not to overcook; the carrots are best when they have a bit of crunch left and are still a bright orange color.

Serves 4-6 as a side dish.

Mixed Heirloom Potato Hashbrowns

We often serve these potatoes to our guests at the B&B as an accompaniment to various breakfast dishes. Using heirloom potatoes from our garden guarantees unbeatable freshness. Use fresh herbs for the recipe if you can.

DIRECTIONS:

Clean the potatoes and cut them into ½ inch cubes. In a large frying pan, combine all ingredients on low-medium heat. Stir the potatoes as you fry them on low heat for about 30 minutes until they are crispy on the outside and soft in the center. Serve hot. *Serves 4-6 as a side dish.*

INGREDIENTS:

3-4 tbsp olive oil (45-60 ml)

6 potatoes (we use a combination of yellow, red and purple) (6)

½ medium onion, diced (½)

1-2 tsp fine sea salt (5-10 ml)

Several dashes ground black pepper

1 tsp dry basil (or three sprigs of fresh basil) (5 ml)

1 tsp dry dill (or three sprigs of fresh dill tops) (5 ml)

GARNISH: sprigs of basil, dill, arugula leaves, flowers

Baked Beets, Parsnips and Carrots with Orange Spice Sauce

*I like to use golden beets for this recipe, as they really brighten
up the dish, although you could use any variety of beet. The tangy citrus
spice sauce complements the earthy flavors of the baked root vegetables.*

INGREDIENTS:

SAUCE:

2 ½ tbsp orange juice (40 ml)

2 tbsp maple syrup (30 ml)

2 tbsp nutritional yeast flakes (30 ml)

2 cloves garlic (2)

½ tsp cinnamon (2 ml)

½ tsp nutmeg (2 ml)

½ tsp paprika (2 ml)

3 tbsp olive oil (45 ml)

1 tbsp fresh gingerroot, grated (15 ml)

2 tbsp tamari (30 ml)

4 cups golden beets, sliced (1,000 ml)

2 cups parsnips, sliced (500 ml)

4 carrots, sliced (4)

DIRECTIONS: 350°F (175°C); 45-55 MINUTES

Prepare the sauce by mixing all of the ingredients in a jar and shaking well. Set aside.

Clean and slice all of the vegetables then place them in a 13-x-9-x-2-inch casserole or baking dish. Pour the sauce over top and stir all of the ingredients together thoroughly. Place the pan in a preheated oven and bake for 45-55 minutes. Stir the vegetables a few times while baking to be sure that they are thoroughly coated with the sauce. Remove from the oven and serve hot. *Serves 6-8 as a side dish.*

Root Vegetable Pot Pie

Friendly Shepherd's Pie

Walnut Basil Rice Casserole

Buckwheat Bean Casserole with Sesame Sauce

Vegetable Mochi Casserole

Portabello Mushroom Tofu Quiche

Vegetable Chocolate Chili Mole

Almond and Vegetable Stuffed Zucchini Boats

Baked Kabocha Squash with Savory Stuffing

Curried Potatoes and Vegetables

Polenta Terrine

Vegetable Kebabs

Root Vegetable Pot Pie

Root vegetables tend to be overlooked, yet they are full of vitamins and minerals and can be grown virtually year-round in our region. The savory root vegetable base with its cobbler-like topping makes an excellent autumn meal.

INGREDIENTS:

ROOT VEGETABLE BOTTOM:

3 tbsp olive oil or other natural oil (45 ml)

3 cups potatoes, cubed (750 ml)

2 cups turnips, cubed (500 ml)

1 cup rutabagas, cubed (250 ml)

2 cups carrots, chopped (500 ml)

½ tbsp fresh gingerroot, grated (7 ml)

5 cloves garlic, diced (5)

¾ tbsp coarse sea salt (12 ml)

½ cup sherry (125 ml)

1 tsp each rosemary and sage (5 ml)

1 tbsp tamari (15 ml)

1 tbsp arrowroot powder (15 ml)

½ cup water (125 ml)

2 cups kale, stems removed
and finely chopped (500 ml)

TOPPING:

2 cups flour (500 ml)

3 tsp baking powder (15 ml)

½ tsp salt (2 ml)

½ cup olive oil or other natural oil (125 ml)

½ cup rice milk (125 ml)

1 tsp apple cider vinegar (5 ml)

DIRECTIONS: 350°F (175 °C); 20-25 MINUTES

For the root vegetable bottom, place a large pot on medium heat. Place the olive oil in the pot and add the potatoes, turnips, rutabagas, carrots, ginger, garlic, salt, sherry and herbs. Stir the ingredients frequently to prevent them from sticking to the bottom of the pot. As the vegetables are cooking, mix the tamari, arrowroot powder and water in a separate cup, stirring until the powder is dissolved. Pour this mixture into the vegetable pot and continue stirring. Cook the vegetables on medium heat for about half an hour, until they begin to soften.

While the vegetables are cooking, begin preparing the topping. In a medium-size mixing bowl, stir the flour, salt and baking powder together. Make a well in the center of the flour mixture, and slowly add the oil, vinegar and water. Carefully mix the wet ingredients together in the well until they are emulsified, then stir them into flour mixture, until a soft dough is formed. Set aside.

After the vegetables have begun to soften, pour them into a large casserole dish. Crumble chunks of the dough over top, covering the entire casserole evenly with the dough. Place in a preheated oven and bake for 20-25 minutes, until the dough turns a golden brown. Remove from oven and serve warm.

Serves 6-8.

Friendly Shepherd's Pie

*This delicious vegetarian version of Shepherd's Pie is loaded with savory vegetables
and ground nuts, providing a wide array of protein, vitamins, calcium and other
minerals. You can substitute almost any vegetable in the filling to suit your palate.*

DIRECTIONS: 350°F (175°C); 45-55 MINUTES

Fill a large pot ¾ full with water and 1 tsp sea salt. Bring to a boil, then add the potatoes and allow them to cook for about 20 minutes, or until they are soft. When the potatoes are soft, drain the water then return them to the pot. Add the olive oil or soy margarine, 1 tsp sea salt, black pepper and soy milk. Mash thoroughly with a masher or electric mixer until a creamy consistency is achieved. Taste and add more salt, pepper, oil or soy milk as necessary to reach the desired consistency. Set aside.

While the potatoes are boiling, in another large pot sauté the onion in the oil on medium heat. Add the carrots, broccoli and celery, stirring regularly. Stir in the tomatoes, mushrooms, nuts, oats, flour and yeast. Stir thoroughly and regularly. Add the water and tamari, continuing to stir. Allow the mixture to cook for several minutes, then remove from heat.

Distribute the filling evenly on the bottom of a large casserole dish, then scoop spoonfuls of the topping onto the filling, gently spreading it evenly over the filling. Sprinkle paprika over the top, then place in a preheated oven and bake for about 45-55 minutes. The top should begin to turn a light golden color. I often rotate the dish halfway through the baking time to ensure even cooking through the entire dish. Remove from the oven and serve hot.
Serves 6-8.

INGREDIENTS:

TOPPING:

8 medium-large potatoes, peeled and cubed (8)

3-4 tbsp olive oil or soy margarine (45-60 ml)

2 tsp coarse sea salt (10 ml)

Several dashes ground black pepper

½ cup soy milk (you may need more) (125 ml)

FILLING:

3 tbsp olive oil or other natural oil (50 ml)

1 large onion, diced (1)

4 medium carrots, grated (4)

1 cup broccoli florets, finely chopped (250 ml)

2 ribs celery, thinly sliced (2)

1½ cups fresh tomatoes, diced (375 ml)

1½ cups mushrooms, thinly sliced (button mushrooms will work, but I often use portabello mushrooms) (375 ml)

⅓ cup each hazelnuts and almonds, finely ground (80 ml)

½ cup quick oats (125 ml)

¼ cup flour (60 ml)

2 tbsp nutritional yeast (30 ml)

¼-½ cup water (60-125 ml)

2-3 tbsp tamari (30-45 ml)

GARNISH: *paprika*

Walnut Basil Rice Casserole

*This is a delicious casserole that is so simple to make and a fantastic way
to use up leftover rice! We grow basil in our greenhouse and harvest fresh walnuts
from our tree, providing an incredibly fresh and aromatic edge to this dish.*

INGREDIENTS:

2 cups brown basmati rice, cooked (500 ml)
1½ cups walnuts (375 ml)
½ cup fresh basil (125 ml)
½ medium onion (½)
2 tbsp tamari or soy sauce (30 ml)
5 tbsp rice milk or soy milk (75 ml)

DIRECTIONS: 325°F (160°C); 50-60 MINUTES

Place all ingredients in a food processor and blend until a coarse consistency is achieved. Spoon the mixture into an oiled loaf pan or small casserole dish and bake in a preheated oven for 50-60 minutes. Allow the casserole to cool for 5-10 minutes before serving slices. *Serves 4-6.*

Buckwheat Bean Casserole with Sesame Sauce

*This nourishing casserole is a quick and easy dish to create,
especially when you have leftover buckwheat and beans. The creamy
sesame sauce on top is a delightful complement to the casserole.
A wonderful dish when you need a boost of protein.*

DIRECTIONS: 325°F (160°C); 35-45 MINUTES

FOR THE SAUCE:

In a small saucepan, bring the rice milk and tahini to a simmer, whisking the ingredients to dissolve the tahini. Add the tamari, yeast and flour, and continue whisking. Bring the mixture to a gentle boil, and whisk continuously for a couple of minutes. Remove from heat and set aside.

Combine all of the casserole ingredients together in a large mixing bowl, stirring thoroughly. Lightly oil a medium-sized casserole dish and spread out the mixture in the dish. Pour the sauce evenly over top of the casserole and sprinkle a few dashes of paprika on top. Place in a preheated oven and bake for about 35-45 minutes. Serve warm with Lemon Sesame Kale (page 91) and Baked Paprika Yam Sticks (page 86).

INGREDIENTS:

SAUCE:

½ cup tahini (125 ml)

1 ½ cups rice milk or soy milk (375 ml)

1 tbsp tamari (15 ml)

2 tbsp nutritional yeast (30 ml)

1 tbsp flour (15 ml)

CASSEROLE:

5 cups buckwheat, cooked and cooled (1,250 ml)

2 cups pinto beans, (or 1 can pinto beans) (500 ml)

½ cup almonds, ground (125 ml)

½ cup walnuts, ground (125 ml)

2 tbsp tamari (30 ml)

2 tbsp olive oil (30 ml)

1 medium onion, diced (1)

1 tbsp fresh gingerroot, grated (15 ml)

⅓ cup flour (kamut or barley are delicious, but any flour will do) (80 ml)

½ cup rice milk or soy milk (125 ml)

Vegetable Mochi Casserole

Although this dish has several steps to it, it is well worth the effort. Mochi is a rice product that traditionally comes from Japan, though you can often find it in grocery stores. When baked it becomes both crispy and chewy and makes an excellent topping on casseroles. This dish is filled with fresh garden vegetables, fried tofu and a creamy sauce, and is one of our family favorites. Try adding other vegetables that are in season, such as green beans, spinach, cabbage or zucchini.

INGREDIENTS:

SAUCE:

4 cups soy milk (1,000 ml)

2 tbsp nutritional yeast (30 ml)

1 tbsp arrowroot powder (15 ml)

1 cup cashew butter (other nut butters and tahini also work well) (250 ml)

2 tbsp tamari (30 ml)

1 tsp dried dill weed (5 ml)

TOPPING:

1 package of mochi, grated (1) (10 oz/-284 g)

2 tbsp tamari (30 ml)

2 tbsp brown rice vinegar (30 ml)

2 tbsp olive oil (30 ml)

2 tbsp tahini (30 ml)

FRIED TOFU:

13 oz package firm tofu (370 g)

2 tbsp olive oil (30 ml)

2 tbsp tamari (30 ml)

2 tbsp nutritional yeast (30 ml)

FILLING:

2 heads broccoli, cut into small florets (2)

6 medium carrots, sliced (6)

1 cup green peas, fresh or frozen (250 ml)

1 cup mushrooms, sliced (250 ml)

3 ribs celery, sliced (3)

1 medium onion, chopped (1)

DIRECTIONS: 350°F (175°C); 35-40 MINUTES

Sauce: In a medium saucepan, place one cup of soy milk along with the yeast, arrowroot powder, cashew butter and tamari. Begin heating the mixture on medium as you whisk the ingredients together to create a creamy consistency. Bring the sauce to a low simmer. As the sauce thickens, gradually incorporate the rest of the soy milk, a little at a time. Remove from heat and set aside.

Topping: Grate the mochi with a hand grater. It is very hard to grate and takes a bit of muscle power, but have patience. Place the grated mochi in a large bowl and stir in the tamari, vinegar, oil and tahini. Combine the ingredients thoroughly and set aside.

Fried Tofu: In a large frying pan, heat the olive oil on medium. Add the tofu and fry for several minutes, stirring occasionally to keep the tofu from burning on the bottom of the pan. Continue frying until the tofu begins to brown on the sides and becomes crispy. Stir in the tamari, then stir in the yeast flakes and fry for 2 more minutes. Remove from heat and set aside.

Filling: Prepare the vegetables and place them in a steamer. Bring the steamer to a boil and steam the vegetables for about 3-5 minutes, just until they begin to soften only slightly. Remove from heat and remove the lid to allow the steam to escape. Set aside.

continued on next page

To assemble the casserole, use a large baking dish, approximately 13 x 9 x 2 inches in size. Place the steamed vegetables in the dish, with the tofu on top. Evenly pour the sauce over the vegetables and tofu, then sprinkle the topping evenly over the entire casserole. Place the casserole in a preheated oven and bake for about 35-40 minutes or until the topping begins to brown and turn crispy. Remove from the oven and serve hot. *Serves 6-8.*

Portabello Mushroom Tofu Quiche

This is a delectable vegan version of quiche with a wonderful flaky crust. It is full of delicious portabello mushrooms, vegetables, fresh basil and a creamy tofu filling.

DIRECTIONS: 350°F (175°C); 20-25 MINUTES

Prepare a half recipe of Flaky Pastry (page 193). Follow the instructions, then press the dough into an oiled 9-inch pie dish. Place the crust in a preheated oven and bake for 10-15 minutes. Remove from oven and set aside.

Prepare the filling by placing the tofu, nutritional yeast, mustard, vinegar, tamari, onion powder and garlic into a food processor. Blend the ingredients for several minutes until a creamy texture is achieved. Set aside.

In a large frying pan, sauté the onion in the olive oil on medium-low heat for about 5 minutes. Stir in the mushrooms and sauté for an additional 5 minutes. Add the basil and peas, then stir in the spinach and tamari and sauté until the spinach wilts, approximately 5 minutes. Stir in the tofu mixture and cook for 5 more minutes. Remove from heat and pour the filling and vegetables into the prepared pie crust. Place the red pepper strips in a circle on top of the quiche. Place the quiche into a preheated oven and bake for 20-25 minutes. Allow the quiche to cool for about 10 minutes before serving.
Serves 6-8.

INGREDIENTS:

½ recipe Flaky Pastry (page 193) (½)

FILLING:

13 oz firm tofu (370 g)

1 tbsp nutritional yeast flakes (15 ml)

1 tsp Dijon mustard (5 ml)

¼ cup brown rice vinegar (60 ml)

1 tbsp tamari (15 ml)

1 tsp onion powder (5 ml)

3 cloves garlic (3)

¾ cup red onion, diced (175 ml)

2 tbsp olive oil (30 ml)

2 portabello mushrooms, cut into thin pieces (2)

¼ cup fresh basil leaves, chopped (60 ml)

1 cup green peas, fresh or frozen (250 ml)

2 tbsp tamari (30 ml)

1 bunch spinach, washed, stems removed and chopped (1)

½ red pepper, thinly sliced (½)

109

Vegetable Chocolate Chili Mole

Mole is a Spanish word describing something that is mashed together. Traditionally, it is a combination of chocolate, spices and chilis. This chili recipe incorporates some of the traditional mole ingredients to create a divine, spicy chili loaded with delicious fresh vegetables. The fresh, sweet garden tomatoes and vegetables are exquisite. As if we need an excuse to eat chocolate!

INGREDIENTS:

3 tbsp olive oil (50 ml)

1 onion, diced (1)

6 cloves garlic, diced (6)

2 bay leaves (2)

1 tsp each thyme, ground cumin and basil (5 ml)

½ tsp each cinnamon and chili flakes (2 ml)

⅛ tsp allspice (0.5 ml)

Several dashes ground black pepper

1 tbsp coarse sea salt (15 ml)

½ cup vegan dark organic chocolate chips or chunks (125 ml)

1½ cups each carrots and celery, chopped (375 ml)

1 each green, red and yellow peppers, stems and seeds removed and chopped (1)

14 oz can each pinto, garbanzo and kidney beans, rinsed (398 ml)

28 oz can diced tomatoes, or 4 cups fresh tomatoes, diced 796 ml)

1 cup corn kernels, fresh, frozen or canned (250 ml)

DIRECTIONS:

In a large pot, warm the olive oil on medium heat. Add the onion, garlic, spices and sea salt, sautéing until the onions begin to turn translucent. Stir in the chocolate until melted. Add the carrots, celery, peppers and beans and sauté for 5-10 minutes. Stir in the tomatoes and corn, and reduce heat to a low simmer. Cover and simmer for about 30 minutes. Serve over a bed of warm rice with fresh bread.

Serves 6-8.

Mandarin Orange
Spice Cake *(page 144)*

Orange Currant
Cranberry Scones
(page 127)

Peppermint Oatmeal Carob
Cookies (page 214), with Triple
Almond Cookies in background

Almond and Vegetable Stuffed Zucchini Boats

Zucchinis tend to be abundant in the summer, and this is an elegant way to serve this summer squash for dinner.

DIRECTIONS: 350°F (175°C); 35-40 MINUTES

Cut the zucchinis in half lengthwise. Using a spoon, scoop out and dice the centers. Reserve the flesh for the stuffing. In a large frying pan, sauté the onion and ginger in the olive oil on medium heat for about 5-10 minutes. Stir in the carrots, mushrooms, broccoli and reserved zucchini flesh, and sauté 5-10 minutes more. Add the almonds and tamari and sauté for 5 more minutes. Remove from heat. Evenly stuff each of the zucchini halves with the sautéed vegetables and place them on a baking sheet. Place the stuffed zucchinis in a preheated oven and bake for 35-40 minutes. Remove from the oven and serve. The zucchini boats can be served on a bed of plain basmati rice, or try serving them with Lemon Cardamom Rice with Green Peas (page 71).

Serves 8.

INGREDIENTS:

4 small zucchinis (4)
1½ cups red onion, diced (375 ml)
3 tbsp olive oil (45 ml)
1 tbsp fresh gingerroot, grated (15 ml)
2 cups carrots, grated (500 ml)
1 cup mushrooms, diced (field mushrooms are fine, or try a wild mushroom variety such as chanterelles) (250 ml)
1 cup broccoli florets, diced (250 ml)
1 cup almonds, finely ground (250 ml)
2 tbsp tamari (30 ml)

Baked Kabocha Squash
with Savory Stuffing

*We grow several varieties of winter squash at our farm and
kabocha squash is by far my favorite. The bright orange color, sweet
flavor and perfect texture make it a fabulous addition to
winter meals, especially when topped with a delicious savory stuffing.*

INGREDIENTS:

¾ cup red onion, diced (175 ml)

3 tbsp olive oil (45 ml)

2 cloves garlic, diced (2)

3 ribs celery, thinly sliced (3)

2 tsp savory (10 ml)

*1 cup field mushrooms, thinly
sliced (250 ml)*

*½ loaf of bread, sliced and chopped into
cubes (½)*

1 cup black olives, sliced (250 ml)

4 tbsp tamari (60 ml)

½ cup walnuts, coarsely chopped (125 ml)

1 kabocha squash (1)

DIRECTIONS: 350°F (175°C); 40-45 MINUTES

In a large frying pan or wok, sauté the red onion in olive oil on medium-low heat. Stir in the garlic, celery, savory, mushrooms and bread cubes, sautéing for an additional 5-10 minutes. Add the olives, tamari and walnuts, stirring all ingredients together thoroughly for a few minutes. Remove from heat and set aside.

Prepare the kabocha squash by cutting it in half, removing the stem and seeds, then slicing the flesh into wedges about one inch wide. The skin of kabocha squash is edible and can be left on. Place the wedges around the edge of a baking dish, then scoop the stuffing into the center of the dish, covering most of the squash. Place the dish into a preheated oven and bake for 35-45 minutes. Check to make sure the squash is done by poking a piece with a fork; it should be soft. If the stuffing looks like it's getting a bit dry, you can place a lid over the dish for the last 10-15 minutes while it's baking. Serve hot.

Serves 6-8.

Curried Potatoes and Vegetables

This simple curried vegetable dish is delicious, and you can use any number of combinations of vegetables depending on what you have available at the time. Try adding eggplant, sweet potato, broccoli, sweet peppers, snow peas, spinach or green beans. Using sweet, new summer potatoes adds an incredible freshness to this dish.

DIRECTIONS:

In a large cooking pot, heat the olive oil and onion on medium. Stir frequently, cooking for a few minutes. Add the chopped potatoes, ginger, salt, turmeric, cumin and mustard seeds, stirring frequently so that the potatoes do not stick to the bottom of the pan. Continue cooking the potatoes for about 10 minutes until they begin to soften. Stir in the carrots, cauliflower and peas. Cook for another 5 minutes, stirring occasionally. Add the water as necessary, to help keep the vegetables from sticking to the bottom of the pan. Cook for an additional 10-15 minutes, until the cauliflower and carrots begin to soften, but still have some crunch in them. Stir in the tamari and remove from heat. Serve hot. This dish is excellent with Spelt Chapatis (page 137) and Raita with Soy Yogurt (page 21). *Serves 6-8.*

INGREDIENTS:

¼ cup olive oil (60 ml)

1 red onion, diced (1)

6 medium red or yellow potatoes, skins on and chopped into cubes (6)

2 tbsp fresh gingerroot, grated (30 ml)

1 tbsp coarse sea salt (15 ml)

½ tbsp turmeric (7 ml)

1 tsp each cumin seed and mustard seed (5 ml)

½ tsp black cardamom seed (2 ml)

4 medium carrots, chopped (4)

1 head cauliflower, chopped (1)

1 cup green peas, fresh or frozen (250 ml)

½-1 cup water (125-250 ml)

2 tbsp tamari (30 ml)

Vegetable Kebabs

*These vegetable kebabs with their tangy marinade are a great way
for vegetarians to participate in a summer barbecue. If you do
not have access to a barbecue, they can be roasted in the oven instead.*

INGREDIENTS:

1 head broccoli, cut into florets (1)

1 carrot, sliced diagonally (1)

10 small tomatoes or cherry tomatoes (10)

10 button or field mushrooms (10)

1 red onion, cut into large
wedges or pieces (1)

2 red peppers, cut into 1-inch cubes (2)

13 oz package firm tofu, cut
into cubes (370 g)

MARINADE:

¼ cup olive oil (60 ml)

¼ cup tamari (60 ml)

3 tbsp fresh gingerroot, grated (45 ml)

¼ cup nutritional yeast flakes (60 ml)

1 tbsp maple syrup (15 ml)

1 tbsp Dijon mustard (15 ml)

DIRECTIONS:

Prepare the marinade first by combining all of the marinade ingredients in a bowl and stirring them together thoroughly. Set aside.

Prepare the kebabs by arranging the prepared vegetables and tofu on 10-12 wooden skewers. Place the skewered vegetables on a baking sheet and drip the marinade evenly over kebabs so that all of the vegetables and tofu are covered. Allow them to sit for 15-20 minutes to absorb some of the marinade. You can scoop up the marinade that drips through onto the pan and pour it back onto the kebabs. To bake the kebabs, place them on a barbecue grill on low heat, grilling and rotating them as they brown (about 10-15 minutes in total), or in a preheated oven at 350°F and bake for about 15-20 minutes. Serve hot.

Serves 10-12.

Polenta Terrine

Though this recipe has a number of steps it is well worth the time. Each of the parts adds something unique to the finished dish. This is best served hot but is also good at room temperature—just be sure that the polenta stays moist. This recipe is a slightly adapted version of a creation from my friend Rebecca Jehn.

DIRECTIONS: 350°F (175°C); 45 MINUTES

Slice the mushrooms, then toss with 3-4 tablespoons of olive oil, oregano, ½ tsp salt and several dashes pepper. Roast in a shallow pan in a 400°F (200°C) oven until browned and firm, turning frequently, about 30-40 minutes. Be sure the mushrooms have lost all of their liquid.

While the mushrooms are roasting, grill the sweet red peppers over a gas flame or hot grill until the skin is blistered and blackened. The flesh will soften but should still have a bit of firmness. Scrape off the blistered skin, remove the stem and seeds and cut into eight pieces. Set aside.

Wash and julienne the chard and steam until wilted. Season with a few dashes of salt and pepper. Set aside.

Prepare the sauce by sautéing the onions in 2-3 tablespoons of olive oil until translucent. Stir in the garlic and sauté for 5 more minutes, being careful it doesn't burn. Add the chopped tomatoes, salt and pepper. Simmer for about 30 minutes or until thickened, then stir in the basil.

Remove from heat and set aside.

While the tomato sauce is thickening, bring the 5 cups of water and 1 tbsp salt to a boil in a large pot for the polenta. Pour in the cornmeal, stirring constantly. Reduce the heat and simmer about 15 minutes until it starts to thicken, then remove from heat. Pour about 1½ cups polenta into the bottom of a lightly oiled 9-inch casserole dish. Layer the mushrooms evenly on top of the polenta. Layer another cup of the polenta evenly on top of the mushrooms. Place the chard on this second surface and then layer the remaining polenta in the same way. Finally, add a layer of grilled peppers. Bake covered in a 350°F oven for about 45 minutes. Remove from the oven and allow the polenta to cool in the dish on a cooling rack for about 5-10 minutes. Invert onto a serving platter. Reheat the tomato sauce and pour over the inverted polenta. Slice into pie shaped wedges and serve on a bed of arugula leaves. *Serves 6-8.*

INGREDIENTS:

10 large field mushrooms (10)
4 tbsp olive oil (60 ml)
1 tsp dried oregano (5 ml)
½ tsp fine sea salt (2 ml)
Several dashes ground black pepper
2 sweet red peppers (2)
1 bunch Swiss chard (1)
2-3 tbsp olive oil (30-45 ml)
1 medium onion, chopped (1)
2-3 cloves garlic, minced (2-3)
3 cups tomatoes, chopped (750 ml)
½ tsp fine sea salt (2 ml)
Several dashes ground black pepper
3 tbsp fresh basil, chopped (45 ml)
5 cups water (1,250 ml)
1 tbsp coarse sea salt (15 ml)
1¾ cups coarse cornmeal (425 ml)
½ cup olive oil (125 ml)

GARNISH: arugula leaves

Brian's French Toast

Pear Cardamom Muffins

Banana Walnut Muffins

Strawberry Jalapeño Corn Muffins

Apple Walnut Spice Muffins

Lemon Lavender Blueberry Muffins

Rhubarb Pecan Muffins

Banana Carob Almond Coconut Muffins

Ginger Anise Peach Muffins

Orange Currant Cranberry Scones

Maple Orange Blueberry Granola

Amasake Pancakes

Fresh Lemon Mint Fruit Salad

Chai Jasmine Rice Pudding

Mom's Basic Dinner Rolls

Easy Biscuits

Basic Bread

Pizza Dough

April's 'Bread Wot is Amazing'

Spelt Chapatis

Red Pepper Hemp Cornbread

Spelt Cinnamon Buns

Vegetable Tofu Scramble

Brian's French Toast

A superb vegan rendition of French toast, this recipe was given to me by my friend Brian. We often serve this to our guests at the farm for breakfast.

INGREDIENTS:

1½ cups soy milk (375 ml)
2 tbsp flour (30 ml)
1 tbsp nutritional yeast (15 ml)
1 tsp sweetener (5 ml)
½ tsp cinnamon (2 ml)
1 tsp arrowroot powder (5 ml)
Dash of salt
8-10 slices bread (8-10)
Oil for frying

DIRECTIONS:

Combine the soy milk, flour, yeast, sweetener, cinnamon and salt in a medium bowl and whisk together to dissolve the flour. Place two slices of bread in the mixture and allow them to soak for a few minutes. Place them in a heated skillet with a couple of tablespoons of oil and allow them to brown on one side before flipping over to brown on the other side. As you place the soaked bread into the frying pan, soak another 2 slices in the mixture and add them to the frying pan as space becomes available. Continue soaking and frying new slices of bread until all of the liquid in the bowl has been used. Serve the French toast hot with maple syrup, jam, fresh fruit salad or frozen rice or soy dessert on top. *Serves 3-4.*

Pear Cardamom Muffins

These tasty muffins have a delicate flavor and a subtle crunch from the poppyseeds.
The pear adds additional sweetness and moisture to the muffins.

DIRECTIONS: 350°F (175°C); 30 MINUTES

Prepare a muffin tray by lightly oiling 10-12 muffin tins. Set aside.

In a medium-size mixing bowl, combine the flour, baking powder, baking soda, salt and cardamom. In a separate bowl, combine the oil, sugar, vanilla, soy milk, poppyseeds, lemon juice and rind, and whisk together until emulsified. Stir the pear into the wet ingredients. Pour the wet ingredients into the dry ingredients and gently stir together, being careful not to overmix.

Scoop spoonfuls of the mixture into prepared muffin tins, filling each tin level. Place the pan in a preheated oven and bake for about 30 minutes. Remove from the oven and allow the muffins to cool for 10-15 minutes in the pan before gently lifting them out of the tins.

Makes 10-12 muffins.

INGREDIENTS:

2 cups whole spelt or wheat flour (500 ml)

1 tsp baking powder (5 ml)

½ tsp each baking soda and fine sea salt (2 ml)

3 tbsp poppy seeds (45 ml)

½ cup canola oil or other natural oil (125 ml)

½ cup cane sugar (125 ml)

1 tsp vanilla extract (5 ml)

1 cup vanilla soy milk (250 ml)

1 tsp cardamom, ground (5 ml)

1 tbsp lemon juice, freshly squeezed (15 ml)

1 tbsp lemon rind (15 ml)

1½ cups pear, grated (375 ml)

119

Banana Walnut Muffins

These tasty muffins are a great way to use up ripe bananas.

INGREDIENTS:

2 cups whole spelt or wheat flour (500 ml)
1 tsp baking powder (5 ml)
*½ tsp each baking soda and
fine sea salt (2 ml)*
1 tsp cinnamon (5 ml)
*½ cup canola oil or other
natural oil (125 ml)*
½ cup cane sugar (125 ml)
1 tsp vanilla extract (5 ml)
1 cup vanilla soy milk (250 ml)
1½ cups mashed bananas (375 ml)
1 tbsp lemon juice, freshly squeezed (15 ml)
½ cup walnuts, chopped (125 ml)

DIRECTIONS: 350°F (175°C); 30 MINUTES

Prepare a muffin tray by lightly oiling 10-12 muffin tins. Set aside.

In a medium-size mixing bowl, combine the flour, baking powder, baking soda, salt and cinnamon. In a separate bowl, combine the oil, sugar, vanilla, soy milk and lemon juice, and whisk together until emulsified. Stir in the banana. Pour the wet ingredients into the dry ingredients and gently stir together, being careful not to overmix. Fold in the walnuts.

Scoop spoonfuls of the mixture into prepared muffin tins, filling each tin level. Place the pan in a preheated oven and bake for about 30 minutes. Remove from the oven and allow the muffins to cool for 10-15 minutes in the pan before gently lifting them out of the tins. Makes 10-12 muffins.

Variation: For Banana Blueberry Muffins, try adding 1 cup of fresh or frozen blueberries folded into the batter.

Strawberry Jalapeno Corn Muffins

*The combination of strawberries, fresh herbs and spicy
jalapenos in this corn flour muffin is exquisite.*

DIRECTIONS: 350°F (175°C); 30 MINUTES

Prepare a muffin tray by lightly oiling 10-12 muffin tins. Set aside.

In a medium-size mixing bowl, combine the flours, baking powder, baking soda, salt and oregano. In a separate bowl, combine the oil, sugar, soy milk, lemon juice, jalapeno and basil, and whisk together until emulsified. Pour the wet ingredients into the dry ingredients and gently stir together, being careful not to overmix. Fold in the strawberries.

Scoop spoonfuls of the mixture into prepared muffin tins, filling each tin level. Place the pan in a preheated oven and bake for about 30 minutes. Remove from the oven and allow the muffins to cool for 10-15 minutes in the pan before gently lifting them out of the tins. *Makes 10-12 muffins.*

INGREDIENTS:

1 cup whole spelt or wheat flour (250 ml)

1 cup corn flour (250 ml)

1 tsp baking powder (5 ml)

*½ tsp each baking soda and
fine sea salt (2 ml)*

1 tsp dried oregano (5 ml)

*½ cup canola oil or other
natural oil (125 ml)*

½ cup cane sugar (125 ml)

1 cup vanilla soy milk (250 ml)

1 tbsp lemon juice, freshly squeezed (15 ml)

1 jalapeno, seeds removed and diced (1)

3 tbsp fresh basil, finely chopped (45 ml)

*1½ cups fresh or frozen strawberries
(if large berries, cut into halves or
quarters) (375 ml)*

Apple Walnut Spice Muffins

The aroma of these spiced muffins filling the house on a Sunday morning is just wonderful. This is a great way to use up extra apples.

INGREDIENTS:

1 cup whole spelt or wheat flour (250 ml)

1 cup white spelt or wheat pastry flour (250 ml)

1 tsp baking powder (5 ml)

½ tsp each baking soda, fine sea salt and cinnamon (2 ml)

¼ tsp each ground cloves and nutmeg (1 ml)

½ cup canola oil or other natural oil (125 ml)

½ cup cane sugar (125 ml)

1 tsp vanilla extract (5 ml)

½ cup vanilla soy milk (125 ml)

½ cup apple juice (125 ml)

1 tsp apple cider vinegar (5 ml)

1½ cups apple, grated (about 2 apples) (375 ml)

½ cup walnuts, coarsely chopped (125 ml)

DIRECTIONS: 350°F (175°C); 30 MINUTES

Prepare a muffin tray by lightly oiling 10-12 muffin tins. Set aside.

In a medium-size mixing bowl, combine the flours, baking powder, baking soda, salt, cinnamon, cloves and nutmeg. In a separate bowl, combine the oil, sugar, vanilla, soy milk, apple juice and vinegar, and whisk together until emulsified. Stir the grated apple into the wet ingredients. Pour the wet ingredients into the dry ingredients and gently stir together, being careful not to overmix. Fold in the walnuts.

Scoop spoonfuls of the mixture into prepared muffin tins, filling each tin level. Place the pan in a preheated oven and bake for about 30 minutes. Remove from the oven and allow the muffins to cool for 10-15 minutes in the pan before gently lifting them out of the tins.

Makes 10-12 muffins.

Lemon Lavender Blueberry Muffins

Lemon and lavender complement each other very well, and the addition of plump blueberries in these moist muffins is truly a treat.

DIRECTIONS: 350°F (175°C); 30 MINUTES

Prepare a muffin tray by lightly oiling 10-12 muffin tins. Set aside.

In a medium-size mixing bowl, combine the flours, baking powder, baking soda and salt. In a separate bowl, combine the oil, sugar, vanilla, soy milk, lemon juice, lemon rind and lavender flowers, and whisk together until emulsified. Pour the wet ingredients into the dry ingredients and gently stir together, being careful not to overmix. Fold in the blueberries.

Scoop spoonfuls of the mixture into prepared muffin tins, filling each tin level. Place the pan in a preheated oven and bake for about 30 minutes. Remove from the oven and allow the muffins to cool for 10-15 minutes in the pan before gently lifting them out of the tins.

Makes 10-12 muffins.

INGREDIENTS:

1 cup whole spelt or wheat flour (250 ml)
1 cup white spelt or wheat pastry flour (250 ml)
1 tsp baking powder (5 ml)
½ tsp each baking soda and fine sea salt (2 ml)
½ cup canola oil or other natural oil (125 ml)
½ cup cane sugar (125 ml)
2 tsp vanilla extract (10 ml)
1 cup vanilla soy milk (250 ml)
⅓ cup lemon juice, freshly squeezed (80 ml)
3 tbsp lemon rind (45 ml)
1 tbsp lavender flowers, dried (15 ml)
1 cup blueberries, fresh or frozen (250 ml)

Rhubarb Pecan Muffins

*When rhubarb abounds, these are great muffins to make,
and the pecans add a wonderful crunch.*

INGREDIENTS:

1½ cups rhubarb stems, sliced (375 ml)

½ cup cane sugar (125 ml)

*2¼ cups white spelt or wheat
pastry flour (560 ml)*

1 tsp baking powder (5 ml)

½ tsp each nutmeg and fine sea salt (2 ml)

1 tsp cinnamon (5 ml)

⅓ cup canola oil or other natural oil (80 ml)

½ cup maple syrup (125 ml)

1 tsp vanilla extract (5 ml)

1 tsp apple cider vinegar (5 ml)

*⅔ cup vanilla soy milk or
rice milk (160 ml)*

1 tbsp lemon rind (15 ml)

½ cup pecans, finely chopped (125 ml)

DIRECTIONS: 350°F (175°C); 30 MINUTES

Prepare a muffin tray by lightly oiling 10-12 muffin tins. Set aside.

In a small bowl, combine the rhubarb and sugar and set aside.

In a medium-size mixing bowl, combine the flour, baking powder, nutmeg, cinnamon and salt. In a separate bowl, combine the oil, maple syrup, vanilla, vinegar, soy milk and lemon rind, and whisk together until emulsified. Pour the wet ingredients into the dry ingredients and gently stir together, being careful not to overmix. Fold in the rhubarb and sugar mixture.

Scoop spoonfuls of the mixture into prepared muffin tins, filling each tin level. Place the pan in a preheated oven and bake for about 30 minutes. Remove from the oven and allow the muffins to cool for 10-15 minutes in the pan before gently lifting them out of the tins.

Makes 10-12 muffins.

Banana Carob Almond Coconut Muffins

The flavors of banana and coconut complement each other well, and the addition of almonds and carob in these moist muffins complete this union.

DIRECTIONS: 350°F (175°C); 30 MINUTES

Prepare a muffin tray by lightly oiling 10 muffin tins. Set aside.

In a medium-sized mixing bowl, combine the flour, baking powder, baking soda, salt and cinnamon. In a separate bowl, combine the oil, sugar, vanilla, soy milk and lemon juice, and whisk together until emulsified. Stir in the bananas. Pour the wet ingredients into the dry ingredients and gently stir together, being careful not to overmix. Fold in the almonds, coconut and carob chips.

Scoop spoonfuls of the mixture into prepared muffin tins, filling each tin level. Place the pan in a preheated oven and bake for about 30 minutes. Remove from the oven and allow the muffins to cool for 10-15 minutes in the pan before gently lifting them out of the tins.

Makes 10-12 muffins.

INGREDIENTS:

2 cups whole spelt or wheat flour (500 ml)

1 tsp baking powder (5 ml)

½ tsp each baking soda and fine sea salt (2 ml)

1 tsp cinnamon (5 ml)

½ cup canola oil or other natural oil (125 ml)

½ cup cane sugar (125 ml)

1 tsp vanilla extract (5 ml)

1 cup vanilla soy milk (250 ml)

1½ cups bananas, mashed (375 ml)

1 tbsp lemon juice, freshly squeezed (15 ml)

½ cup almonds, chopped (125 ml)

½ cup dried medium-sized coconut flakes (125 ml)

½ cup carob chips (125 ml)

Ginger Anise Peach Muffins

These are great muffins to make in the summer when fresh peaches are sweet and juicy. The subtle flavors of the ginger and anise spices enhance the sweet flavor of the peaches in these delicious, moist muffins.

INGREDIENTS:

1 cup whole spelt (250 ml)
1 cup white spelt flour (250 ml)
1 tsp baking powder (5 ml)
½ tsp each baking soda and fine sea salt (2 ml)
1 tsp anise seeds, ground (5 ml)
½ cup canola oil or other natural oil (125 ml)
½ cup cane sugar (125 ml)
2 tsp vanilla extract (10 ml)
1 cup vanilla soy milk (250 ml)
2 tbsp lemon juice, freshly squeezed (30 ml)
2 tbsp gingerroot, fresh grated (30 ml)
1 cup peaches, peeled and chopped into small pieces (250 ml)

DIRECTIONS: 350°F (175°C); 30 MINUTES

Prepare a muffin tray by lightly oiling 10 muffin tins. Set aside.

In a medium-size mixing bowl, combine the flour, baking powder, baking soda and salt. In a separate bowl, combine the anise, oil, sugar, vanilla, soy milk, lemon juice and gingerroot, and whisk together until emulsified. Stir in the peaches. Pour the wet ingredients into the dry ingredients and gently stir together, being careful not to overmix.

Scoop spoonfuls of the mixture into prepared muffin tins, filling each tin level. Place the pan in a preheated oven and bake for about 30 minutes. Remove from the oven and allow the muffins to cool for 10-15 minutes in the pan before gently lifting them out of the tins.

Makes 10-12 muffins.

Orange Currant Cranberry Scones

*This is a delightfully flaky scone that is delicious as a
breakfast item or a treat with afternoon tea.*

DIRECTIONS: 375°F (190°C); 20 MINUTES

In a small bowl, combine the cranberries, currant, and orange juice and set aside.

In a medium mixing bowl, combine the flour, baking powder, salt and cinnamon. Cut the margarine into the flour mixture with a fork until it is the texture of a coarse meal. Make a well in the center of the ingredients and pour the syrup, zest and soy milk into the well. Stir the currants, cranberries and orange juice into the well, then mix until the dough is thoroughly combined.

Shape the dough into a large ball, place on a floured surface and cut into eight equal portions. Roll each of these portions into a round ball and place on a lightly oiled baking sheet, allowing 1-2 inches between each scone. Place in a preheated oven and bake for about 20 minutes, until the scones begin to brown. Serve warm with jams, jellies, flax oil or nut butters. *Makes 8 scones.*

INGREDIENTS:

*⅓ cup each dried cranberries
and currants (80 ml)*

⅓ cup orange juice, freshly squeezed (80 ml)

*3⅓ cups sifted spelt or wheat
pastry flour (830 ml)*

1 tbsp baking powder (15 ml)

½ tsp sea salt (2 ml)

¼ tsp cinnamon (1 ml)

½ cup soy margarine (125 ml)

½ cup maple syrup (125 ml)

1 tsp orange rind zest (5 ml)

¾ cup soy milk or rice milk (175 ml)

Maple Orange Blueberry Granola

Granola makes a delightful breakfast treat and is also delicious over soy yogurt, frozen soy desserts or as a layer in a parfait. Experiment!

INGREDIENTS:

7 cups large rolled oats (1,750 ml)
1½ cups almonds, coarsely chopped (375 ml)
¾ cup walnuts, coarsely chopped (175 ml)
1 tbsp vanilla extract (15 ml)
4 tbsp orange juice, freshly squeezed (60 ml)
2 tbsp orange rind, grated (30 ml)
¾ cup maple syrup (175 ml)
½ cup olive or canola oil (125 ml)
½ tsp sea salt (2 ml)
1½ cups dried blueberries (375 ml)

DIRECTIONS: 350°F (175°C) 30 MINUTES

In a large bowl, combine the oats, nuts and salt. Make a well in the center of the bowl and pour the vanilla, orange juice and rind, maple syrup and oil into the well. Stir the dry ingredients into the wet ones and mix until they are thoroughly combined. Spread half of the granola mixture onto an ungreased cookie sheet and place on the top rack of a preheated oven for 15 minutes. Remove the sheet from the oven and stir the granola around on the sheet. Place the cookie sheet back in the oven and bake for another 15 minutes. Remove from the oven and let cool. Bake the remaining half of the mixture in the same manner. When all of the granola has cooled, stir in the dried blueberries. You can store this granola in glass jars or canisters.

Makes 8-10 servings.

Amasake Pancakes

These incredible crepe-like pancakes were developed by my friend Geoff and are a legend unto themselves. Many of our guests enjoy these delicious, fluffy pancakes for their morning fare. For extra-fluffy pancakes, the batter is best prepared the night before. Amasake is a beverage made from rice and can be found in many health food stores and a growing number of grocery stores. There are many flavors available and any of them will work for this recipe.

DIRECTIONS:

Combine the ingredients in a large bowl, whisking them together thoroughly. Cover with a cloth and allow the batter to sit overnight, if possible.

To prepare the pancakes, heat a frying pan on medium-low, adding a small amount of oil to make sure the pan is seasoned. Scoop about ¹/₂ cup of batter into the center of the frying pan and gently tip the pan in a circular motion so that the batter spreads into a thin circle. Allow the pancake to cook on one side for several minutes until it begins to brown, then gently flip it over and cook the other side. Continue cooking the rest of the pancakes the same way. You should not have to add more oil between pancakes unless they really begin to stick. Serve them hot with your favorite toppings such as maple syrup, jams, fresh berries and sliced fruits or frozen sorbets. We often have a few frying pans going at one time for quicker production. You can also place the finished pancakes on a plate in the oven on low heat to keep them warm and then serve them together once the pancakes are all made.

Makes about 15 pancakes.

INGREDIENTS:

3 ½ cups amasake rice drink (875 ml)
*2 cups whole spelt flour or
wheat flour (500 ml)*
⅛ tsp fine sea salt (0.5 ml)

Fresh Lemon Mint Fruit Salad

In the height of the summer, there is nothing like the sweet and juicy combinations
of sun-ripened fruit in a lovely fruit salad for breakfast. Almost any combination
of fresh fruits will work with this recipe. Try whatever you have available
at the time. Apples, grapes, pears, blackberries, oranges, grapefruit, and raspberries
are delicious additions. Pomegranate seeds add a beautiful splash of color and
crunch while the fresh lemon and mint sprigs add an unforgettable zing!

INGREDIENTS:

2 apricots, cut into quarters (2)
1 peach, sliced (1)
1 nectarine, sliced (1)
1 banana, sliced (1)
1 cup strawberries, sliced (250 ml)
2 kiwis, peeled and sliced (2)
1 cup fresh blueberries (250 ml)
½ pomegranate, cut open and seeds
carefully removed (½)
2 tbsp lemon juice,
freshly squeezed (30 ml)
⅛ tsp stevia powder (0.5 ml)
3-4 sprigs fresh mint, finely diced (3-4)

DIRECTIONS:

Prepare the fruit and gently combine it in a large bowl. In a separate dish, dissolve the stevia in the lemon juice and stir in the mint. Pour this over the fruit and fold together gently so as not to bruise the fruit. Chill or serve immediately. Garnish with fresh sprigs of mint.

Serves 4-6.

Chai Jasmine Rice Pudding

Jasmine rice has a delightful scent when cooking and makes a wonderful rice pudding base. This combination of chai spices and orange rind makes for a fragrant treat that is fabulous as a dessert and doubles as a nutritious spin on breakfast cereal.

DIRECTIONS:

In a large pot, place 6 cups of soy milk, rice, orange rind, syrup, raisins, spices, vanilla and salt. Bring to a boil, then reduce heat to low and allow it to gently simmer for about one hour (or until the rice has sufficiently softened). Stir occasionally to keep the rice from sticking to the bottom of the pot. Remove from heat and stir in the remaining 2 cups of soy milk. Delicious when served warm. Garnish with grated orange rind and calendula or shungiku flowers.
Serves 6-8.

INGREDIENTS:

8 cups vanilla soy milk (2,000 ml)
1 cup white jasmine rice (250 ml)
1 tbsp orange rind (15 ml)
3 tbsp maple syrup (45 ml)
1 cup raisins (250 ml)
⅛ tsp each cinnamon, cardamom, cloves, allspice and nutmeg (0.5 ml)
2 tbsp vanilla extract (30 ml)
½ tsp sea salt (2 ml)

GARNISH: grated orange rind, calendula or shungiku flowers

131

Mom's Basic Dinner Rolls

*This recipe is adapted from one that my mother used to make
delicious dinner rolls for festive family occasions.*

2 tsp dry yeast (10 ml)

¼ cup warm water (60 ml)

1 cup soy milk, heated (250 ml)

¼ cup maple syrup (60 ml)

¼ cup olive oil or other natural oil (60 ml)

1 tsp sea salt (5 ml)

1 tsp vinegar (5 ml)

*3 ½ cups flour (I use whole spelt, but
most flours will work) (875 ml)*

DIRECTIONS: 400°F (200°C); 12-15 MINUTES

In a small bowl, combine yeast and water and set aside. In a separate large bowl, combine soy milk, maple syrup, oil, salt and vinegar. Mix 1½ cups flour into the soy milk mixture, stirring thoroughly. Add the yeast mixture, combining all ingredients together. Add the remaining 2 cups of flour, stirring to form a soft dough. Place the dough into an oiled bowl, making sure all of the dough is lightly oiled. Cover with a towel and let rise in a warm place until it doubles in size, about 1½-2 hours. Press down the dough and divide into halves. Roll out one half at a time on a floured board in a circular shape. With a knife, cut the dough into 12 even pie slices. Take each slice and roll it from the wide end towards the pointed end. Place the rolls on an oiled cookie sheet, curving them slightly into a crescent shape as you place them on the sheet. Repeat the process with the remaining half of the dough. Let the rolls rise until double in size, about 35-40 minutes. Place into a preheated oven and bake for 12-15 minutes. Makes 24 rolls.

Variation: Roll veggie dogs or slices of soy cheese into the centre of each roll for treats for children.

Easy Biscuits

*This is a quick and easy recipe. Whip up some warm biscuits to
serve with a hot bowl of soup or savory pâté. I got this recipe from
a friend years ago and it never fails. These biscuits are also fun to
make with children using cookie cutters for different shapes.*

DIRECTIONS: 400°F (200°C); 20 MINUTES

In a medium mixing bowl, stir together the flour, salt and baking powder. If you're using any of the optional ingredients, stir those in now as well. Add the oil to the flour mixture and thoroughly mix it in. Stir in the water until a dough is formed. Form the dough into a ball, then cut it in half. Roll one half of the dough out on a lightly floured surface with a rolling pin, to about 1/2 to 3/4 inch thickness. Using the rim of a glass or cup, press down on the dough to cut out round biscuit shapes. Place the biscuits on a lightly oiled baking sheet. Add the scraps of the dough back into the second ball of dough and continue with the same procedure, rolling out the dough and cutting shapes. Once the tray is full and all the dough has been used, place the baking pan in a preheated oven and bake for about 20 minutes. Remove from the oven and serve with warm bowls of soup or various dips and spreads.
Makes 20-25 biscuits.

INGREDIENTS:

*4 cups spelt flour (or try half spelt or
wheat flour with half barley, rice or
kamut flour) (1,000 ml)*

1 tsp sea salt (5 ml)

1 tbsp baking powder (15 ml)

½ cup olive oil or other natural oil (125 ml)

1½ cups water (375 ml)

*OPTIONAL (try adding one of
the following to alter the recipe):*

¼ diced onion (¼)

2 cloves garlic, minced (2)

1 tsp basil or oregano (5 ml)

2 tbsp sesame seeds (30 ml)

Basic Bread

*This is quite a simple recipe that makes either two loaves of bread or
three thin pizza crusts. There's just something about the smell of fresh bread
out of the oven that makes everyone want to stay for dinner.*

INGREDIENTS:

2 cups warm water (500 ml)
2 tbsp baking yeast (30 ml)
2 tbsp brown rice syrup (30 ml)
2 tbsp coarse sea salt (30 ml)
4 tbsp olive oil (60 ml)
4 cups whole spelt flour (1,000 ml)
2 cups light spelt flour (500 ml)

DIRECTIONS: 375°F (190°C); 50 MINUTES

Pour the warm water into a bowl and add the yeast. Stir in the brown rice syrup and set aside for 5 minutes. Add the oil and salt and stir together. Set aside.

In a large bowl, combine the flours together, creating a well in the center.

Pour the yeast mixture into the centre of the flour well and slowly stir together until a soft dough is formed. Use your hands to knead the dough for 5-10 minutes. Get your hands wet as necessary to keep the dough from sticking to your fingers. Make a round ball with the dough and place it back in the large bowl. Dribble some olive oil over it and rub it around to coat the ball of dough. Place a wet towel over the bowl and set it in a warm place to rise for about 2 hours. When the dough has risen, punch it down with your fists, then knead it again into a ball.

To make two loaves of bread, separate the dough into halves, then form them into logs the length of your bread pans. Using lightly oiled bread pans, place the logs of dough into each pan and gently press the dough down into the pan. Cover both pans with a towel and let rise in a warm place for another 1-2 hours. When the bread dough has risen just over the edges of the pan, place it in a preheated oven at 375°F and bake for 45-50 minutes. Check to make sure the tops of the loaves are golden brown. Remove from heat and set on a wire rack in the loaf pans until the bread has cooled. When cool, turn each pan upside down and gently shake the bread out. If it sticks a bit, you may need to run a knife around the edge of the pan to loosen it.

Pizza Dough

This is the same bread recipe that also makes three thin pizza crusts.

DIRECTIONS: 375°F (190°C); 30 MINUTES

To make 3 thin pizza crusts, follow the bread recipe directions on the previous page, but after the first rising, punch the dough down and separate it into three equal parts. Knead each part into a ball then place some flour on a flat surface and begin rolling one ball of dough with a rolling pin. You can make round or rectangular pizzas, depending on the shape of your baking trays. When you have rolled the dough to the thickness and size that you want, gently lift it onto a lightly oiled baking sheet. Place the sheet in a preheated oven. Bake the dough for about 3-4 minutes. Remove from heat and set aside on the baking sheet. Repeat the process with the remaining two pieces of dough. When the dough is all prebaked you can add you favorite toppings and then bake each pizza again for 20-25 minutes. The dough can also be frozen after it has been prebaked for the first time, and saved for another day.

INGREDIENTS:

2 cups warm water (500 ml)

2 tbsp baking yeast (30 ml)

2 tbsp brown rice syrup (30 ml)

2 tbsp coarse sea salt (30 ml)

4 tbsp olive oil (60 ml)

4 cups whole spelt flour (1,000 ml)

2 cups light spelt flour (500 ml)

April's 'Bread Wot is Amazing'

My friend April gave me this amazingly simple-to-create bread loaf recipe. It is a delicious yeast-free bread that uses up leftover rice. There are never any leftovers when I serve this unique bread, and many people ask for the recipe.

INGREDIENTS:

1 cup cornmeal (250 ml)

4 cups spelt flour (1,000 ml)

2 tbsp olive, corn, sesame or other natural oil (30 ml)

3-4 cups brown rice, cooked and cooled (750-1,000 ml)

1 ¼ tsp fine sea salt (6 ml)

1 ½ cups (or more) water (375 ml)

DIRECTIONS: 350°F (175°C) DO NOT PREHEAT OVEN; 60 MINUTES

In a large bowl, combine the cornmeal, flour and salt, and rub in the oil with your fingertips. Work the rice with your fingers until all of the grains are separated. Add enough water to make a dough that you can knead. You may need more water, depending on the wetness of the rice you use.

Shape the dough into 2 even, round loaves. Place the sesame seeds on a plate then roll each loaf in the sesame seeds until they are completely covered. Sprinkle some sesame seeds on a baking sheet, then place each loaf on the sheet. Put the baking sheet with both loaves in a cold oven, then turn the oven on to 350°F and bake for one hour. Remove from the oven and allow the loaves to cool. Use a long bread knife to cut thin slices of bread and serve with a soup.

Yields 2 round, hearty loaves.

Spelt Chapatis

*Chapatis are an East Indian flat bread. They are quite simple to
make and a delicious addition to a meal. I use white spelt flour for this
recipe, though a wheat pastry flour would work as well.*

DIRECTIONS:

Place the flour and salt in a large mixing bowl. Add the 5 tbsp of oil and mix it into the flour thoroughly. Begin stirring in the water, a few tablespoons at a time. When all of the water is added, use your hands to form the dough into a ball. The dough can be a bit tough at first, but continue to knead it for several minutes until it becomes more pliable. Form the dough into a round ball, then cut it into 8 equal portions.

Place a large cast-iron skillet on a burner on medium-low heat to begin warming the pan.

Take one of the portions of dough and form it into a small ball. Roll it around in the palms of your hands for a minute to get a round shape forming, then press the ball flat between your hands so it is pressed into the shape of a pancake. Place the dough on a floured surface and, using a rolling pin, roll the dough to about a thickness of ¼ inch. Try to keep the dough in a round shape, spinning it on the floured surface as you roll it. Add 1 tsp of olive oil to the preheated skillet, then place the rolled chapati into the skillet. Spin the chapati occasionally to allow it to cook thoroughly on the one side. After about 1-2 minutes it should start to turn a golden brown color (make sure the chapati does not burn). Flip it over and allow the second side to brown lightly for 1-2 minutes. While the first chapati is in the pan cooking, continue to roll out the remaining chapatis. Cook the chapatis in the pan one at a time. As each chapati is cooked, remove it from the pan and place it on a plate. Cover with a clean cloth to keep them warm. You should not need to add more oil between each chapati, but if you find they are sticking, you may add additional oil. Serve warm.
Makes 8 chapatis.

INGREDIENTS:

3 cups light spelt flour (750 ml)
1 tsp fine sea salt (5 ml)
5 tbsp olive oil (75 ml)
12 tbsp cold water (180 ml)
1 tsp olive oil for pan (5 ml)

Red Pepper Hemp Cornbread

Hemp seeds are a great source of vegetarian protein and Omega
fatty acids. They make a wonderful addition to this
cornbread recipe topped with a colorful garnish of red pepper.

INGREDIENTS

¾ cups corn flour (175 ml)
¾ cups hulled hemp seeds or
hemp meal (175 ml)
¾ cups whole spelt flour (175 ml)
1 tsp baking powder (5 ml)
½ tsp each baking soda and
fine sea salt (2 ml)
½ cup olive oil or other
natural oil (125 ml)
⅓ cup cane sugar (80 ml)
1 tbsp lemon juice, freshly squeezed (15 ml)
1 cup soy milk (250 ml)
1 tsp each dried oregano and basil (5 ml)
½ cup sweet red pepper, diced (125 ml)
½ cup corn kernels, fresh
or frozen (125 ml)

GARNISH: thin strips of red pepper (10)

DIRECTIONS: 350°F (175°C); 40-45 MINUTES

Lightly oil a pie plate and set aside.

In a medium mixing bowl, combine the corn flour, hemp meal, spelt flour, baking powder, baking soda, salt, basil and oregano. In a separate bowl, combine the oil, sugar, soy milk, lemon juice, diced red pepper and corn kernels, and whisk together until emulsified. Pour the wet ingredients into the dry ingredients and gently stir together, being careful not to overmix.

Pour the mixture into the oiled pie plate, then gently place the strips of red pepper on top of the dough in a circular pattern. Place the pan in a preheated oven and bake for 40-45 minutes or until the edges begin to lightly brown. Remove from oven and allow the cornbread to cool for 15-20 minutes in the pan. Slice the cornbread into pie wedges and serve.
Makes 1 pie-shaped loaf.

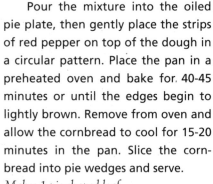

Spelt Cinnamon Buns

Everybody loves cinnamon buns! Use the recipe for Basic Bread (page 134)
or Pizza Dough (page 135) for the bun portion of this recipe.

DIRECTIONS: 350°F (175°C); 30 MINUTES

For the filling, combine the flour, maple syrup, oil and cinnamon together thoroughly. Remove ½ cup of this mixture and set aside; it will be used later as a topping for the cinnamon buns.

Prepare one recipe of Basic Bread Dough, following the recipe directions until the dough has risen once and you have punched it down with your fists.

From this point, knead the dough into a ball, then divide it into two even balls. Using one of the balls, roll out the dough on a lightly floured surface trying to keep it in the shape of a large square. The dough should be about ½ inch thick. Spread half of the filling evenly over the dough, then sprinkle on half of the raisins and walnuts. Starting at one edge, begin rolling the dough into a large tube shape. Slice the tube into 12 even rounds, and gently place each round flat on a prepared baking sheet. Repeat the process with the remaining ball of dough. When all of the buns are placed on the baking sheet, evenly spread the reserved ½ cup of filling on top of each bun. Set the baking sheet in a warm area to allow the dough to rise for an additional 30 minutes or until double in size.

When the dough has risen, place the buns in a preheated oven for about 30 minutes. Remove from the oven and serve warm.
Makes 24 rolls.

INGREDIENTS:

1 recipe Basic Bread (page 134) or
Pizza Dough (page 135) (1)

FILLING:
1 cup whole spelt flour (250 ml)
1 cup maple syrup (250 ml)
½ cup oil (125 ml)
1 tbsp cinnamon (15 ml)
1 cup raisins (250 ml)
1 cup walnuts, finely chopped (250 ml)

Vegetable Tofu Scramble

*My son loves having this vegan version of scrambled eggs
with vegetables for breakfast in the morning. Full of protein
and vitamins, it is a great way to start the day.*

INGREDIENTS:

2 tbsp olive oil (30 ml)
½ leek, diced (½)
½ tsp turmeric (2 ml)
2 cloves garlic, diced (2)
5 sprigs fresh basil, chopped (5)
½ medium tomato, diced (½)
*½ cup purple sprouting broccoli shoots
or regular broccoli florets chopped into
small pieces (125 ml)*
13 oz firm tofu (370 g)
½ cup arugula, chopped (125 ml)
4 button mushrooms (4)
½ sweet red pepper, diced (½)
2 tbsp tamari (30 ml)

DIRECTIONS:

In a large skillet, sauté the leek in the olive oil until lightly brown. Stir in the turmeric, garlic and basil. Add the tomatoes, broccoli and tofu and cook for several minutes more. Stir in the arugula, mushrooms, red pepper and tamari, and continue sautéing and stirring for several minutes. Remove from heat and serve hot.
Serves 2-4.

PART II

Dessert Island

Cakes

Mandarin Orange Spice Cake

Chocolate Lavender Cake

Chocolate Red Velvet Cake

Lemon Soy Yogurt Cake

Blueberry Lime Cake

Rose Petal Cake

Chocolate Almond Kahlua Cake

Hazelnut Pear Cake

Carrot Pineapple Cake

Not Quite Coffee Cake

Lemon Poppyseed Cake

Chocolate Jalapeño Cake

Mandarin Orange Spice Cake

This recipe was created after having several leftover Mandarin oranges during the holiday season. The spices enhance the orange, and the maple syrup creates an incredibly moist and delicious cake. Use regular navel oranges instead of Mandarins at any other time of the year. Top with Creamy Mandarin Orange Icing (page 158).

INGREDIENTS:

1¾ cups spelt flour (425 ml)

1 tsp baking soda (5 ml)

½ tsp fine sea salt (2 ml)

1 tsp cinnamon (5 ml)

⅛ tsp each nutmeg, cloves and allspice (0.5 ml)

⅔ cup maple syrup (160 ml)

4 tbsp canola oil or other natural oil (60 ml)

3 tbsp Mandarin orange juice, freshly squeezed (about 3 mandarins) (45 ml)

1 tbsp Mandarin orange rind, grated (15 ml)

1 tsp fresh gingerroot, grated (5 ml)

¾ cup rice milk or soy milk (175 ml)

1 recipe Creamy Mandarin Orange Icing (page 158) (1)

DIRECTIONS: 350°F (175°C); 35-40 MINUTES

In a large bowl, combine the flour, baking soda, salt, cinnamon, nutmeg, cloves and allspice. In a smaller bowl, combine the maple syrup, oil, orange juice, orange rind, ginger and soy milk, whisking together to emulsify the wet ingredients. Make a well in the center of the flour mixture and pour in the wet ingredients. Mix with a fork gently; do *not* beat. Pour into a lightly oiled and floured 8-x-8-inch cake pan, a Bundt pan, or an 8-inch springform pan. Bake 35-40 minutes. Check to see if cake is done by inserting a toothpick into the center of cake; it should come out clean. Let cool on a rack before removing from the pan. Decorate the cake with Creamy Mandarin Orange Icing and garnish with edible flowers such as tangerine gems or calendula.

Chocolate Lavender Cake

The flavors of lavender and chocolate seem to complement each other well.
This cake is a rich, sophisticated ending to a lovely evening dinner party.

DIRECTIONS: 350°F (175°C); 45-50 MINUTES

Combine the flour, cocoa powder, baking soda and salt in a large mixing bowl. In a separate bowl, combine the maple syrup, soy milk, oil, vinegar and vanilla and whisk until emulsified. Pour the wet ingredients into the dry and gently stir them together. Fold in the lavender flowers. Pour the batter evenly into 2 lightly oiled and floured 8-inch springform or other round cake pans. Place in the oven for 45-50 minutes. Test for doneness with a toothpick; it should come out clean when the cake is ready. Let cakes cool on racks before removing from the pans.

This cake goes nicely with Holy Chocolate Icing (page 158). Spread half of the icing on one of the cakes. Place the second cake on top of the first one and spread the remaining icing on top. Garnish with a few sprigs of lavender in the center and a sparse sprinkle of lavender flowers around the top edge of the cake.

INGREDIENTS:

3 cups whole spelt flour (750 ml)
6 tbsp cocoa powder (90 ml)
2 tsp baking soda (10 ml)
¾ tsp salt (3 ml)
1 ½ cup maple syrup (375 ml)
1 ½ cup vanilla soy milk (375 ml)
½ cup canola oil or other natural oil (125 ml)
2 tbsp apple cider vinegar (30 ml)
1 tbsp vanilla extract (15 ml)
4 tbsp dried lavender flowers (60 ml)

Chocolate Red Velvet Cake

This moist, rich, spongy cake is stunningly offset with
Creamy Fuschia Icing (page 159), and the novelty of beets and
chocolate together will surprise and delight any guest!

INGREDIENTS:

2 ½ cups sifted spelt pastry flour (625 ml)
½ tsp fine sea salt (2 ml)
4 tbsp cocoa powder (60 ml)
2 tsp baking soda (10 ml)
5 tbsp beet powder (75 ml)
1 ½ cups chopped, boiled beets (375 ml)
1 ½ cup water (use water from
boiling beets, if possible) (375 ml)
2 tsp vanilla extract (10 ml)
8 tbsp canola oil or other
natural oil (120 ml)
1 ½ cups maple syrup (375 ml)
2 tbsp apple cider vinegar (30 ml)

GARNISH: *cocoa powder, chocolate shavings*

DIRECTIONS: 350°F (175°C); 50 MINUTES

Boil beets in several cups of water for 10-15 minutes and let the water reduce down to about 1¹/2 cups. Keep this water for later.

In a large bowl, combine flour, salt, cocoa, baking soda and beet powder. In a medium bowl combine vanilla, oil, maple syrup and vinegar. Whisk vigorously until the ingredients are emulsified. Place beets and remaining 1¹/2 cups beet water in a blender and blend until smooth. Pour the beet mixture into the wet ingredients and combine thoroughly. Pour the wet mixture into the center of the dry ingredients and stir gently until thoroughly mixed. Pour mixture evenly into 2 oiled and floured 8-inch springform pans. Place pans in oven on middle rack and bake for about 50 minutes. Test to see if they are done by poking a toothpick into the center of each cake; it should come out clean. Let cakes cool in pans on a rack before removing from pans. Use icing as desired. Creamy Fuschia Icing goes particularly well with this cake, as the bright pink color contrasts with the dark color of the cakes. Garnish with chocolate shavings or sift cocoa powder lightly on top.

Lemon Soy Yogurt Cake

This tangy, moist cake is delicious with Lemon Almond Yogurt Topping (page 160) dripped over top and garnished with slivered almonds. Perfect for an afternoon treat with a cup of tea.

DIRECTIONS: 350°F (175°C); 45 MINUTES

Combine the flour, baking soda, baking powder and salt in a large mixing bowl. In a separate bowl, stir together the oil, maple syrup, soy yogurt, lemon juice and lemon rind. Pour the wet ingredients into the dry ingredients and gently stir them together. Fold in the almonds. Pour the batter into an oiled and floured 9-inch baking pan and place in a preheated oven for 45 minutes. Test doneness with a toothpick; it should come out clean when the cake is ready. Place the cake in the pan on a cooling rack until fully cooled. Remove from pan and place on a serving tray. Spread Lemon Almond Yogurt Icing over the top and let the icing drip down the sides of the cake. Sprinkle with chopped almonds and chill in the fridge until ready to serve.

INGREDIENTS:

1½ cups whole spelt flour (375 ml)
¾ tsp baking soda (3 ml)
1 tsp baking powder (5 ml)
¼ tsp salt (1 ml)
2 tbsp canola oil or other natural oil (30 ml)
¾ cup maple syrup (175 ml)
1½ cups plain soy yogurt (375 ml)
2 tbsp lemon juice, freshly squeezed (30 ml)
1 tbsp lemon rind (15 ml)
½ cup chopped almonds (125 ml)
1 recipe Lemon Almond Yogurt Icing (1)

GARNISH: ½ cup chopped almonds (60 ml)

Blueberry Lime Cake

*I have always loved the combination of blueberries and lime, and
this moist cake is a great way to unite those flavors. Top with Maple
Lime Glaze (page 161) or Blueberry Lime Sauce (page 164).*

INGREDIENTS:

3 cups whole spelt flour (750 ml)

3 tsp baking soda (15 ml)

½ tsp salt (2 ml)

*⅔ cup canola oil or other
natural oil (160 ml)*

4 tsp apple cider vinegar (20 ml)

1 tbsp vanilla extract (15 ml)

¾ cup vanilla soy milk (175 ml)

1 cup maple syrup (250 ml)

¼ cup lime juice, freshly squeezed (60 ml)

1 tbsp lime rind, grated (15 ml)

⅔ cup blueberries, fresh or frozen (160 ml)

1 recipe Maple Lime Glaze (page 161) (1)

*1 recipe Blueberry Lime Sauce
(page 164) (1)*

DIRECTIONS: 350°F (175°C); 35 MINUTES

In a large mixing bowl, combine flour, baking soda and salt. In a separate bowl, vigorously whisk together the oil, vinegar, vanilla, soy milk, syrup, lime juice and rind. Pour the wet mixture into the dry ingredients and gently combine them together, stirring just until the batter is fully mixed. Pour the batter evenly into 2 oiled and floured 8-inch springform pans. Using ⅓ cup of blueberries per cake, arrange them gently on the top of the batter in a decorative pattern. Place the pans in the preheated oven and bake for 35 minutes. Test doneness with a toothpick, poking it into the center of the cakes; the toothpick should come out clean when the cake is ready.

Tips for decorating Blueberry Lime Cakes (Layered or Single Cake):

For glazing the cakes, follow the Maple Lime Glaze recipe, then spoon the mixture over the tops of two cooled Blueberry Lime Cakes, spreading it carefully over the entire surface of each cake. Let the cakes chill. This glaze creates a beautiful shine.

For a double layer cake, the Blueberry Lime Sauce can be placed on one of the glazed Blueberry Lime Cakes, and the second glazed cake can be placed on top, creating a layered cake. Alternatively, each of the glazed Blueberry Lime Cakes can be served separately as a single layer cake, and the Blueberry Lime Sauce can be spooned onto each serving.

Rose Petal Cake

Have you ever smelled a rose and wanted to take a bite out of it? This gorgeous cake has the most beautiful, delicate flavor of roses and the deep red Rose Icing (page 160) is absolutely stunning. This makes a glorious presentation for Valentine's Day, especially if you have heart-shaped cake pans. You can find rose water in health food stores, herbal stores or Mediterranean specialty stores.

DIRECTIONS: 350°F (175°C); 35 MINUTES

Place rose petals in a small bowl and pour boiling water over them. Cover and let sit.

In a large mixing bowl, combine flour, baking soda, baking powder, and salt. In a separate bowl, combine soy milk, vanilla, lemon juice, maple syrup and rose water, and whisk until emulsified. Pour the wet mixture into the dry ingredients and gently stir them together. Fold in the roses and water. Pour the mixture evenly into 2 oiled and floured 8-inch springform pans. Bake in a preheated oven for 35 minutes. Remove from oven and allow cakes to cool in pans on top of cooling racks. Remove from pans when cool.

This cake is lovely with Rose Icing. Spread the icing on top of the first cake, then place the second cake layer on top. Spread the remaining icing on the top and sides of the cake. Garnish with dried rose florets in the center of the cake.

INGREDIENTS:

¾ cup dried rose petals, all stems removed (175 ml)

½ cup boiling water (125 ml)

1¾ cup whole spelt flour (425 ml)

½ tsp baking soda (2 ml)

1 tsp baking powder (5 ml)

½ tsp salt (2 ml)

½ cup canola oil or other natural oil (125 ml)

½ cup vanilla soy milk (125 ml)

1 tsp vanilla extract (5 ml)

1 tbsp lemon juice, freshly squeezed (15 ml)

⅔ cup maple syrup (160 ml)

2½ tbsp rose water (40 ml)

1 recipe of Rose Icing (1)

GARNISH: several dried rose florets

Chocolate Almond Kahlua Cake

Top this wonderful cake with Chocolate Almond Kahlua Icing (page 161).
Chocolate and coffee make a wonderful marriage. Need I say more?

INGREDIENTS:

2 cups whole wheat or
spelt flour (500 ml)
½ tsp sea salt (2 ml)
3 tbsp cocoa powder (50 ml)
1 tsp baking soda (5 ml)
1 cup maple syrup (250 ml)
1 tsp vanilla extract (5 ml)
1 tbsp apple cider vinegar (15 ml)
5 tbsp canola oil or other
natural oil (75 ml)
¾ cup rice milk or soy milk (175 ml)
1 tsp almond extract (5 ml)
¼ cup Kahlua (coffee liqueur) (60 ml)
1 recipe Chocolate Almond
Kahlua Icing (page 161) (1)

DIRECTIONS: 350°F (175°C); 35 MINUTES

In a large, bowl mix the flour, salt, cocoa and baking soda, then set aside. In a smaller bowl, combine the maple syrup, vanilla, vinegar, oil, soy milk, almond extract and Kahlua, stirring vigorously until emulsified. Make a well in the center of the dry ingredients and pour in the wet ingredients. Mix thoroughly, but do not overmix.

Pour into an oiled and floured 8-x-8-inch baking pan. Bake for 35-40 minutes. Insert toothpick into center of cake to see if it is finished baking; the toothpick should come out clean. Let cake cool on rack before removing from pan. Top with Chocolate Almond Kahlua Icing.

Hazelnut Pear Cake

*This sweet, moist cake has a lovely hazelnut topping. I like to make
this cake in the fall when pears are ripe and at their peak.*

DIRECTIONS: 350°F (175°C); 40-45 MINUTES

Combine the flour, salt, baking soda and nutmeg in a medium bowl. In a large bowl, thoroughly combine the oil, grated pear, soy milk, lemon juice and maple syrup. Pour the wet ingredients into the dry ingredients and mix together with a fork gently; do not beat. Pour the batter into an oiled and floured 8-inch springform pan.

Sprinkle the topping evenly over the cake batter and then arrange the pear slices around the edge of the cake in a circle. Bake in a preheated oven for 40-45 minutes. Test with a toothpick; the toothpick should come out clean if the cake is done. Let cool slightly on a rack then remove springform pan rim and serve.

INGREDIENTS

1¾ cup whole spelt flour (425 ml)

½ tsp sea salt (2 ml)

1 tsp baking soda (5 ml)

½ tsp nutmeg, freshly ground (2 ml)

4 tbsp canola oil or other
natural oil (60 ml)

1 cup pear, sliced into quarters,
cored and grated) (250 ml)

⅔ cup vanilla soy milk (160 ml)

2 tbsp lemon juice, freshly squeezed (30 ml)

¾ cup maple syrup (175 ml)

TOPPING:

¼ cup hazelnuts, finely ground (60 ml)

¼ cup organic sugar cane (60 ml)

⅛ tsp nutmeg, freshly ground (0.5 ml)

GARNISH: ½ pear, pealed and sliced
into thin wedges

Carrot Pineapple Cake

This recipe makes two small round cakes, in 8-inch or less springform pans.
If you use 8-inch springform pans the cakes will be fairly thin.
The coconut and pineapple add a refreshing tropical taste to this cake.
This cake goes well with Cashew Cream (page 163).

INGREDIENTS:

½ cup canola oil or other natural oil (125 ml)

1 cup maple syrup (250 ml)

2 tsp apple cider vinegar (10 ml)

¼ cup vanilla soy milk (60 ml)

1 tsp vanilla extract (5 ml)

1 cup carrot, grated (250 ml)

1½ cup chopped pineapple, canned (425g can) or fresh (375 ml)

½ cup dried coconut flakes (125 ml)

1½ cup light spelt flour (375 ml)

½ tsp fine sea salt (2 ml)

1 tsp cinnamon (5 ml)

1 tsp baking powder (5 ml)

½ cup walnuts (optional) (125 ml)

1 recipe Cashew Cream (page 163) (1)

GARNISH: ½ cup coconut flakes, walnuts and/or pineapple

DIRECTIONS: 350°F (175°C); 40 MINUTES

In a medium size bowl, combine first five ingredients until mixed together. Add grated carrots, pineapple and coconut and stir until thoroughly combined.

In a large bowl combine flour, salt, cinnamon, baking powder and walnuts, if using. Make a well in the center of these dry ingredients and then pour the wet ingredients into the well and stir gently until all of the ingredients are combined thoroughly. Scoop the mixture into 2 small oiled and floured springform pans. Place in a preheated oven and bake for 40 minutes. Poke a toothpick or skewer into the center of the cakes to make sure they are done; the skewer should come out clean.

Let the cakes cool on a rack in the pans before removing. Sometimes these cakes stick a little because of the pineapples. I usually remove the sides of the pan and then slide a knife under the cake first to separate it from the bottom of the springform pan before flipping it onto a plate. The beauty of springform pans is that the bottom tray can be used as a serving plate if desired.

Once the cakes are thoroughly cooled, spread Cashew Cream onto the bottom layer of the cake, then add the top layer, and continue to spread the remaining cream over the tops and sides. Garnish the top of the cake with coconut flakes and chopped walnuts or pineapple chunks. If you have made one square cake, simply spread the icing on top after the cake has thoroughly cooled, then sprinkle the coconut, walnuts and pineapple on top.

Not Quite Coffee Cake

A slightly adapted version from a recipe given to me by a friend years ago, this is a simple cake that is well received on a sunny afternoon with a cup of tea or a scoop of vanilla soy or rice frozen dessert.

DIRECTIONS: 375°F (190°C); 40 MINUTES

For the topping, combine the flour, spices and sugar in a medium bowl. Add the oil and crumble the mixture together with your fingers until all of the ingredients are thoroughly combined. Set this mixture aside.

For the cake, combine the flour, spices, salt, coffee substitute and baking powder in a large mixing bowl. In a separate bowl, combine the syrup, soy milk, vanilla and oil, and stir these together rapidly. Pour the wet ingredients into the dry ones and stir the batter together gently. Pour mixture into an oiled and floured 8-inch springform pan or an 8-x-8-inch cake pan. Sprinkle the topping evenly over the cake batter in the pan. Place the pan in a preheated oven and bake for about 40 minutes. Use a toothpick to test for doneness; it should come out clean when the cake is ready.

INGREDIENTS:

CAKE:

2½ cups whole spelt flour (625 ml)
1 tsp each cinnamon and nutmeg (5 ml)
½ tsp each allspice and cloves (2 ml)
¼ tsp salt (2 ml)
4 tbsp powdered coffee substitute (60 ml)
1 tsp baking powder (5 ml)
1 tsp baking soda (5 ml)
¾ cup maple syrup (175 ml)
¾ cup vanilla soy milk (175 ml)
2 tsp vanilla extract (10 ml)
½ cup canola oil or other natural oil (125 ml)
1 tsp apple cider vinegar (5 ml)

TOPPING:

½ cup whole spelt flour (125 ml)
¼ tsp each cinnamon and nutmeg (1 ml)
⅛ tsp each allspice and cloves (0.5 ml)
¼ cup organic sugar (60 ml)
2 tbsp canola oil or other natural oil (30 ml)

153

Lemon Poppyseed Cake

This moist, tangy cake is delightful with the subtle crunch from the poppyseeds.
Spread Lemon Icing (page 164) over the cooled cakes for a delectable dessert.

INGREDIENTS:

4 tsp lemon rind (20 ml)
¼ cup lemon juice, freshly squeezed (60 ml)
1¼ cups soy milk or rice milk (310 ml)
3 cups whole spelt flour (750 ml)
2 tsp baking soda (10 ml)
¾ tsp fine sea salt 3 ml
⅔ cup canola oil or other natural oil (160 ml)
2 tbsp poppy seeds (30 ml)
1½ cups maple syrup (375 ml)
½ tsp vanilla extract (2 ml)
1 recipe Lemon Icing (page 164) (1)

DIRECTIONS: 350°F (175°C); 30-35 MINUTES

In a small bowl, combine lemon rind, lemon juice and soy milk, then set aside.

In a large mixing bowl, combine the flour, baking soda and salt. Set aside.

In a separate mixing bowl, combine the oil, poppyseeds, maple syrup and vanilla. Stir in the soy milk and lemon mixture. Pour the wet ingredients into the flour mixture and stir together until a smooth consistency is achieved. Pour the batter evenly into 2 oiled and floured 9-inch round cake pans. Place in a preheated oven and bake for 30-35 minutes. Use a toothpick to test the doneness by poking a small hole into the center of the cakes. The toothpick should come out clean when the cakes are done. Allow the cakes to cool on a rack before removing them from the pans.

Chocolate Jalapeño Cake

The combination of spicy jalapeños and dark chocolate yields a wonderful culinary surprise. This rich, moist cake is sublime when topped with Holy Chocolate Icing (page 158).

DIRECTIONS: 350°F (175°C); 45 MINUTES

Melt the chocolate in a double boiler on medium heat, then set aside.

In a large bowl, combine the flour, salt, baking soda, baking powder, cocoa powder and cinnamon. Set aside. In a second large bowl, combine the oil, jalapeños, syrup, soy milk, vanilla and vinegar. Stir or whisk together vigorously until emulsified. Stir in the melted chocolate, again mixing vigorously. Pour the wet ingredients into the dry ingredients and combine thoroughly. Pour the batter into a lightly oiled 8-x-8-inch cake pan. Place in a preheated oven and bake for about 45 minutes. Check to see if the cake is done by poking a toothpick in the centre of the cake. The toothpick should come out clean.

INGREDIENTS:

½ cup vegan dark chocolate, chips or chunks (125 ml)

2 cup whole spelt flour (500 ml)

½ tsp fine sea salt (2 ml)

1 tsp baking soda (5 ml)

1 tsp baking powder (5 ml)

3 tbsp cocoa powder (45 ml)

½ tsp cinnamon (2 ml)

½ cup canola oil or other natural oil (125 ml)

3 jalapeños, seeds removed and diced (3)

¾ cup maple syrup (175 ml)

1 cup vanilla soy milk (250 ml)

1 tbsp vanilla extract (15 ml)

1 tsp apple cider vinegar (5 ml)

1 recipe Holy Chocolate Icing (page 158) (1)

Icings and Glazes

Creamy Mandarin Orange Icing

Holy Chocolate Icing

Chocolate Frosting

Creamy Fuschia Icing

Lemon Almond Yogurt Icing

Rose Icing

Chocolate Almond Kahlua Icing

Maple Lime Glaze

Cherry Glaze

Lavender Lemon Glaze

Cashew Cream

Coffee Glaze

Blueberry Lime Sauce

Lemon Icing

Creamy Mandarin Orange Icing

*This icing is particularly rich and creamy and should satisfy any
non-vegan icing fiend, as it closely resembles traditional creamy,
buttery icings. The orange flavor adds a nice touch. It can
be used to decorate Mandarin Orange Spice Cake (page 144).*

INGREDIENTS:

½ cup soy margarine (125 ml)
¼ cup maple syrup (60 ml)
¾ cup organic powdered sugar (175 ml)
¼ cup cashew butter (60 ml)
1 tbsp Mandarin orange rind (15 ml)

DIRECTIONS:

Blend all ingredients in a food processor on high for several minutes until very creamy and thoroughly combined. Chill icing for 1-2 hours. Spread onto thoroughly cooled cake and decorate with grated orange rind and calendula flowers. Keep cake chilled until serving.

Variation: Add ½-1 tsp each of beet powder and turmeric to dye the icing an orange color. Add a small portion of each at a time as you blend the icing, until you reach a desired color.

Holy Chocolate Icing

*Unlike the Chocolate Frosting (page 159), which thickens to a
spreadable consistency for decorating a cake, this satiny icing is poured
warm over top of a cake or brownies in a pan and then left to set.*

INGREDIENTS:

*1 cup vegan dark chocolate,
chips or chunks (250 ml)*
⅓ cup soy margarine (80 ml)

DIRECTIONS:

In a double boiler, place the chocolate and margarine and heat on medium until both melt completely. Stir the mixture thoroughly, then remove from heat and pour over a cooled cake or brownies that are still in their baking pan. Place the pan in the fridge until the icing sets.

Chocolate Frosting

*This frosting is akin to a ganache. You can add slightly
more soy milk to reach your desired consistency.*

DIRECTIONS:

Melt the chocolate in a double boiler. Add the margarine and stir until melted. Pour in the soy milk and whisk until thoroughly incorporated. Remove from heat and pour into a bowl. Chill in the fridge until thickened, or place in the freezer if you are in a hurry. Vigorously stir the icing just before spreading it on the cake to be sure it is a creamy texture. If you wish to ice the sides of the cake as well, then double the recipe.

INGREDIENTS:

*¾ cup vegan dark chocolate,
chips or chunks (175 ml)*

½ cup soy margarine (125 ml)

½ cup vanilla soy milk (125 ml)

Creamy Fuschia Icing

*The color of this icing is absolutely incredible, as the beet powder
transforms it into a brilliant shade of fuschia. Experiment with the quantity of
beet powder used to create the color you desire. Wonderful for a Valentine's
cake and scrumptious on Chocolate Red Velvet Cake (page 146).*

DIRECTIONS:

Blend all ingredients in a food processor on high for several minutes until very creamy and thoroughly combined. Chill icing for 1-2 hours. Spread onto thoroughly cooled cake. Keep cake chilled until ready to serve. This recipe makes enough to ice two round cakes, with icing on the top of the cake and between the layers. I like to leave the sides of the cake without icing, but if you prefer to cover the whole cake, make 1½ times the recipe.

INGREDIENTS:

¾ cup soy margarine (175 ml)

⅓ cup maple syrup (80 ml)

2 tsp vanilla extract (10 ml)

1 cup organic powdered sugar (250 ml)

⅓ cup cashew butter (80 ml)

2 tsp beet powder (10 ml)

Lemon Almond Yogurt Topping

*This topping is wonderful over Lemon Soy Yogurt Cake (page 147),
or can be added on top of granola and fresh fruit.*

INGREDIENTS:

1 cup plain soy yogurt (250 ml)
2 tbsp lemon juice, freshly squeezed (30 ml)
⅛ tsp stevia powder (0.5 ml)
½ cup almond butter, smooth (125 ml)
1 tbsp arrowroot powder (15 ml)

DIRECTIONS:

Place the soy yogurt, lemon juice, and stevia into a food processor and blend briefly. Add the almond butter and arrowroot powder and blend again until all ingredients are thoroughly combined. Pour into a bowl and chill for a couple of hours to thicken. Spread over cake and serve.

Rose Icing

*The rose water makes this aromatic icing the perfect
complement to Rose Petal Cake (page 149).*

INGREDIENTS:

1 cup cashew butter (250 ml)
½ cup soy margarine (125 ml)
1 tsp vanilla extract (5 ml)
4 tsp beet powder (20 ml)
½ cup maple syrup (125 ml)
1 tbsp rose water (15 ml)

DIRECTIONS:

Blend all ingredients for several minutes on high in a food processor, scraping down the sides with a spatula as needed. Process on high until a creamy consistency is reached. Chill for about 1 hour before spreading over cakes.

Chocolate Almond Kahlua Icing

This incredibly decadent icing richly complements the
Chocolate Almond Kahlua Cake (page 150).

DIRECTIONS:

Melt chocolate in a double boiler, taking care that no water gets into the chocolate. Place almond butter in a separate bowl. Pour melted chocolate into almond butter and mix thoroughly until creamy. Add Kahlua and continue to mix thoroughly. The icing should thicken up quickly. Spread over top of cooled chocolate cake and sprinkle with finely chopped almonds.

INGREDIENTS:

1 cup smooth almond butter (250 ml)
1 cup vegan dark chocolate,
chunks or chips (250 ml)
2 tbsp Kahlua (30 ml)
2 tbsp almonds, finely chopped (30 ml)

Maple Lime Glaze

This tangy glaze complements the Blueberry Lime Cake (page 148).

DIRECTIONS:

In a small saucepan, combine the lime juice and maple syrup. Bring this to a low simmer. In a small bowl, combine the water and agar agar, stirring until the powder is dissolved. Pour the water mixture into the simmering lime mixture and stir the ingredients together thoroughly. Remove from heat and spoon the mixture over the tops of two Blueberry Lime Cakes, carefully spreading it evenly around to cover the entire surface of each cake. Let the cakes chill. This glaze gives cakes a beautiful shine.

INGREDIENTS:

2 tbsp lime juice, freshly squeezed (30 ml)
4 tbsp maple syrup (60 ml)
3 tbsp water (45 ml)
½ tsp agar agar powder (2 ml)

Cherry Glaze

*This simple glaze with a base of black cherry juice is a lovely
complement to frozen desserts, such as sorbets or vanilla soy ice cream.
You can try pouring it over fresh fruit salads as well.*

INGREDIENTS:

1 cup black cherry juice (250 ml)

1 tbsp cornstarch (15 ml)

½ cup maple syrup (125 ml)

¼ tsp almond extract (1 ml)

1 tbsp olive oil or other natural oil (15 ml)

DIRECTIONS:

In a small saucepan, combine juice, syrup and cornstarch until the cornstarch is dissolved. Turn on heat and bring to a simmer, whisking in the almond extract and oil until the ingredients are emulsified and thickened. Serve warm over frozen dessert.

Lavender Lemon Glaze

*This zesty glaze provides an attractive topping for
Lavender Lemon Cheesecake (page 174).*

INGREDIENTS:

3 tbsp lemon juice, freshly squeezed (45 ml)

1 tsp lemon rind, grated (5 ml)

½ tbsp lavender flowers, dried (7 ml)

1 tbsp maple syrup (15 ml)

1 tbsp water (15 ml)

¼ tsp agar agar powder (1 ml)

DIRECTIONS:

Place all ingredients in a small pot and whisk together. Bring the mixture to a low boil while whisking, then remove from heat. Spoon the glaze evenly over the prepared Lavender Lemon Cheesecake and place in the refrigerator to chill until the glaze is set.

Cashew Cream

*This creamy topping is delicious on top of fruit
or granola, or as a dollop on top of pies.*

DIRECTIONS:

Place the cashews and water in a bowl and let sit overnight. In the morning, strain the cashews, reserving the liquid. Place the cashews in a food processor with the vanilla and brown rice syrup and blend on high for several minutes until light and creamy. Add some of the reserved water to the food processor and blend again to reach a desired consistency.

INGREDIENTS:

1 ½ cups cashews, raw (375 ml)
1 ½ cups water (375 ml)
2 tbsp brown rice syrup (30 ml)
1 tsp vanilla (5 ml)

Coffee Glaze

*This glaze gives a wonderful shine as a topping
to Coffee Cheesecake (page 177).*

DIRECTIONS:

Place all ingredients in a small saucepan and stir until the powders have dissolved. Bring to a boil and then reduce to a simmer for a couple of minutes while stirring. Remove from heat and pour the glaze over a cooled Coffee Cheesecake. Garnish the cake with pecans and chill until the glaze sets.

INGREDIENTS:

1 ½ tbsp maple syrup (20 ml)
¼ cup water (60 ml)
1 tbsp coffee substitute or instant coffee powder (15 ml)
¼ tsp agar agar powder (1 ml)

Blueberry Lime Sauce

*Blueberries and limes are a zesty and refreshing combination, and this
sauce complements the Blueberry Lime Cake (page 148), as a sauce
in between two layers, or as a dollop on a serving from a single layer cake.*

INGREDIENTS:

2 cups blueberries, fresh or frozen (500 ml)
2 tbsp lime juice, freshly squeezed (30 ml)
2 tbsp maple syrup (30 ml)

DIRECTIONS:

Place the blueberries in a medium saucepan over medium heat, stirring them until they begin to break down. Add the lime juice and maple syrup, stirring thoroughly. Remove from heat.

Place the mixture into a blender and whiz on high for several minutes until the mixture is smooth. Pour into a bowl and chill the mixture for about an hour before using.

Lemon Icing

*This creamy icing is the perfect topping for the
moist Lemon Poppyseed Cake (page 154).*

INGREDIENTS:

1 cup soy margarine (250 ml)
3 cups organic powdered sugar (750 ml)
2 tbsp lemon juice, freshly squeezed (30 ml)
1 tbsp lemon rind (15 ml)

DIRECTIONS:

Place all ingredients in a food processor and blend on high for several minutes until a creamy consistency is achieved. Transfer the icing to a bowl and chill for 1-2 hours before icing the thoroughly cooled cakes.

Pies and "Cheesecakes"

Simple Strawberry Pie

Cherry Pie

Creamy Chocolate Pecan Pie

Almond Tofu Cheesecake

Banana Maple Whisky Pie

Lemon Maple Blueberry Pie

Raspberry Blueberry Amasake Pie

Cognac Cherry Cheesecake

Lavender Lemon Cheesecake

Butternut Brandy Pie

Brandied Peach Streusel Pie

Coffee Cheesecake

Creamy Peach Cardamom Pie

Leah's Blueberry Lavender Tarts

Simple Strawberry Pie

This is a wonderfully refreshing summer pie, and so guilt-free when sweetened with stevia! Try adding Cashew Cream (page 163) on top.

INGREDIENTS:

1 prebaked pie crust, 9-inch (1)

3 cups strawberries, whole and raw (750 ml)

4 cups strawberries, cooked and mashed (1,000 ml)

2 tbsp arrowroot (30 ml)

½ tsp agar agar powder (2 ml)

½ tsp stevia powder (2 ml)

1 cup water (250 ml)

GARNISH: strawberries, sliced and splayed

DIRECTIONS:

Place 3 cups of whole, uncooked strawberries into a cooled, prebaked pie crust, pointy ends up. In a medium saucepan, place 4 cups of strawberries and bring to a simmer. Mash the berries as they soften. In a small bowl, combine water, arrowroot powder, agar agar and stevia powders, and whisk so that all dry ingredients are dissolved in the water. Pour this mixture into mashed strawberries and bring to a boil, stirring and mashing ingredients together as it thickens to create a sauce. Pour this sauce over the strawberries in the pie crust and place in the refrigerator until set, approximately 2-3 hours. Garnish with a sliced and splayed strawberry in the center of the pie.

Cherry Pie

*There's just something about cherries in this simple
pie that is truly mouth-watering! Taking the time to
pit the fresh cherries is well worth the effort.*

DIRECTIONS:

Place the whole pitted cherries in a large cooking pot. Simmer on low heat for 10-15 minutes until juices emerge. Add stevia powder and whisk into the cherries.

In a separate small bowl or cup, combine soy milk, arrowroot powder and agar agar powder, making sure the powders are thoroughly dissolved. Pour this mixture into the simmering cherries and whisk quickly for a few minutes until the cherry juice thickens a little. Remove from heat and pour into prebaked and cooled pie crust. Place the pie in the refrigerator to chill until set.

INGREDIENTS:

1 prebaked pie crust, 9-inch (1)

4½-5½ cups cherries, fresh or frozen and pitted (1,125-1,375 ml)

½ tsp stevia powder (2 ml)

3 tbsp vanilla soy milk or rice milk (45 ml)

1 tbsp arrowroot powder (15 ml)

1 tsp agar agar powder (5 ml)

Creamy Chocolate Pecan Pie

This is a truly rich and scrumptious pie. The creamy texture is mouth watering and is particularly enhanced by a dollop of frozen vanilla rice or soy dessert.

INGREDIENTS:

1 unbaked pie crust, 8-inch (1)

1 cup vegan dark chocolate, chunks or chips (250 ml)

¼ cup soy margarine (60 ml)

2½ cups pecans (625 ml)

⅛ tsp fine sea salt (0.5 ml)

1 cup brown rice syrup (250 ml)

½ cup vanilla soy milk (125 ml)

¼ tsp cinnamon (1 ml)

1 tsp vanilla extract (5 ml)

1 tsp agar agar powder (5 ml)

GARNISH: *pecans, whole and/or chopped, chocolate shavings*

DIRECTIONS: 350°F (175°C); 25-30 MINUTES

Prepare one 8-inch unbaked pie crust, such as the Buckwheat Hazelnut Crust (page 184).

In a small double boiler, combine chocolate and soy margarine. Cook on element until ingredients are melted and thoroughly combined. (If you do not have a double boiler, place a small pot inside a larger pot that has some water in it and bring water to a boil. Be sure that none of the water can get into the smaller pot where the ingredients are).

In a food processor, combine pecans and salt and blend until pecans are fairly well ground. Add the brown rice syrup and continue to blend with the pecans. This mixture will get quite thick. In a small bowl, combine the soy milk, agar agar powder, cinnamon and vanilla and stir until the agar agar powder is dissolved. Add this to the pecan mixture and blend thoroughly. Pour the chocolate mixture from the double boiler into the food processor

continued on next page

and once again, blend all ingredients together.

Scoop this mixture into an unbaked pie crust. Place the pie in the oven for 15 minutes. Remove the pie from the oven and decorate the top with a few pecans as you like. Put the pie back into the oven and cook for an additional 10-15 minutes. Let the pie cool and thoroughly chill it for several hours before serving.

Almond Tofu Cheesecake

*This creamy tofu cheesecake is full of wonderful almond flavor.
Try it with the Almond Oat Crust (page 183).*

DIRECTIONS: 350°F (175°C); 60 MINUTES

Place all ingredients in a food processor and blend on high for several minutes until a creamy, smooth consistency is reached. Scrape the sides of the food processor down as necessary to make sure all of the ingredients are incorporated. Pour the mixture into an unbaked, prepared pie crust. Sprinkle the chopped almonds on top. Place the pie in the preheated oven and bake for about one hour. Remove from oven and let cool on a rack for 10-15 minutes, then place in the refrigerator to chill for several hours until firmly set. Serve chilled.

INGREDIENTS:

1 unbaked pie crust, 8- or 9-inch (1)
13 oz package firm tofu (370g)
¾ cup smooth almond butter (175 ml)
1 tsp vanilla extract (5 ml)
⅔-¾ cup brown rice syrup (depending on your sweet tooth) (150-175 ml)
1 tsp almond extract (5 ml)

GARNISH: 1 tbsp almonds, finely chopped (15 ml)

Banana Maple Whisky Pie

*This creamy banana pie is fabulous with the combinations of
maple syrup and whisky. There is never a piece left in the pan!
Try an Almond Oat Crust (page 183) for this pie.*

INGREDIENTS:

1 prebaked pie crust, 8- or 9-inch (1)
1 cup vanilla soy milk (250 ml)
⅔ cup maple syrup (160 ml)
1 cup vanilla soy milk (250 ml)
⅛ tsp fine sea salt (0.5 ml)
1 tsp vanilla (5 ml)
2 tsp agar agar powder (10 ml)
1 tbsp cornstarch (15 ml)
2 tbsp whisky or rum (optional) (30 ml)
4 bananas, sliced (4)

DIRECTIONS:

In a saucepan, mix 1 cup of soy milk and maple syrup. Bring to a boil while stirring. In a bowl, mix the next six ingredients thoroughly, making sure the agar agar powder is dissolved. Pour the ingredients from the bowl into the saucepan and continue stirring until thickened. Remove from heat.

Place sliced bananas into prebaked pie crust. Pour saucepan mixture over bananas until pie crust is full. Chill until set.

Lemon Maple Blueberry Pie

*This pie is particularly delightful in the summer when
fresh plump blueberries are in season. The lemon
and maple flavors add a summery freshness to this pie.*

DIRECTIONS:

Prepare prebaked pie crust. Try Almond Oat Crust (page 183).

Rinse blueberries and set aside. If using frozen blueberries, set them aside in a bowl to thaw out as you prepare the rest of the pie.

In a small saucepan, combine 1 cup of soy milk and maple syrup. Bring to a boil and reduce to low simmer, stirring occasionally. In a separate small bowl or cup, combine remaining 1/2 cup soy milk, lemon juice, salt, agar agar powder, cornstarch and lemon rind. Mix together thoroughly to ensure that powders are dissolved. Pour this mixture into the pot with the soy milk and maple syrup and whisk all ingredients together for several minutes as it begins to thicken. Remove from heat. Place blueberries into prebaked and cooled pie crust, then pour the hot mixture over the blueberries until the pie is full. Place the pie in the refrigerator until it sets. Garnish with borage flowers and/or grated lemon rind.

INGREDIENTS:

1 prebaked pie crust, 8- or 9-inch (1)

3 cups blueberries, fresh or frozen (750 ml)

1 cup vanilla soy milk (250 ml)

2/3 cup maple syrup (160 ml)

1/2 cup vanilla soy milk (125 ml)

1/8 tsp fine sea salt (0.5 ml)

1/3 cup lemon juice, freshly squeezed (80 ml)

1 tsp agar agar powder (5 ml)

2 tsp cornstarch (10 ml)

1 tsp lemon rind (5 ml)

GARNISH: several borage flowers and/or grated lemon rind

Raspberry Blueberry Amasake Pie

This pie is very simple to make and the raspberries combined with the blueberries provide both an extraordinary color and flavor combination. The stevia and amasake help to sweeten the fruit, but allow the subtle tartness of the berries to come through. Try it in the Almond Oat Crust (page 183) or the Pumpkin Seed Rice Flour Crust (page 182). A lovely summer pie for a picnic!

INGREDIENTS:

1 prebaked pie crust, 9-inch (1)

3 cups raspberries, frozen or fresh (750 ml)

3 cups blueberries, frozen or fresh (750 ml)

½ tsp stevia powder (2 ml)

1 cup hazelnut amasake (or soy milk if you cannot find amasake) (250 ml)

1 tbsp arrowroot powder (15 ml)

1 tsp agar agar powder (5 ml)

GARNISH: raspberries, blueberries and/or borage flowers

DIRECTIONS:

Place raspberries and blueberries in a large saucepan and simmer until raspberries begin to break down. In a small bowl, place amasake, stevia, arrowroot powder and agar agar powder. Thoroughly mix these together, making sure the powders dissolve. Pour this mixture into the simmering pot of berries and whisk all ingredients together for a few minutes. Remove from heat and pour mixture into cooled prebaked pie crust. Decorate top of pie with fresh raspberries, blueberries and borage flowers. Chill until set.

Cognac Cherry Cheesecake

This vegan cherry cheesecake made with tofu has a wonderfully subtle hint of cognac, and complements a gracious summer evening meal when the cherries are in their peak season. Almond Oat Crust (page 183) is delicious with this recipe.

DIRECTIONS:

Prepare the pie crust of choice. Do not bake, but set aside in pie plate.

In a food processor, place the first five ingredients and blend on high for several minutes until a creamy and smooth texture is achieved. Scrape down the sides of the food processor with a spatula as needed. Pour the mixture into the unbaked pie crust (the pie should only be about half full) and place it in a preheated oven for 45-55 minutes. The filling will turn a light golden color at the edges when ready. Remove from the oven and let the pie cool on a wire rack. When cooled, place pie in refrigerator to chill until filling is set.

Meanwhile, place cherries in a large saucepan and bring to a low simmer. Stir the cherries as necessary at the beginning so that they do not stick to the bottom of the pan. As they cook, the cherries will release their juices, preventing them from sticking. Pour out about ⅓ cup of the cherry juice from the pot into a small bowl and set aside to cool. Once the cherries have softened (approximately 10-15 minutes), mash them in the pot with a masher so that they break down a bit, but not so much as to turn it into a puree. Continue to simmer the cherries. Once the reserved cherry juice has cooled, add the stevia and agar agar powders and mix thoroughly in the juice until the powders are dissolved. Pour this juice into the pot of cherries and stir while simmering. Remove pot from heat. Pour the cherries over the chilled pie and filling. Place in the refrigerator again and chill until the cherries have set, approximately 2-3 hours. Garnish with several borage flowers. Serve chilled.

INGREDIENTS:

1 unbaked pie crust, 8- or 9-inch (1)

10 oz (or 1-1½ cups) firm tofu (300 g)

1 tsp vanilla extract (5 ml)

½-⅔ cup brown rice syrup (125-150 ml)

3 tbsp cognac (45 ml)

1½ tbsp lemon juice, freshly squeezed (20 ml)

2½ cups cherries, fresh or frozen, pitted (625 ml)

¼ tsp stevia powder (1 ml)

¼ tsp agar agar powder (1 ml)

GARNISH: *Borage flowers*

Lavender Lemon Cheesecake

*The use of turmeric in this recipe creates a lovely yellow color
that is accentuated by the purple lavender flowers in the
cheesecake. Try it with Almond Lavender Crust (page 187).*

INGREDIENTS:

1 unbaked pie crust, 8- or 9-inch (1)

3 cups firm tofu (750 ml)

1 cup maple syrup (250 ml)

⅓ cup brown rice syrup (80 ml)

1½ tsp turmeric (7 ml)

1 tbsp lemon rind (15 ml)

*4 tbsp lemon juice,
freshly squeezed (60 ml)*

*1 recipe Lavender Lemon
Glaze (page 162) (1)*

DIRECTIONS: 350°F (175°C); 1 HOUR

Place all of the ingredients in a food processor and blend on high for several minutes until they reach a smooth consistency. Pour the mixture on top of the unbaked pie crust in a spring-form pan. Gently give the pan a shake to let the mixture settle into the pan. Place the pan into a preheated oven and bake for about one hour. Remove from the oven and let the cake thoroughly cool.

When the cake is cool, prepare one recipe of Lavender Lemon Glaze and spoon the glaze evenly over the top of the cake. Place the cheesecake into the refrigerator and chill thoroughly before serving.

Butternut Brandy Pie

*Spicy pies made from fresh winter squash have always been one of my
favorites and typify a classic autumn harvest dessert. Even those
who think they don't like traditional pumpkin pie often love this rendition.*

DIRECTIONS: 350°F (175°C) 30-35 MINUTES

Peel squash, remove seeds and chop into small pieces. Steam or boil the squash until soft. Drain any liquid from the squash. Place the steamed squash into a blender with the remaining ingredients and blend for several minutes until a smooth consistency is achieved. You may need to scrape down the sides of the blender occasionally. Pour the mixture into a prepared, unbaked pie crust and give the pie plate a gentle shake to settle the pie filling. Place the pie in a preheated oven and bake for 15 minutes. Rotate the pie 180 degrees and bake for an additional 15-20 minutes. The sides of the crust should brown lightly. Remove pie from the oven and let cool, then place in a refrigerator and chill for several hours until set.

INGREDIENTS:

1 unbaked pie crust, 8 or 9 inch (1)

*5 cups cubed butternut squash (most
any winter squash will do) (1,250 ml)*

½ tbsp fresh gingerroot, grated (10 ml)

¾ cup brown rice syrup (175 ml)

½ tsp cinnamon (2 ml)

*¼ tsp each powdered cloves
and nutmeg (1 ml)*

1 tbsp vanilla extract (15 ml)

3 tbsp brandy (45 ml)

½ tsp agar agar powder (2 ml)

Brandied Peach Streusel Pie

*Fresh summer peaches are packed with flavor and make this pie
a wonderful and elegant finale to a meal. For a scrumptious touch,
serve warm with a dollop of frozen vanilla soy dessert!*

INGREDIENTS:

1 unbaked pie crust, 9-inch (1)

FILLING:

10 ripe peaches, peeled, pitted
and sliced into wedges (10)

4 tbsp maple syrup (60 ml)

4 tbsp cognac (60 ml)

¼ tsp nutmeg (1 ml)

2 tsp arrowroot powder (10 ml)

¼ tsp agar agar powder (1 ml)

⅛ tsp salt (0.5 ml)

1 tbsp canola oil or other natural oil (15 ml)

TOPPING:

½ cup whole spelt flour (125 ml)

½ cup almonds, ground (125 ml)

½ cup large rolled oats,
coarsely ground (125 ml)

⅛ tsp each cinnamon,
nutmeg and cloves (0.5 ml)

pinch sea salt

3 tbsp canola oil or other natural oil (45 ml)

3 tbsp maple syrup (45 ml)

½ tsp vanilla extract (2 ml)

DIRECTIONS: 325°F (160°C); 25 MINUTES

For the filling, place all of the ingredients into a large saucepan and stir together gently to dissolve the powders. Bring to a boil and then simmer for about 5 minutes. Pour the peaches into the prepared, unbaked pie crust and set aside.

For the topping, combine the flour, almonds, oats, salt and spices in a medium bowl. Make a well in the center of the bowl and combine the oil, syrup and vanilla in the well. Next, stir the dry ingredients into the wet ones until thoroughly combined. Sprinkle the topping evenly over the peach filling. Place the pie in a preheated oven and bake for 25 minutes. Remove from the oven and allow the pie to cool on a wire rack.

Coffee Cheesecake

This smooth, rich dessert will satisfy the coffee lover. It is equally delicious made from coffee substitute, for those who do not wish to have the added caffeine. Pecan Barley Coffee Crust (page 192) is perfect for this cheesecake. Top it with Coffee Glaze (page 163).

DIRECTIONS: 350°F (175°C); 45-50 MINUTES

Place tofu, vanilla, cashew butter, syrup, coffee and salt in a food processor and blend on high for several minutes until a creamy consistency is achieved. Pour the mixture onto the prepared, unbaked Pecan Barley Coffee Crust. Gently give the pan a shake to settle the mixture evenly. Place the pan in a preheated oven and bake for 45-50 minutes. Gently remove the pan from the oven and place on a wire rack to cool. When cooled, prepare one recipe of Coffee Glaze and then pour it evenly over the cake and sprinkle the top with chopped pecans for garnish.

INGREDIENTS:

1 unbaked pie crust, 8-inch (1)
14 oz (about 1 block) firm tofu (400 g)
1 tbsp vanilla extract (15 ml)
½ cup cashew butter (125 ml)
1 cup brown rice syrup (250 ml)
4 tbsp coffee substitute or instant coffee powder (60 ml)
Pinch of salt
1 recipe Coffee Glaze (1)

GARNISH: *several coarsely chopped pecans*

Creamy Peach Cardamom Pie

*Cardamom and peaches are a delightful flavor combination and
they make this pie a refreshing, light summer dessert when peaches are ripe.
Pumpkin Seed Rice Flour Crust (page 182) lends a wonderful texture
to this pie, though any number of crusts would work well.*

INGREDIENTS:

1 prebaked pie crust, 9-inch (1)
10 peaches, pitted, peeled and sliced (10)
⅛ tsp cardamom (0.5 ml)
1 cup soft dessert tofu (220 g)
⅓ cup maple syrup (80 ml)
½ tsp agar agar powder (2 ml)
⅛ tsp stevia powder (0.5 ml)
1 tsp vanilla extract (5 ml)
Pinch of salt

DIRECTIONS:

Prepare peaches by slicing them, peeling the skins, and removing the pits. Place the prepared peaches into a medium saucepan with the cardamom and bring to a low simmer. Stir as necessary so they do not stick to the bottom of the pan.

While the peaches are simmering, place the remaining ingredients in a food processor and process on high for several minutes until a smooth texture is reached. Pour this mixture into the pan with the peaches and bring to a simmer, stirring. Gently pour the contents into a cooled, prebaked pie crust. Be careful not to pour too quickly or the mixture may splash over the sides of the pie. Chill the pie in the refrigerator until set.

Leah's Blueberry Lavender Tarts

*My friend Leah, who had the brilliant idea to combine lavender and
blueberries in these delicious tarts, can take credit for this recipe.
Use the Flaky Pastry (page 193) as the base and form into tart shells.*

DIRECTIONS:

In a large saucepan, begin cooking the
blueberries on medium heat. As the
juice from the berries is released, whisk
in the remaining ingredients. Continue
to stir as the berry mixture thickens,
then remove from heat and allow the
mixture to cool for 10-15 minutes.
Scoop the filling into the prepared tart
shells, then chill to allow the berry filling to set, about 20-30 minutes.
Makes 20-25 tarts.

INGREDIENTS:

*1 recipe Flaky Pastry (page 193), made
into prebaked tart shells (1)*
*5 cups blueberries, fresh
or frozen (1,250 ml)*
1 tbsp lavender flowers, dried (15 ml)
¼ tsp stevia powder (1 ml)
1 tbsp arrowroot powder (15 ml)
½ tsp agar agar powder (2 ml)

Pie Crusts

Pumpkin Seed Rice Flour Crust

Almond Oat Crust

Buckwheat Hazelnut Crust

Barley Coconut Crust

Cocoa Walnut Crust

Almond Lavender Crust

Ginger Bread Crust

Toasted Walnut Date Crust

Toasted Pecan Apricot Crust

Pumpkin Seed Fig Crust

Pecan Barley Coffee Crust

Flaky Pastry

Pumpkin Seed Rice Flour Crust

The texture of this crust is absolutely wonderful! It also provides a tasty gluten-free crust alternative. It goes particularly well with Butternut Brandy Pie (page 175) and Raspberry Blueberry Amasake Pie (page 172), but could accompany any other pie recipe as well.

INGREDIENTS:

1 ¼ cups brown rice flour (310 ml)

1 ¼ cups pumpkin seeds, finely ground (310 ml)

⅛ tsp fine sea salt (0.5 ml)

2 tbsp brown rice syrup (30 ml)

6-8 tbsp canola oil or other natural oil (90-120 ml)

DIRECTIONS: 325°F (160°C); 30 MINUTES

Mix the brown rice flour, ground pumpkin seeds and salt into a large bowl. Make a well in the center of the ingredients. In the well, put brown rice syrup and oil, combining these two ingredients together first. Then slowly incorporate the dry ingredients into the wet until all are thoroughly mixed together. The brown rice syrup can be very sticky, so this may take a few minutes. When this is done, grab a handful of the mixture in your hand and squeeze it together; the dough should be sticky enough to hold its form, but still be fairly crumbly. If it does not loosely hold its shape, continue to add another tablespoon or two of oil as needed until you reach the proper consistency. Press dough into an oiled 8-inch or 9-inch pie plate.

For recipes that call for a pre-baked pie crust, place the pie plate with dough into a preheated oven for 15 minutes. Rotate the pie plate a half turn and bake for another 15 minutes. The edges will be golden when finished. Be careful not to overbake!

Almond Oat Crust

This crust is one of my favorites and can be used for almost any pie recipe. The almond and oat flavors are wonderful together, and provide a delicious option for wheat-free pie crust. It's only ever had rave reviews.

DIRECTIONS: 325°F (160°C); 30 MINUTES

Mix almonds, oats and salt in a large bowl. Make a well in the center of the ingredients. In the well, put the brown rice syrup and oil, combining these two ingredients together first. Then slowly incorporate the dry ingredients into the wet until all are thoroughly mixed together. The brown rice syrup can be very sticky, so it may take a few minutes to work all of the ingredients together. When this is done, grab a handful of the mixture in your hand and squeeze it together; the dough should be sticky enough to hold its form, but still fairly crumbly. If it does not loosely hold its shape, continue to add another tablespoon or two of oil as needed until you reach the proper consistency. Press dough into an oiled 8-inch or 9-inch pie plate.

For recipes that call for a pre-baked pie crust, place the pie plate with dough into a preheated oven for 15 minutes. Rotate the pie plate a half turn then place back in oven for another 15 minutes. The edges will be golden when finished. Be careful not to overbake!

INGREDIENTS:

2 cups almonds, finely ground (500 ml)

1 cup oats, finely ground, or oat flour (250 ml)

⅛ tsp fine sea salt (0.5 ml)

2 tbsp brown rice syrup (30 ml)

4-6 tbsp canola oil or other natural oil (60-90 ml)

Buckwheat Hazelnut Crust

This crust has a rich taste from the stronger flavors of both the buckwheat and the hazelnuts. This is another excellent gluten-free pie crust that augments any number of pie recipes.

INGREDIENTS:

1¼ cups hazelnuts, finely ground (310 ml)

1¼ cups buckwheat groats, finely ground, or buckwheat flour (310 ml)

⅛ tsp fine sea salt (0.5 ml)

6-8 tbsp canola oil or other natural oil (90-120 ml)

2 tbsp brown rice syrup (30 ml)

DIRECTIONS: 325°F (160°C); 30 MINUTES

Mix buckwheat flour, ground hazelnuts and salt into a large bowl. Make a well in the center of the ingredients. In the well, put brown rice syrup and oil, combining these two ingredients together first. Slowly incorporate the dry ingredients into the wet until all are thoroughly mixed together. The brown rice syrup can be very sticky, so it may take a few minutes to work all of the ingredients together. When this is done, grab a handful of the mixture in your hand and squeeze it together; the dough should be sticky enough to hold its form, but still fairly crumbly. If it does not loosely hold its shape, continue to add another tablespoon or two of oil as needed until you reach the proper consistency. Press dough into an oiled 8-inch or 9-inch pie plate.

For recipes that call for a pre-baked pie crust, place the pie plate with dough into a preheated oven for 15 minutes. Rotate the pie plate a half turn, then bake for an additional 15 minutes. The edges will be golden when finished. Be careful not to overbake!

Barley Coconut Crust

*Barley flour makes a wonderful crust, and the
coconut adds a unique twist to the pastry.*

Directions: 325°F (160°C); 30 minutes

Mix flour, coconut and salt in a large bowl. Make a well in the center of the ingredients. In the well, put brown rice syrup and oil, combining these two ingredients together first. Slowly incorporate the dry ingredients into the wet until all are thoroughly mixed together. The brown rice syrup can be very sticky, so it may take a few minutes to work all of the ingredients together. When this is done, grab a handful of the mixture in your hand and squeeze it together; the dough should be sticky enough to hold its form, but still fairly crumbly. If it does not loosely hold its shape, continue to add another tablespoon or two of oil as needed until you reach the proper consistency. Press dough into an oiled 8-inch or 9-inch pie plate.

For recipes that call for a pre-baked pie crust, place the pie plate with dough into a preheated oven for 15 minutes. Rotate the pie plate a half turn then place back in oven for another 15 minutes. The edges will be golden when finished. Be careful not to overbake!

Ingredients:

1 ½ cups barley flour (375 ml)
1 ½ cups medium coconut, dried (375 ml)
¼ tsp salt (1 ml)
2 tbsp brown rice syrup (30 ml)
*2-4 tbsp canola oil or other
natural oil (30-60 ml)*

185

Cocoa Walnut Crust

*This crust goes well with chocolate pies of any sort and
the walnuts add texture and a rich flavor.*

INGREDIENTS:

*1¼ cups flour (spelt, barley,
brown rice, etc.) (310 ml)*
¾ cup walnuts, ground (175 ml)
¼ cup cocoa powder (60 ml)
¼ tsp salt (1 ml)
2 tbsp brown rice syrup (30 ml)
*2-5 tbsp canola oil or other
natural oil (30-75 ml)*

DIRECTIONS: 325°F (160°C); 30 MINUTES

Mix flour, walnuts, cocoa and salt in a large bowl. Make a well in the center of the ingredients. In the well, put brown rice syrup and oil, combining these two ingredients together first. Then slowly incorporate the dry ingredients into the wet until all are thoroughly mixed together. The brown rice syrup can be very sticky, so it may take a few minutes to work all of the ingredients together. When this is done, grab a handful of the mixture in your hand and squeeze it together; the dough should be sticky enough to hold its form, but still fairly crumbly. If it does not loosely hold its shape, continue to add another tablespoon or two of oil as needed until you reach the proper consistency. Press dough into an oiled 8-inch or 9-inch pie plate.

For recipes that call for a pre-baked pie crust, place the pie plate with dough into a preheated oven for 15 minutes. Rotate the pie plate a half turn then place back in oven for another 15 minutes. The edges will be golden when finished. Be careful not to overbake!

Almond Lavender Crust

*This crust was created for Lavender Lemon Cheesecake (page 174),
but adds a subtle lavender flavor to fruit pies as well.*

DIRECTIONS: 325°F (160°C); 30 MINUTES.

Mix the flour, ground almonds and salt into a large bowl. Make a well in the center of the ingredients. In the well, put maple syrup, lavender flowers, and oil, combining these three ingredients together in the centre. Slowly incorporate the dry ingredients into the wet until all are thoroughly mixed together. When this is done, grab a handful of the mixture in your hand and squeeze it together; the dough should be sticky enough to hold its form, but still fairly crumbly. If it does not loosely hold its shape, continue to add another tablespoon or two of oil as needed until you reach the proper consistency. Press dough into an oiled 8-inch or 9-inch pie plate.

For recipes that call for a pre-baked pie crust, place the pie plate with dough into a preheated oven for 15 minutes. Rotate the pie plate a half turn and bake for another 15 minutes. The edges will be golden when finished. Be careful not to overbake!

INGREDIENTS:

1½ cups almonds, finely ground (375 ml)
1 cup brown rice flour (250 ml)
¼ tsp sea salt (1 ml)
½ tbsp dried lavender flowers (7 ml)
*6 tbsp canola oil or other
natural oil (90 ml)*
2 tbsp maple syrup (30 ml)

Ginger Bread Crust

This crust is a wonderful, spicy addition to Butternut Brandy Pie (page 175).

INGREDIENTS:

2 cups whole spelt flour (500 ml)
¼ tsp sea salt (1 ml)
⅛ tsp cinnamon (0.5 ml)
1 tbsp fresh gingerroot, grated (15 ml)
1 tbsp molasses (15 ml)
1 tbsp maple syrup (15 ml)
6-8 tbsp canola oil or other natural oil (90-120 ml)

DIRECTIONS: 325°F (160°C); 30 MINUTES

Mix the flour, cinnamon and salt in a large bowl. Make a well in the center of the ingredients. In the well, put molasses, maple syrup, ginger and oil, combining these ingredients together first in the center. Slowly incorporate the dry ingredients into the wet until all are thoroughly mixed together. The sweeteners can be very sticky, so it may take a few minutes to work all of the ingredients together. When this is done, grab a handful of the mixture in your hand and squeeze it together; the dough should be sticky enough to hold its form, but still fairly crumbly. If it does not loosely hold its shape, continue to add another tablespoon or two of oil as needed until you reach the proper consistency. Press dough into an oiled 8-inch or 9-inch pie plate.

For recipes that call for a pre-baked pie crust, place the pie plate with dough into a preheated oven for 15 minutes. Rotate the pie plate a half turn then place back in oven for another 15 minutes. The edges will be golden when finished. Be careful not to overbake!

Toasted Walnut Date Crust

This superb no-bake crust is ideal for those without
an oven, or for those summer days when you'd
really like a pie, but feel too hot to fire up the oven.

DIRECTIONS:

Toast the walnuts in a skillet for several minutes on medium high heat, stirring frequently until the edges begin to brown. Remove from heat. Place the walnuts and the remaining ingredients in a food processor and blend until the mixture reaches a coarse, mealy texture. Scoop the mixture into an 8-inch ungreased pie pan and press it down with your fingers so that it covers the surface and sides of the pie pan evenly.

Any pie filling that does not need to be baked can be used in this pie crust. You can keep the crust chilled until you are ready to use it.

INGREDIENTS:

1½ cups walnuts (375 ml)
1 cup fresh dates, pitted (250 ml)
1 tsp vanilla (5 ml)
¼ tsp sea salt (1 ml)

Toasted Pecan Apricot Crust

This is a delicious gluten-free, no-bake pie crust that goes particularly well with fruit pies. Great for those with no oven or no time!

Ingredients:

1 ½ cups pecans (375 ml)
1 cup dried, unsulphured apricots (250 ml)
1 tsp vanilla (5 ml)
¼ tsp sea salt (1 ml)

Directions:

Toast the pecans in a skillet for several minutes on medium high heat, stirring frequently until the edges begin to brown. Remove from heat. Place the pecans and the remaining ingredients in a food processor and blend until the mixture reaches a coarse, mealy texture. Scoop the mixture into an 8-inch ungreased pie pan and press it down with your fingers so that it covers the surface and sides of the pie pan evenly.

Any pie filling that does not need to be baked can be used in this pie crust. You can keep the crust chilled until you are ready to use it.

Pumpkin Seed Fig Crust

This wonderful no-bake crust is ideal for anyone eating a raw food diet, or for those who do not have access to an oven but are craving a pie!

DIRECTIONS:

Toast the pumpkin seeds in a skillet for several minutes on medium high heat, stirring frequently until the edges begin to brown. Remove from heat. Place the pumpkin seeds and the remaining ingredients in a food processor and blend until the mixture reaches a coarse, mealy texture. Scoop the mixture into an 8-inch ungreased pie pan and press it down with your fingers so that it covers the surface and sides of the pie pan evenly.

Any pie filling that does not need to be baked can be used in this pie crust. You can keep the crust chilled until you are ready to use it.

INGREDIENTS:

1½ cups pumpkin seeds, hulled (375 ml)
1 cup Calimyrna figs (250 ml)
1 tsp vanilla extract (5 ml)
¼ tsp sea salt (1 ml)

Pecan Barley Coffee Crust

This tasty crust is a great complement to Coffee Cheesecake (page 177).

Ingredients:

⅔ cup pecans, ground (160 ml)

¾ cup barley flour (175 ml)

¼ tsp sea salt (1 ml)

2 tbsp coffee substitute or
instant coffee (30 ml)

2 tbsp brown rice syrup (30 ml)

4 tbsp canola oil or other
natural oil (60 ml)

Directions: 325°F (160°C); 30 minutes

Mix the flour, ground pecans, coffee and salt into a large bowl. Make a well in the center of the ingredients. In the well, put syrup and oil, combining these two ingredients together in the center. Slowly incorporate the dry ingredients into the wet until all are thoroughly mixed together. When this is done, grab a handful of the mixture in your hand and squeeze it together; the dough should be sticky enough to hold its form, but still fairly crumbly. If it will not loosely hold its shape, continue to add another tablespoon or two of oil as needed until you reach the proper consistency. Press dough into an oiled 9-inch springform pan or pie plate, depending on which pie you are creating.

For recipes that call for a pre-baked pie crust, place the pie plate with dough into a preheated oven at 325° for 15 minutes. Rotate the pie plate a half turn and bake for another 15 minutes. The edges will be golden when finished. Be careful not to over-bake! Cool on rack.

Flaky Pastry

The use of coconut oil for this pastry was a trick I learned from my friend Leah. It makes an incredible flaky vegan pastry, delicious for both sweet and savory recipes.

DIRECTIONS: 325°F (160°C); 15-25 MINUTES

In a large mixing bowl, combine the flour and salt. Cut the coconut oil into the flour mixture with a pastry cutter or mash with a masher or fork. Use coconut butter that is at room temperature for ease of mixing. Once most of the coconut butter is cut into the flour, use your fingers to break up any remaining bits. Stir in the ice water one tablespoon at a time. Use your hands to form a ball of dough.

For Pie Crusts: Press the dough into an oiled pie plate. For prebaked pie crusts, place the crust in a preheated oven and bake for about 25-30 minutes. The edges should be a golden brown.

For Tart Shells: Take small handfuls of dough, about the size of a golf-ball, and shape them into small tart shapes. Place the tarts on an oiled baking sheet. For recipes that call for prebaked tart shells, place them in a preheated oven and bake for about 20-25 minutes. The edges should be a golden brown. Let the pastries cool before adding the filling. Makes about 20-25 small tart shells.

For Shortcakes: Divide the dough into two balls. Roll out one ball at a time on a floured surface with a rolling pin to about 1/2 inch thick. Use a round cookie cutter or the rim of a glass to cut out circular shortcakes. Set each of the shortcakes on a greased baking sheet, place them in a preheated oven and bake for about 15 minutes. Remove from oven and transfer the shortcakes to a wire rack for cooling before assembling.

For a half recipe (if only making one single bottom pie crust): Use 1 1/2 cups (375 ml) white spelt flour, 1/4 tsp (1 ml) fine sea salt, 1/3 cup (80 ml) coconut butter, and 5 tbsp (75 ml) ice water. Follow the directions above and roll out dough or press dough into a greased pie pan.

INGREDIENTS:

3 cups white spelt flour (750 ml)
1/2 tsp fine sea salt (2 ml)
3/4 cup coconut oil (175 ml)
10-15 tbsp ice water (150-225 ml)

Apricot Crème Pudding

Triple Chocolate Kahlua Velvet Pudding
and Variations: Mint Chocolate, Almond Chocolate
and Orange Chocolate

Almond Amasake

Butternut Spice Bread Pudding

Cardamom Pear Pudding

Simple Apple Apricot Delight

Geoffs Peach Pear Gel

Raspberry Mousse

Apricot Crème Pudding

This pudding is sweet and delicious and full of apricot flavor!

INGREDIENTS:

1 cup dried apricots (250 ml)
1½ cups apple juice (375 ml)
3 cups vanilla soy milk (750 ml)
4 tbsp tapioca starch (60 ml)
2½-3 tsp agar agar powder (10-15 ml)

DIRECTIONS:

In a medium bowl, soak the dried apricots in apple juice for several hours or overnight. Place in a pot and bring to boil. Turn down to simmer and whisk the apricots; after awhile they will begin to break down as they absorb the liquid. Once most of the liquid has been absorbed and evaporated, mix soy milk with tapioca starch and the agar agar powder in a small bowl and stir until the starch is dissolved. Pour this liquid into the pot with the apricot mixture and continue to whisk for several minutes while simmering as the liquid thickens. Whisk vigorously to break down the apricots as much as possible. Remove from heat and pour mixture into a food processor. Whiz on high for several minutes until the pudding is creamy and smooth. Pour into six small dessert dishes and garnish with long, thin slivers of dried apricot in the center of the bowl. Chill until set. Delicious served warm or chilled. *Serves 6.*

Triple Chocolate Kahlua Velvet Pudding

This pudding is truly out of this world, and the combination of chocolate and Kahlua in a rich, creamy, satin texture is sublime.

DIRECTIONS:

Melt chocolate chunks in a double boiler, being sure to simmer the water and not boil it. Set aside.

In a medium saucepan, whisk 1²/3 cup soy milk with the brown rice syrup and bring to a simmer. In a separate bowl, combine the remaining 1 cup of soy milk, agar agar, salt, Kahlua, cocoa powder and cornstarch. Whisk until the agar agar, cocoa and cornstarch are dissolved. Pour this mixture into the saucepan and whisk all of these ingredients together while simmering. The mixture will thicken somewhat. Remove from heat and pour in the remaining melted chocolate. Whisk mixture together thoroughly and then pour into a large bowl and place in the refrigerator to chill and thoroughly set until firm, usually at least a few hours. When the pudding is firm, transfer it into a food processor and blend on high for several minutes until the pudding is a smooth and creamy consistency. Scoop into serving bowls and garnish with thin shavings of chocolate. Makes about four small but sinful servings.

Variations:

Mint Chocolate Velvet Pudding: Omit Kahlua and replace with 1/2 tsp (2 ml) peppermint extract. Garnish with mint leaves.

continued on next page

INGREDIENTS:

1²/3 cup chocolate soy milk (400 ml)

²/3 cup brown rice syrup (160 ml)

1 cup chocolate soy milk (250 ml)

2 tsp agar agar powder (10 ml)

1/8 tsp fine sea salt (0.5 ml)

3 tbsp Kahlua (optional) (45 ml)

2 tbsp cocoa powder (30 ml)

3 tsp cornstarch (15 ml)

1/3 cup vegan dark chocolate, chunks or chips (80 ml)

GARNISH: chocolate shavings

Almond Chocolate Velvet Pudding:
Omit Kahlua and replace with ½ tsp
(2 ml) almond extract. Garnish with
slivered almonds.

Orange Chocolate Velvet Pudding:
Omit Kahlua and replace with the
juice and grated rind of 1 orange.

Almond Amasake Bread Pudding

*This creamy bread pudding has a rich almond flavor and is best served
warm out of the oven. It can be created as a gluten-free dessert if the
bread you use is gluten free. It's also a great way to use up old, stale bread.*

INGREDIENTS:

5 cups cubed, dried bread (1,250 ml)
4 cups almond amasake (1,000 ml)
2 tsp almond extract (10 ml)
1 tbsp arrowroot powder (15 ml)
Pinch of salt
1 cup vanilla soy milk or rice milk (250 ml)
½ cup almonds, chopped (125 ml)
½ cup almonds, ground (125 ml)

DIRECTIONS: 350°F (175°C); 1 HOUR

Place dried bread cubes in a large casserole or baking dish. In a medium-size mixing bowl, combine amasake, almond extract, salt and arrowroot powder, stirring thoroughly to dissolve the arrowroot powder. Pour this mixture over the bread and let sit for 2-3 hours.

After the bread has absorbed most of the amasake mixture, add the soy milk and chopped almonds and stir. Sprinkle the ground almonds on top and place the dish into a preheated oven and bake for about 1 hour. Remove from the oven and serve warm. This bread pudding is very satisfying with a dollop of vanilla soy or rice dessert.

Serves 6-8.

Butternut Spice Bread Pudding

Bread puddings are a great way to use up bread that is on the verge of becoming stale. Chop up the bread that you are unable to use and leave it out in open air to harden. You can save these dried cubes of bread until you have enough for a recipe. Just make sure they remain in the open air so they do not mould.

DIRECTIONS: 350°F (175°C); 60 MINUTES

Place stale bread into large casserole baking dish and set aside.

Remove the seeds, stem and skin from the butternut squash and cut the flesh into small cubes. Place the cubes into a medium saucepan with about an inch of water. Boil until soft. Drain the liquid from the squash. Place the squash in a blender with the soy milk, vanilla, spices, cornstarch and syrup. Blend together until a smooth consistency is achieved. Pour the mixture over the bread in the casserole dish and let it sit for about an hour. After an hour, if the bread has absorbed all of the liquid, pour a little more soy milk on top and gently stir it in. Just before placing the casserole dish in the preheated oven, sprinkle the top with the pecans. Bake for about one hour.

Serves 6-8.

INGREDIENTS:

*5 cups cubed, stale bread (about
1-inch pieces) (1,250 ml)*

1½ cups butternut squash (375 ml)

3½ cups vanilla soy milk (875 ml)

1 tsp vanilla extract (5 ml)

1½ tsp ground cinnamon (7 ml)

1 tbsp fresh gingerroot, grated (5 ml)

*½ tsp each allspice, cloves
and nutmeg (2 ml)*

1 tbsp cornstarch (15 ml)

⅔ cup maple syrup (160 ml)

⅔ cup pecans, finely chopped (160 ml)

Cardamom Pear Pudding

*This creamy, light pudding is a wonderful finalé to a meal. It is very
quick and easy to make, and always pleases the guests. This is a wonderful
recipe for using ripe pears that are bountiful in the fall.*

INGREDIENTS:

4 medium pears, ripe (4)

1½ cup vanilla soy milk (375 ml)

2 tsp vanilla extract (10 ml)

½ cup maple syrup (125 ml)

*2½ tbsp whole or sifted spelt flour (or any
other flour works well also) (40 ml)*

2 tsp arrowroot powder (10 ml)

⅛ tsp cardamom, ground (0.5 ml)

DIRECTIONS:

Peel, core, and slice the pears into thin, bite-size pieces. Place them in a medium saucepan and sauté on medium heat, stirring the pears so that they do not stick to the pan. Be sure to use ripe pears, as they will help provide enough juice to keep the pears from sticking. Add the ground cardamom and continue to stir.

In a separate bowl, place the remaining ingredients and whisk them together thoroughly. Pour this mixture into the saucepan with the pears and whisk together. Bring the mixture to a boil, then reduce to a simmer and continue whisking for about 5 minutes. Remove from heat and pour the mixture evenly into 4 small dessert serving bowls. Chill the pudding for a couple of hours until set.

Serves 4.

Simple Apple Apricot Delight

*This simple dessert is naturally sweetened by the fruit and has a
wonderful flavor from the apple and apricot combination. It is a light,
elegant dessert that can be easily prepared for guests when time
is running short. Try serving it with a splash of soy milk over top.*

DIRECTIONS:

Peel and core the apples, then slice them into thin bite-size pieces. Dice up the dried apricots. Place the apples and apricots into a medium saucepan and heat on medium, stirring the fruit so that it does not stick to the pan. As the fruit begins to soften, add the soy milk and continue to stir until the apricots have begun to dissolve and the apples have softened. If there is not enough liquid, add a bit more soy milk to reach your desired texture. Serve this dessert warm in individual dessert bowls with a splash of soy milk on top.

Serves 4-6.

INGREDIENTS:

5 apples (5)
6 dried apricots (6)
¼ cup vanilla soy milk or rice milk (60 ml)

Geoff's Peach Pear Gel

*This is a wonderful, light dessert for a summer evening, and it is
very simple to prepare. For a festive splash, add a dollop of vanilla frozen
rice dessert or fruit sorbet on the top of each bowl before serving.*

DIRECTIONS:

Place the pears in a medium saucepan and cook on medium heat, simmering until they become quite soft. Mash the pears in the pan. Add the peach slices and cook with the pears for a few minutes until they soften slightly. Stir in the maple syrup and agar agar powder until it dissolves. Scoop the dessert into four serving bowls and chill until set.

Serves 4.

INGREDIENTS:

4 pears, peeled and finely chopped (4)
4 peaches, peeled and sliced (4)
2 tbsp maple syrup (30 ml)
½ tsp agar agar powder (2 ml)

201

Raspberry Mousse

*The color of this dessert is so lovely, and the refreshing raspberry
flavor an enhancement to this wonderful summer dessert.*

INGREDIENTS:

1½ cups vanilla soy milk (375 ml)

1 tbsp agar agar powder (15 ml)

⅛ tsp salt (0.5 ml)

*2½ cups raspberries, fresh
or frozen (625 ml)*

1½ cups soft dessert tofu (310 ml)

1 tsp vanilla extract (5 ml)

½ cup maple syrup (125 ml)

½ tsp stevia powder (2 ml)

*GARNISH: a few raspberries, mint
sprigs and/or borage flowers*

DIRECTIONS:

In a medium saucepan, whisk the soy milk, agar agar, and salt. Bring to a simmer and stir for several minutes. Remove from heat and pour the mixture into a food processor with the remaining ingredients. Blend the mixture on high for several minutes then pour into a large serving bowl and chill for several hours before serving. Garnish the center of the dessert with a few raspberries and some borage flowers or mint sprigs.
Serves 6.

Cookies

Lavender Chocolate Chunk Cookies

Orange Hazelnut Cookies

Triple Almond Cookies

Anise Almond Poppyseed Cookies

Mocha Hazelnut Spice Cookies

Pistachio Coconut Cardamom Cookies

Oatmeal Coconut Pumpkin Seed Cookies

Carob Pecan Cookies

Orange Candied Ginger Cookies

Crunchy Peanut Butter Cookies

Peppermint Oatmeal Carob Cookies

Maple Pecan Cookies

Oatmeal Lemon Fig Cookies

Chocolate Rum Pecan Balls

Mom's Thumbprint Cookies

Carob Coconut Balls

Chocolate Peppermint Pecan Barley Cookies

Almond Apricot Rice Flour Cookies

Chocolate Chocolate Almond Cookies

Kahlua Chocolate Almond Cookies

Chocolate Orange Hazelnut Cookies

Lavender Chocolate Chunk Cookies

*These are for the daredevil cookie eater. If you've never eaten
lavender, you may want to use only one tablespoon of flowers for
this recipe. If you love lavender, you'll love these cookies!*

INGREDIENTS:

*½ cup canola oil or other
natural oil (125 ml)*

1 tsp apple cider vinegar (5 ml)

1 tsp vanilla extract (5 ml)

¾ cup organic sugar (175 ml)

*1-2 tbsp dried lavender flowers (depending
on how adventurous you are) (15-30 ml)*

¼ cup maple syrup (60 ml)

*1½ cups whole wheat or
whole spelt flour (375 ml)*

½ tsp sea salt (2 ml)

1 tsp baking soda (5 ml)

1 tsp baking powder (5 ml)

*½ cup vegan dark chocolate,
chunks or chips (125 ml)*

DIRECTIONS: 350°F (175°C); 12-15 MINUTES

Combine the oil, vinegar, water, vanilla, sugar and lavender flowers in a medium-size bowl, mixing thoroughly. In a large bowl, combine flour, salt, baking soda and baking powder. Make a well in the center of the dry ingredients and pour the wet ingredients into the well. Mix all ingredients together thoroughly. Fold in chocolate chunks. Roll dough into approximately 1-inch balls and place on an oiled cookie sheet, about two inches apart. Bake for 12-15 minutes.

Makes approximately 20 cookies.

Orange Hazelnut Cookies

These crunchy cookies are delightful with a cup of tea. The rich taste of hazelnuts and citrus make a delectable combination.

DIRECTIONS: 350°F (175°C): 15 MINUTES

Combine the sugar, maple syrup, oil, ground hazelnuts, orange rind and vanilla together in a medium bowl. In a larger bowl, combine the flour, baking soda, baking powder and salt. Pour the wet ingredients into the dry ingredients and mix them together thoroughly. Roll small amounts of dough onto an oiled cookie sheet. Bake for 15 minutes. Continue to bake the remaining cookies in the same fashion.

Makes 30-35 small cookies.

INGREDIENTS:

¼ cup organic sugar (60 ml)

¾ cup maple syrup (175 ml)

¼ cup canola oil or other natural oil (60 ml)

¾ cup hazelnuts, finely ground (175 ml)

1 tbsp orange rind, grated (15 ml)

1 tbsp vanilla extract (15 ml)

1½ cup whole wheat or spelt flour (375 ml)

1 tsp baking soda (5 ml)

1 tsp baking powder (5 ml)

½ tsp fine sea salt (2 ml)

½ cup hazelnuts, coarsely chopped (125 ml)

Triple Almond Cookies

Most often peanut butter is used for a nut cookie, but this recipe is a tasty change from peanuts, especially for those who have allergies. Using almond butter, almond extract and raw almonds, these cookies emanate that rich nutty flavor.

INGREDIENTS:

2 cups whole spelt flour (500 ml)

½ tsp fine sea salt (2 ml)

1 tsp baking soda (5 ml)

1 tsp baking powder (5 ml)

⅔ cup crunchy almond butter (160 ml)

¾ cup canola oil or other natural oil (175 ml)

¾ tsp almond extract (3 ml)

¾ cup organic sugar (175 ml)

2 tsp apple cider vinegar (10 ml)

2 tbsp water (30 ml)

½ cup almonds, coarsely chopped (125 ml)

DIRECTIONS: 350°F (175°C); 15 MINUTES

Combine the flour, salt, baking soda and baking powder in a large bowl. In a medium-bowl, combine the almond butter, oil, almond extract, sugar, vinegar and water, and stir rapidly with a fork until the ingredients are thoroughly mixed. Pour the wet ingredients into the bowl of dry ingredients and gently mix all ingredients together into a dough. Roll dough into 1-inch balls and set about 2 inches apart on 2 lightly oiled cookie sheets. Bake for 15 minutes. Remove the cookie sheets from the oven and allow the cookies to cool on the sheet for 3-5 minutes before placing on a cooling rack. These cookies are fairly fragile so be gentle with them when moving them. These will keep for several days in a cookie jar. *Makes 30-35 cookies.*

Anise Almond Poppyseed Cookies

*The almond and spicy anise flavors go very well together
and are enhanced by the subtle crunch of poppy seeds.*

DIRECTIONS: 350°F (175°C); 12-15 MINUTES

Combine the flour, poppy seeds, salt, anise and almonds in a large mixing bowl. In a medium bowl, combine the syrup, oil, vinegar, almond and vanilla extracts, rapidly stirring them together until emulsified. Pour the wet ingredients into the dry ingredients and gently stir until all ingredients are thoroughly combined. Using a heaping teaspoon amount of dough, roll dough into small balls and place 1½ inches apart on an oiled cookie sheet. Bake in a preheated oven for 12-15 minutes. Leave cookies on cookie sheets for several minutes to cool, then transfer to a cooling rack.

Makes 50 cookies.

INGREDIENTS:

2¼ cups whole spelt flour (560 ml)

3 tbsp poppy seeds (45 ml)

¼ tsp salt (1 ml)

2 tsp ground anise (10 ml)

1 cup almonds, finely chopped (250 ml)

¾ cup maple syrup (175 ml)

½ cup canola oil or other
natural oil (125 ml)

1 tsp apple cider vinegar (5 ml)

2 tsp almond extract (10 ml)

1 tsp vanilla extract (5 ml)

Mocha Hazelnut Spice Cookies

Chunks of hazelnut and a spicy snap make these cookies a favorite among friends.

INGREDIENTS:

2 cups whole spelt flour (500 ml)
1 tsp baking soda (5 ml)
1 tsp baking powder (5 ml)
½ tsp salt (2 ml)
1 tsp each cinnamon,
nutmeg and cloves (5 ml)
½ tsp allspice (2 ml)
2 tbsp cocoa powder (30 ml)
¾ cup maple syrup (175 ml)
½ cup canola oil or other
natural oil (125 ml)
1 tbsp vanilla extract (15 ml)
1 tsp apple cider vinegar (5 ml)
4 tbsp powdered coffee substitute (60 ml)
1 cup hazelnuts, chopped (250 ml)

DIRECTIONS: 375°F (190°C); 12 MINUTES

Combine the flour, baking soda, baking powder, salt, spices and cocoa powder in a large mixing bowl. In a separate bowl, combine the syrup, oil, vanilla, vinegar and coffee substitute, whisking vigorously to emulsify the ingredients. Add the hazelnuts to the wet mixture and stir them in. Pour the wet ingredients into the dry and stir together gently. Drop small spoonfuls of dough onto the prepared cookie sheets, spacing the cookies about 1½ inches apart. Bake one tray at a time in a preheated oven for 12 minutes. Remove from cookie sheet and let cookies cool on cooling rack.

Makes 30-35 cookies.

Pistachio Coconut Cardamom Cookies

A delicious light, crunchy cookie that is accented by a subtle combination of cardamom and pistachio nuts.

DIRECTIONS: 350°F (175°C); 15 MINUTES

In a large bowl, combine flours, baking powder, baking soda, salt and cardamom. In a separate bowl, whisk together vigorously the oil, syrup, vanilla and vinegar. Stir in the coconut. Pour the wet ingredients into the dry ones and combine. Fold in the pistachio nuts. Drop tablespoonfuls onto oiled cookie sheets, about 1½ inches apart. Place one cookie sheet in a preheated oven and bake for about 15 minutes. Remove cookies from oven and place them on a cooling rack to cool. Bake the next set of cookies the same way.

Makes about 45 cookies.

INGREDIENTS:

1 cup whole spelt flour (250 ml)

1 cup brown rice flour (250 ml)

1 tsp baking powder (5 ml)

1 tsp baking soda (5 ml)

¼ tsp salt (1 ml)

½ tsp cardamom, ground (2 ml)

½ cup canola oil or other natural oil (125 ml)

¾ cup maple syrup (175 ml)

3 tsp vanilla extract (15 ml)

1 tsp apple cider vinegar (5 ml)

⅔ cup dried coconut, shredded (160 ml)

1 cup pistachio nuts, chopped (250 ml)

Oatmeal Coconut Pumpkin Seed Cookies

These cookies are delicious and disappear very quickly. The sweet combination of oats, coconut and maple syrup is delightful!

INGREDIENTS:

1 ¾ cups brown rice flour (425 ml)

¾ tsp fine sea salt (3 ml)

1 tsp baking soda (5 ml)

1 tsp baking powder (5 ml)

½ cup canola oil or other natural oil (125 ml)

¾ cup maple syrup (175 ml)

¼ cup sugar (60 ml)

1 tsp vanilla extract (5 ml)

1 tsp apple cider vinegar (5 ml)

⅔ cup dried coconut (160 ml)

⅔ cup oats (160 ml)

¾ cup pumpkin seeds (175 ml)

DIRECTIONS: 350°F (175°C); 15 MINUTES

Combine flour, salt, baking soda and baking powder in a large mixing bowl. In a separate medium-size bowl, combine oil, syrup, vanilla, vinegar and coconut, whisking vigorously until the mixture is emulsified. Pour the wet mixture into the dry mixture and stir together until all ingredients are thoroughly mixed. Fold in the oats until evenly combined. Drop 1 tablespoonful of dough onto oiled cookie sheet, spreading cookies about 2 inches apart. Bake in a preheated oven for 15 minutes. Gently remove cookies from sheet and place on cooling rack. They can be crumbly when hot out of the oven, so handle them carefully. *Makes about 30 cookies.*

Carob Pecan Cookies

The maple syrup in these cookies brings out the carob flavor
and the pecans add a nice crunch to the cookie.

DIRECTIONS: 350°F (175°C); 10-12 MINUTES

In a large bowl, combine the flour, carob powder, baking soda, baking powder, salt, cinnamon and nutmeg. In a medium bowl mix the oil, syrup, vinegar, water and vanilla. Stir or whisk vigorously until the mixture is emulsified. Pour the wet mixture into the center of the dry mixture and stir together until all dry ingredients are incorporated. Fold in the pecans. The dough will be quite sticky and soft. Drop tablespoonfuls onto a greased cookie sheet about 2 inches apart. Place on middle rack of a preheated oven and bake for 12 minutes. Remove from the oven and allow cookies to cool on a rack.
Makes 25-30 cookies.

INGREDIENTS:

1⅔ - 2 cups sifted spelt flour (400-500 ml)

4 tbsp carob powder (60 ml)

1 tsp baking soda (5 ml)

1 tsp baking powder (5 ml)

¾ tsp fine sea salt (3 ml)

1 tsp cinnamon (5 ml)

½ tsp nutmeg (2 ml)

¾ cup canola oil or other natural oil (175 ml)

½ cup maple syrup (125 ml)

½ cup sugar (125 ml)

1 tsp apple cider vinegar (5 ml)

1 tbsp water (15 ml)

1 tsp vanilla extract (5 ml)

⅔ cup chopped pecans (160 ml)

⅔ cup carob chips (160 ml)

Orange Candied Ginger Cookies

These ginger cookies have a delightful chewy texture from the candied ginger and a zesty flavor from the addition of orange, making them very hard to stop eating!

INGREDIENTS:

2 cups whole spelt flour (500 ml)

1 tsp baking soda (5 ml)

1 tsp baking powder (5 ml)

¼ tsp salt (1 ml)

¼ tsp cream of tartar (1 ml)

2 tsp dry ginger powder (10 ml)

½ cup maple syrup (125 ml)

¼ cup sugar (60 ml)

⅓ cup molasses (80 ml)

3 tbsp fresh gingerroot, grated (45 ml)

½ cup canola oil or other natural oil (125 ml)

1 tbsp vanilla (15 ml)

1 tsp apple cider vinegar (2 ml)

1 tbsp orange rind (15 ml)

· ⅔ cup candied ginger, cut into thin slices (160 ml)

DIRECTIONS: 350°F (175°C); 12 MINUTES

In a large bowl combine the flour, baking soda, baking powder, salt, cream of tartar and ginger powder. In a separate bowl, combine maple syrup, sugar, molasses, ginger, oil, vanilla, vinegar and orange rind, whisking until emulsified. Pour the wet ingredients into the dry ingredients and combine without overmixing. Fold in the candied ginger.

Drop teaspoonfuls of dough onto 2 oiled cookie sheets, about 2 inches apart. Bake in a preheated oven for 12 minutes. Remove from the oven and leaves cookies on cookie sheets for a few minutes before transferring them to a cooling rack.

Makes about 50 cookies.

Crunchy Peanut Butter Cookies

*The flakes of cereal in these cookies add a delightful
crunch to these tasty favorites.*

DIRECTIONS: 350°F (175°C); 15 MINUTES

In a medium mixing bowl, combine the oil, maple syrup, vanilla, peanut butter and vinegar. Whisk these together vigorously until the mixture is emulsified. In a separate large mixing bowl, combine the flour, baking powder and salt. Pour the wet mixture into the dry ingredients and stir together. Fold in the cereal flakes. Roll dough into 1-inch balls and place on the greased cookie sheets about 1½ inches apart. Press the cookies down with fork tines in a crisscross pattern so that the cookies are slightly flattened. With your fingers, smooth the edges of each cookie, as they may split apart a bit after you flatten them. Place in the preheated oven for about 12 minutes. Remove from oven and place cookies on a wire cooling rack to cool.

Makes 45-50 cookies.

INGREDIENTS:

⅓ cup canola oil or other
natural oil (80 ml)

1 cup maple syrup (250 ml)

1 tbsp vanilla extract (15 ml)

⅔ cup crunchy peanut butter (160 ml)

1 tsp apple cider vinegar (5 ml)

2 cups whole spelt flour (500 ml)

1 tsp baking powder (5 ml)

½ tsp salt (2 ml)

1½ cups oat bran cereal flakes
(almost any variety of cereal
flakes will work) (375 ml)

Peppermint Oatmeal Carob Cookies

These cookies are my favorite, as I am very fond of all things minty.

INGREDIENTS:

2 cups whole spelt flour (500 ml)

1 tsp baking soda (5 ml)

1 tsp baking powder (5 ml)

½ tsp salt (2 ml)

½ cup canola oil or other natural oil (125 ml)

¾ cup maple syrup (175 ml)

1 tsp vanilla extract (5 ml)

¾ tsp peppermint extract (3 ml)

1 tsp apple cider vinegar (5 ml)

¾ cup large rolled oats (175 ml)

1 cup sweetened carob chips (250 ml)

DIRECTIONS: 350°F (175°C); 12 MINUTES

In a large mixing bowl, combine the flour, baking soda, baking powder and salt. In a separate medium-size mixing bowl, mix the oil, syrup, vanilla, peppermint and vinegar, whisking until these ingredients are thoroughly combined. Pour this mixture into the dry ingredients and gently stir them together. Fold in the oats and carob chips. The dough will be quite sticky. Drop small spoonfuls onto 2 oiled cookie sheets. Bake one sheet at a time in a preheated oven for 12 minutes. Remove the cookies from the sheet and place on a cooling rack. Continue with the same procedure for the remaining cookie dough.

Makes 40-45 cookies.

Maple Pecan Cookies

There's just something about the flavor of maple syrup and pecans together that creates a gastronomic epiphany.

DIRECTIONS: 350°F (175°C); 12-15 MINUTES

In a large bowl, combine the sugar, maple syrup, oil, vinegar, lemon rind and vanilla, and whisk or stir rapidly until the ingredients are emulsified.

In a separate large mixing bowl, combine the flour, nutmeg, salt, baking soda and baking powder. Pour the wet ingredients into the flour mixture and gently stir them together thoroughly. Fold in the coarsely chopped pecans. The dough will be fairly sticky.

Roll small amounts of dough into balls and place on 2 oiled cookie sheets. Use the additional whole pecans and place one on top of each mound of cookie dough. Bake one cookie sheet at a time in a preheated oven for 12-15 minutes. Remove from the oven and transfer the cookies to a wire rack to cool. Continue to bake the remaining cookies in the same fashion.

Makes 45 cookies.

INGREDIENTS:

¼ cup organic sugar (60 ml)

¾ cup maple syrup (175 ml)

½ cup canola oil or other natural oil (125 ml)

1 tsp apple cider vinegar (5 ml)

2 tbsp lemon rind (30 ml)

1 tbsp vanilla extract (15 ml)

2 cups whole spelt flour (500 ml)

1 tsp fresh nutmeg, grated (5 ml)

½ tsp fine sea salt (2 ml)

1 tsp baking soda (5 ml)

1 tsp baking powder (5 ml)

1½ cup pecans, coarsely chopped (375 ml)

Additional whole pecans for placing on top of each cookie

Oatmeal Lemon Fig Cookies

Move over raisins—the chewy chunks of dried figs in these cookies are fabulous!

INGREDIENTS:

2 cups whole spelt flour (500 ml)
1 tsp baking soda (5 ml)
1 tsp baking powder (5 ml)
½ tsp sea salt (2 ml)
1 tsp cinnamon (5 ml)
½ cup canola oil or other natural oil (125 ml)
½ cup maple syrup (125 ml)
1 tsp vanilla extract (5 ml)
3 tbsp lemon rind (45 ml)
½ cup organic sugar (125 ml)
⅔ cup large rolled oats (160 ml)
1½ cup calimyrna figs, chopped into small pieces (375 ml)

DIRECTIONS: 350°F (175°C); 12 MINUTES

In a large mixing bowl, combine the flour, baking soda, baking powder, salt and cinnamon. In a separate medium-size mixing bowl, mix the oil, syrup, vanilla, lemon rind and sugar, whisking until these ingredients are thoroughly combined. Pour this mixture into the dry ingredients and gently stir them together. Fold in the oats and figs. The dough will be quite sticky. Roll small balls of dough onto 2 oiled cookie sheets. Bake one sheet at a time in a preheated oven for 12-15 minutes. Remove the cookies from the sheet and place on a cooling rack. Continue using the same procedure with the remaining cookie dough.
Makes 45-50 cookies.

Chocolate Rum Pecan Balls

*These are a nice, festive cookie to make for special occasions,
rich with rum, chocolate and ground pecans.*

DIRECTIONS: 350°F (175°C); 10-12 MINUTES

In a large bowl, combine the flour, salt cinnamon, and cocoa. In a separate medium-size bowl, combine the vanilla, rum, oil, sugar, grain beverage and pecans, whisking together until the ingredients are thoroughly combined. Pour the wet ingredients into the flour mixture and combine together thoroughly. Roll dough into small balls and place on 2 cookie sheets 1/2 inch apart. Bake one sheet at a time for 10-12 minutes. Remove from oven and transfer balls to a wire rack to cool. Bake the remaining cookies in the same fashion.

Makes about 60 small balls.

INGREDIENTS:

2 cups spelt flour (500 ml)

¼ tsp sea salt (1 ml)

½ tsp cinnamon (2 ml)

⅓ cup cocoa powder (or carob powder) (80 ml)

2 tbsp vanilla extract (30 ml)

½ cup dark or light rum (125 ml)

½ cup canola oil or other natural oil (125 ml)

1 cup organic sugar (250 ml)

2 tbsp powdered grain beverage (coffee substitute) (30 ml)

⅔ cup pecans, finely ground (160 ml)

Mom's Thumbprint Cookies

These wonderful cookies are an adapted recipe of a childhood favorite that my mother used to make. Choose your favorite jam for the filling.

INGREDIENTS:

2 cups whole or light spelt flour (500 ml)

¼ tsp sea salt (1 ml)

½ cup canola oil or other natural oil (125 ml)

¾ cup organic sugar (175 ml)

¼ cup maple syrup (60 ml)

1 tsp vanilla extract (5 ml)

1 tsp apple cider vinegar (5 ml)

½ cup almonds, pecans or walnuts, finely chopped (125 ml)

GARNISH: ¼ cup or more jam (60 ml)

DIRECTIONS: 350°F (175°C); 15 MINUTES

In a large bowl, combine the flour and salt. In a medium-size bowl, combine the oil, sugar, maple syrup, vanilla and vinegar, mixing together thoroughly. Pour the wet ingredients into the flour mixture and stir them together. Roll the dough into small balls and roll each of the balls into the chopped nuts. Place the balls on an oiled cookie sheet, about 1½ inches apart. Bake for 10 minutes then remove the cookies from the oven and press your thumb into the center of each cookie gently, making a small depression. Place the cookies back into the oven for an additional 5 minutes. Remove from the oven and allow the cookies to cool on a wire rack. When cooled, place small spoonfuls of jam in the center depression of each cookie.

Makes 40-45 cookies.

Carob Coconut Balls

These no-bake sweet treats are packed with energy and taste delicious!

DIRECTIONS:

Place the raisins in a bowl and pour the boiling water over them. Cover and set aside.

In a double boiler, melt the carob chips and set aside.

In a large bowl, combine the peanut butter, syrup, almonds, vanilla, salt and melted carob. Stir together thoroughly. Stir in the puffed cereal and 1/2 cup of coconut. Drain the raisins and reserve the water. Stir the raisins into the mixture. If it is too dry, add some of the raisin water. If it is too wet, add some more cereal or almonds. Roll the mixture into small balls, then roll each ball in the remaining coconut so that the outside of the balls are evenly coated. Balls can be placed in a container and chilled or eaten while still gooey!

Makes 40-50 balls.

INGREDIENTS:

1½ cups raisins (375 ml)

⅔ cup boiling water (160 ml)

⅔ cup peanut butter (160 ml)

½ cup brown rice syrup (125 ml)

1½ cups almonds, toasted and chopped (375 ml)

1 tsp vanilla extract (5 ml)

Dash sea salt

2 cups carob chips (500 ml)

1½ cups puffed cereal (millet, rice, kamut, etc.) (375 ml)

1 cup large coconut flakes, dried (250 ml)

219

Chocolate Peppermint Pecan Barley Cookies

*Chocolate and peppermint are a wonderful combination, and
the pecans add a bit of a crunch to these cookies. I also really
enjoy the flavor and texture of these barley flour cookies.*

INGREDIENTS:

2 cups barley flour (500 ml)

1 tsp baking soda (5 ml)

1 tsp baking powder (5 ml)

½ tsp sea salt (2 ml)

*½ cup canola oil or other
natural oil (125 ml)*

¾ cup maple syrup (175 ml)

1 tsp vanilla extract (5 ml)

¾ tsp peppermint extract (3 ml)

1 tsp apple cider vinegar (5 ml)

½ cup large rolled oats (125 ml)

*1 cup vegan dark chocolate,
chunks or chips (250 ml)*

½ cup pecans, coarsely chopped (125 ml)

DIRECTIONS: 350°F (175°C); 12 MINUTES

In a large mixing bowl, combine the flour, baking soda, baking powder and salt. In a separate medium-size mixing bowl, mix the oil, syrup, vanilla, peppermint and vinegar, whisking until these ingredients are thoroughly combined. Pour this mixture into the dry ingredients and gently stir them together. Fold in the oats, chocolate and pecans. The dough will be quite sticky. Drop small spoonfuls onto 2 oiled cookie sheets. Bake one sheet at a time in a preheated oven for 12 minutes. Remove the cookies from the sheet and place on a cooling rack. Continue with the same procedure with the remaining cookie dough.

Makes 40-45 cookies.

Almond Apricot Rice Flour Cookies

*These perennially crumbly rice flour cookies are delicious
and make a great gluten-free cookie!*

DIRECTIONS: 350°F (175°C); 12 MINUTES

In a large mixing bowl, combine the flour, baking soda, baking powder and salt. In a separate medium-size mixing bowl, mix the oil, syrup, vanilla, almond extract and vinegar, whisking until these ingredients are thoroughly combined. Pour this mixture into the dry ingredients and gently stir them together. Fold in the oats, apricots and almonds. The dough will be quite sticky. Drop small spoonfuls onto 2 oiled cookie sheets. Bake one sheet at a time in a preheated oven for 12 minutes. Remove the cookies from the sheet and place on a cooling rack. Continue with the same procedure with the remaining cookie dough.
Makes 40-45 cookies.

INGREDIENTS:

2 cups brown rice flour (500 ml)

1 tsp baking soda (5 ml)

1 tsp baking powder (5 ml)

½ tsp sea salt (2 ml)

*½ cup canola oil or other
natural oil (125 ml)*

¾ cup maple syrup (175 ml)

1 tsp vanilla extract (5 ml)

1 tsp almond extract (5 ml)

1 tsp apple cider vinegar (5 ml)

¼ cup large rolled oats (60 ml)

*¾ cup dried, unsulphured apricots, sliced
widthwise into thin slices (175 ml)*

½ cup almonds, coarsely chopped (125 ml)

Chocolate Chocolate Almond Cookies

Any recipe that has "Chocolate Chocolate" in the title is worth a try.

INGREDIENTS:

1½ cups whole spelt flour (375 ml)

¾ cup sifted white spelt flour (175 ml)

1 tsp baking soda (5 ml)

1 tsp baking powder (5 ml)

½ tsp sea salt (2 ml)

¼ tsp cream of tartar (1 ml)

¼ cup cocoa powder (60 ml)

½ cup canola oil or other natural oil (125 ml)

¾ cup maple syrup (175 ml)

1 tsp apple cider vinegar (5 ml)

1 tsp vanilla extract (5 ml)

1 tsp almond extract (5 ml)

1 cup vegan dark chocolate, chips or chunks (250 ml)

½ cup almonds, coarsely chopped (125 ml)

DIRECTIONS: 350°F (175°C); 12 MINUTES

In a large mixing bowl, combine the flours, baking soda, baking powder, salt, cream of tartar and cocoa powder. In a separate medium-size mixing bowl, mix the oil, syrup, vinegar and vanilla, whisking until these ingredients are thoroughly combined. Pour this mixture into the dry ingredients and gently stir them together. Fold in the chocolate chips and hazelnuts. The dough will be quite sticky. Drop small spoonfuls (about 1 tablespoonful) onto 2 oiled cookie sheets. Bake one sheet at a time in a preheated oven for 12 minutes. Remove the cookies from the oven and allow them to remain on the cookie sheet for a couple of minutes before transferring them to a wire rack for cooling. Continue with the same procedure for the remaining cookie dough.

Makes 50 cookies.

Kahlua Chocolate Almond Cookies

Wow! What are you waiting for? The flavors of chocolate, almond and Kahlua come together in this recipe to create a wonderfully rich and satisfying cookie. Just try them!

DIRECTIONS: 375°F (190°C); 12-13 MINUTES

In a large bowl, combine the flour, baking soda, baking powder, salt and cocoa powder. Set aside.

In a separate large mixing bowl, combine the oil, maple syrup, sugar, vanilla, almond extract, vinegar and Kahlua. Whisk or stir the ingredients together rapidly until they are emulsified. Pour the wet ingredients into the flour mixture and gently stir them together thoroughly. Fold in the coarsely chopped almonds and chocolate chips.

The dough will be fairly sticky. Allow the dough to sit for 5 minutes before continuing. Drop small spoonfuls of dough onto 2 oiled cookie sheets. Bake one cookie sheet at a time in a preheated oven for 12-13 minutes. Remove from the oven and transfer the cookies to a wire rack to cool. Continue to bake the remaining cookies in the same fashion.

Makes 45 cookies.

INGREDIENTS:

2 cups white spelt flour (500 ml)

1 tsp each baking soda and baking powder (5 ml)

½ tsp fine sea salt (2 ml)

¼ cup cocoa powder (60 ml)

½ cup canola oil or other natural oil (125 ml)

¼ cup maple syrup (60 ml)

½ cup organic sugar (125 ml)

1 tbsp vanilla extract (15 ml)

1 tsp each almond extract and apple cider vinegar (5 ml)

3 tbsp Kahlua (45 ml)

¾ cup each chopped almonds and vegan dark chocolate chips (175 ml)

Chocolate Orange Hazelnut Cookies

*The subtle citrus flavor combined with the richness of the chocolate
and the chunks of hazelnuts makes a superb cookie.*

INGREDIENTS:

2 cups whole spelt flour (500 ml)
¾ cups ground hazelnuts (175 ml)
⅓ cup cocoa powder (80 ml)
1 tsp baking soda (5 ml)
1 tsp baking powder (5 ml)
½ tsp salt (2 ml)
½ tsp cinnamon (2 ml)
*½ cup canola oil or other
natural oil (125 ml)*
¼ cup maple syrup (60 ml)
¾ cup sugar (175 ml)
1 tsp apple cider vinegar (5 ml)
1 tbsp vanilla extract (15 ml)
3 tbsp orange juice, freshly squeezed (45 ml)
1 tbsp orange rind (15 ml)
½ cup hazelnuts, chopped (125 ml)
*¾-1 cup vegan dark chocolate,
chunks or chips (175-250 ml)*

DIRECTIONS: 350°F (175°C); 12 MINUTES

In a large mixing bowl, combine the flour, ground hazelnuts, cocoa powder, baking soda, baking powder, salt and cinnamon. In a separate medium mixing bowl, combine the oil, syrup, vinegar, vanilla, orange juice and rind, whisking them together until the mixture is emulsified. Pour this mixture into the dry ingredients and gently stir them together thoroughly. Fold in the chopped hazelnuts and chocolate. Drop loose spoonfuls of dough onto 2 greased cookie sheets. Place one sheet in the oven and bake for 12 minutes. Remove cookies from cookie sheet and place on cooling rack. Continue to bake the remainder of the cookies in the same manner.

Makes about 70 cookies.

SWEET LOAVES, BROWNIES, COBBLERS, CRUMBLES, AND ODDBALLS

Yam Pecan Cranberry Loaf

Zucchini Lemon Poppyseed Loaf

Chocolate Banana Walnut Brownies

Berry Streusel

Vegan Baklava

Strawberry Shortcake with Coconut Cream

Cardamom Mochi Fruit Crumble

Strawberry Rhubarb Cobbler

Banana Hazelnut Pâté

Roasted Pears in Sherry with Hazelnuts

Rhubarb Bars

Chocolate Truffles

Yam Pecan Cranberry Loaf

*This delicious sweet loaf is a welcome addition to a
Thanksgiving meal, but can be served any other time of year
as a scrumptious breakfast loaf or with afternoon tea.*

Ingredients:

*1 cup yams or sweet potatoes,
cooked and mashed (250 ml)*

*½ cup canola oil or other
natural oil (125 ml)*

¾ cup maple syrup (175 ml)

1 tsp vanilla extract (5 ml)

1 tsp apple cider vinegar (5 ml)

½ cup vanilla soy milk (125 ml)

*5 tbsp orange juice,
freshly squeezed (75 ml)*

3 tbsp orange rind, grated (45 ml)

2 cups whole spelt flour (500 ml)

3 tsp baking powder (15 ml)

½ tsp fine sea salt (2 ml)

½ cup dried sweetened cranberries (125 ml)

½ cup pecans, coarsely chopped (125 ml)

Directions: 350°F (175°C); 60 minutes

Steam or boil the yams in water in a medium saucepan and cook until soft. Strain the yams and mash them with a masher. Add the oil, syrup, vanilla, vinegar, soy milk, orange juice and orange rind to the yams and mash the ingredients together thoroughly.

In a large mixing bowl, combine the flour, baking powder and salt. Pour the yam mixture into the flour mixture and gently stir them together until all of the flour is incorporated into the wet mixture. Fold in the cranberries and pecans. Scoop the mixture into an oiled and floured bread pan. Place the pan in a preheated oven and bake for about one hour. Use a toothpick to test doneness; this loaf is done when the toothpick comes out clean. Let the loaf cool in the bread pan on a wire rack before removing.

Makes 1 loaf.

Zucchini Lemon Poppyseed Loaf

This tasty, moist loaf is an ideal way to utilize the copious quantities of zucchinis that abound in our gardens at the end of the summer.

DIRECTIONS: 350°F (175°C); 60 MINUTES

In a large bowl, combine the flour, baking powder, salt and poppyseeds. In a medium bowl, combine the oil, syrup, vinegar, lemon rind and lemon juice, stirring rapidly until emulsified. Stir the zucchini into the wet mixture and then pour this into the dry ingredients. Gently stir all of the ingredients together and then pour the mixture into an oiled and floured loaf pan. Place the pan in a preheated oven for about one hour. Remove from the oven and let cool in the pan on a rack before removing the loaf. To help ease the loaf out of the pan, run a knife around the inside of the pan to loosen the loaf from the edges, then invert the pan and gently shake the loaf out onto a rack.

Makes 1 loaf.

INGREDIENTS:

2 cups whole spelt flour (500 ml)
3 tsp baking powder (15 ml)
½ tsp sea salt (2 ml)
3 tbsp poppyseeds (45 ml)
½ cup canola oil or other natural oil (125 ml)
¾ cup maple syrup (175 ml)
1 tsp apple cider vinegar (5 ml)
2 tbsp lemon rind (30 ml)
3 tbsp lemon juice, freshly squeezed (45 ml)
1 cup zucchini, grated (250 ml)

Chocolate Banana Walnut Brownies

These moist and rich brownies are fabulously complemented
by the sweet banana flavor and chunks of walnuts. Top them with
Holy Chocolate Icing (page 158) and they will disappear very fast!

INGREDIENTS:

2 cups whole spelt flour (500 ml)
¾ cups cocoa powder (175 ml)
½ tsp sea salt (2 ml)
1 tsp baking soda (5 ml)
3 bananas, mashed with a fork (3)
⅔ cup canola oil or other
natural oil (160 ml)
1 tbsp vanilla extract (15 ml)
⅔ cup vanilla soy milk or rice milk
(160 ml)
1 cup maple syrup (250 ml)
1 tsp apple cider vinegar (5 ml)
¾ cup chocolate chips, melted (175 ml)
½ cup walnuts, coarsely chopped (125 ml)
1 recipe Holy Chocolate Icing (page 158) (1)

DIRECTIONS: 350°F (175°C); 40 MINUTES

In a large bowl, combine the flour, cocoa, salt and baking soda thoroughly. Set aside.

Place the chocolate chips in a double boiler and heat on medium until they have melted completely. Set aside.

In a separate large bowl, mash the bananas with a fork. Add the oil vanilla, soy milk, maple syrup and vinegar. Pour in the melted chocolate and stir these ingredients so they are thoroughly combined. Pour the wet mixture into the dry mixture and gently stir the ingredients together to form a batter. Pour the batter evenly into an oiled 9-x-13-inch baking pan. Place the pan in a preheated oven and bake for 20 minutes. Rotate the pan 180 degrees and bake for an additional 20 minutes. Remove from the oven and allow the brownies to cool in the pan on a wire rack.

When the brownies have cooled, pour on one recipe portion of Holy Chocolate Icing and set the pan in the refrigerator until the icing has set.
Cut into 20 squares and serve.

Berry Streusel

*A slightly adapted version from a recipe given to me by a friend
years ago, this is a simple cake that is well received on a sunny afternoon
with a cup of tea or a scoop of vanilla soy or rice frozen dessert.*

DIRECTIONS: 375°F (190°C); 40 MINUTES

For the topping, combine the flour, spices and sugar in a medium bowl. Add the oil and crumble the mixture together with your fingers until all of the ingredients are thoroughly combined. Set this mixture aside.

For the cake, combine the flour, spices, salt and baking powder in a large mixing bowl. In a separate bowl, combine the syrup, soy milk, vanilla and oil, and stir these together rapidly.

Pour the wet ingredients into the dry ones and stir the batter together gently. Fold in 1 cup of berries. Pour mixture into an oiled and floured 8-inch cake pan. Sprinkle the topping evenly over the cake batter in the pan. Place the pan in the preheated oven and bake for about 40 minutes. Use a toothpick to test for doneness; it should come out clean when the cake is ready.

INGREDIENTS:

CAKE:

2½ cups whole spelt flour (625 ml)
1 tsp each cinnamon and nutmeg (5 ml)
½ tsp each allspice and cloves (2 ml)
½ tsp sea salt (2 ml)
1 tsp baking powder (5 ml)
1 tsp baking soda (5 ml)
¾ cup maple syrup (175 ml)
¾ cup vanilla soy milk (175 ml)
2 tsp vanilla extract (10 ml)
½ cup olive oil or other natural oil (125 ml)
1 tsp apple cider vinegar (5 ml)
1 cup blueberries, blackberries
or raspberries (250 ml)

TOPPING:

½ cup whole spelt flour (125 ml)
¼ tsp each cinnamon and nutmeg (1 ml)
⅛ tsp each allspice and cloves (0.5 ml)
¼ cup sucanat or organic sugar (60 ml)
2 tbsp canola oil or other natural oil (30 ml)
1½ cups blueberries, blackberries
or raspberries (375 ml)

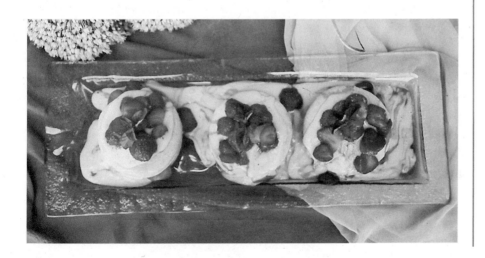

Vegan Baklava

*Baklava is a traditional Middle Eastern dessert usually made with honey.
This delicious vegan version uses brown rice syrup to replace the honey.
The flaky phyllo pastry combined with layers of walnuts, spices and a
lemony syrup creates a sinfully satisfying dessert. Phyllo pastry can be tricky
to handle as it is very fragile. Be careful to follow the instructions on
the package and allow the pastry to thaw for a couple of hours before using.*

INGREDIENTS:

*4 cups walnuts, coarsely
chopped (1,000 ml)*

½ cup organic sugar (125 ml)

1 tbsp cinnamon (15 ml)

¼ tsp cloves (1 ml)

16 oz phyllo pastry (450 mg)

1¼ cup soy margarine (310 ml)

SYRUP:

2 cups brown rice syrup (500 ml)

1 tbsp lemon zest (15 ml)

*1 tbsp lemon juice,
freshly squeezed (15 ml)*

1 tbsp vanilla extract (15 ml)

DIRECTIONS: 350°F (175°C); 35-40 MINUTES

In a large bowl, combine the chopped walnuts, sugar, cinnamon and cloves. Set aside.

Melt the soy margarine on low heat in a small pot and set aside. Using a pastry brush, lightly oil the 13-x-9-x-2-inch baking pan with some of the melted margarine. Remove the sheets of phyllo from their packaging and place them under a damp towel or cloth to prevent them from drying out. Take one sheet of phyllo and gently fold it in half so that it is the same size as the baking pan. Place the folded phyllo in the bottom of the baking pan and gently brush some of the melted margarine over top. Repeat the steps layering one folded phyllo sheet at a time brushed with margarine between each layer until there are 8 layers of phyllo sheets in the pan. Evenly sprinkle half of the walnut mixture over the phyllo pastry, then layer four more sheets of folded phyllo over the nuts, brushing each sheet with some of the margarine as you layer. Sprinkle the remaining half of the walnut mixture evenly over the phyllo pastry again, and follow with another 8 layers of pastry, brushing between each layer with margarine. Place the dish in a preheated oven and bake for 35-40 minutes.

Just before the pastry is ready to come out of the oven, begin preparing the sauce. In a large saucepan,

continued on next page

thoroughly melt the brown rice syrup with the lemon zest and vanilla on medium heat. Bring to a gentle boil and remove from heat. Stir in the lemon juice, then pour the hot syrup over the baklava when it has finished baking. Place the pan on a cooling rack and allow the baklava to thoroughly cool before serving. Use a sharp knife to cut squares or diamonds for serving.

Makes about 20 squares.

Strawberry Shortcake with Coconut Cream

This is a wonderful summer dessert when strawberries are flourishing. The flaky pastry makes a lovely shortcake, and the coconut cream is exquisite when drizzled over top of the sweet berries and pastries. Use Flaky Pastry (page 193) and form into shortcakes.

DIRECTIONS:

Prepare the coconut cream the evening before, if possible. Combine the coconut milk and icing sugar in a large bowl and whisk them together for several minutes. Place in the refrigerator and chill for several hours or overnight.

Prepare the shortcakes by following the directions in the Flaky Pastry recipe. Thoroughly cool the shortcakes and set aside.

Place the berries in a bowl. Gently stir in the maple syrup and set aside.

To assemble, place a shortcake on a serving plate, scoop some coconut cream over the top and then spoon on some of the strawberries. Add another layer of shortcake on top and repeat with the coconut cream and strawberries. Garnish with a sprig of fresh mint and serve. Repeat this process with the remaining shortcakes. This recipe makes enough for eight double shortcake servings. They could be served as single shortcakes as well.

INGREDIENTS:

COCONUT CREAM:

14 oz can coconut milk (be sure to find a coconut milk that does not have water added, avoid light coconut milk as it is not thick enough) (400 ml)

4 cups organic icing sugar (1,000 ml)

1 recipe Flaky Pastry (page 193), made into shortcakes (1)

1 pint strawberries, stems removed and thinly sliced (500 ml)

1-2 tbsp maple syrup (15-30 ml)

GARNISH: sprigs of fresh mint and Johnny Jump-ups or other violets

Cardamom Mochi Fruit Crumble

If you have never had mochi (made by pounding cooked rice), you may find this dessert peculiar. The mochi topping is more chewy and gooey than what one would normally expect in a crumble. But it is a delightful gluten-free alternative to the usual oat crumble toppings and can be found in many specialty Japanese stores and health food stores. However, one may add oats to this recipe as well for additional texture and substance.

INGREDIENTS:

1 package Raisin Cinnamon Mochi, grated (10 oz/284 g) (1)

¾ cup brown rice syrup (175 ml)

¼ cup canola oil or other natural oil (60 ml)

⅔ cup almonds, chopped (160 ml)

1 tsp vanilla extract (5 ml)

⅛ tsp fine sea salt (0.5 ml)

⅔ cup rolled oats (optional) (160 ml)

4-6 medium apples, peeled and sliced (4-6)

2-4 pears, peeled and sliced (2-4)

4-6 plums or apricots, sliced (4-6)

¾ cup strawberries or blueberries, fresh or frozen (175 ml)

Juice of 1 lemon

Dash stevia powder

¼ tsp cinnamon (1 ml)

¼ tsp nutmeg (1 ml)

⅛ tsp cardamom (0.5 ml)

DIRECTIONS: 350°F (175°C); 40-50 MINUTES

Grate the block of mochi and place it into a large bowl. Mochi is very tough to grate and may take some muscle power! Combine the salt with the mochi. Pour the oil and brown rice syrup into the grated mochi, then stir the ingredients together thoroughly. This becomes quite sticky and you may find it easier to use your fingers to work the syrup and oil into the mochi. Stir in the almonds and add the oats, if you are using them. Set aside.

Place the prepared fruit into a medium-size casserole dish (about 8-x-8-inch) with a lid. Juice the lemon and stir a dash of stevia into the juice. Pour this over the fruit and add the cinnamon, nutmeg and cardamom as well, making sure all of the fruit is coated with the juice and spices. Flatten the fruit down gently into the casserole dish and then scoop the mochi topping onto the fruit. Place in a preheated oven with the lid on for 15 minutes. Remove the lid and bake for an additional 25-35 minutes, depending on desired crispness.

Remove from the oven and let cool a bit before serving. This dessert is extraordinary with a scoop of vanilla rice or soy dessert on top. Enjoy! Makes 6-8 servings.

Strawberry Rhubarb Cobbler

This is a slightly adapted version of a cobbler that my mother used to make when I was a child. It always seemed like there was never enough to go around!

Directions: 400°F (200°C); 20-25 minutes

For the topping, combine the flour, baking soda and salt in a medium bowl. Make a well in the center and combine the oil, syrup, soy milk and vinegar in the well. Mix the wet ingredients into the dry ones and stir until all ingredients are moistened. Set aside.

For the filling, place all the ingredients in a medium-size saucepan and bring to a boil, stirring for a couple of minutes. Be sure to stir the cornstarch in well so that it dissolves. Pour the hot filling into an 8-inch round baking dish, usually with five mounds around the perimeter and one mound in the center. Spoon six even mounds of the dough on top of the filling. Place in a preheated oven and bake for 20-25 minutes. Remove from the oven and cool for about 10 minutes before serving. Can be eaten warm or cooled.
Serves 6.

Ingredients:

Topping:

1 cup whole or sifted spelt flour (250 ml)

1½ tsp baking soda (7 ml)

¼ tsp sea salt (1 ml)

¼ cup canola oil or other
natural oil (60 ml)

2 tbsp maple syrup (30 ml)

¼ cup soy milk (60 ml)

½ tsp apple cider vinegar (2 ml)

Filling:

½ cup soy milk (125 ml)

2 tbsp cornstarch (30 ml)

¼ tsp cinnamon (1 ml)

3 cups rhubarb, chopped into
1-inch slices (750 ml)

1½ cups strawberries, sliced (375 ml)

1 tbsp olive oil or other natural oil (15 ml)

3 tbsp maple syrup (45 ml)

Banana Hazelnut Pâté

*This pâté makes a lovely sweet spread on crackers or bread
and is a nice alternative to the usual savory pâté flavors.*

INGREDIENTS:

10 pitted medjhool dates (10)
½ cup dried coconut (125 ml)
2 bananas (2)
Dash stevia powder
½ cup vanilla soy milk (125 ml)
1 tsp vanilla extract (5 ml)
Dash sea salt
1 cup hazelnuts, finely ground (250 ml)

DIRECTIONS: 350°F (175°C); 50-60 MINUTES

Place the first seven ingredients in a blender and blend until smooth in texture, scraping the sides down with a spatula as needed. Add the ground hazelnuts and blend again until thoroughly combined. Scoop into an oiled 6-inch baking dish and bake in a preheated oven for about 50-60 minutes, making sure the edges do not burn. Remove from the oven and cool before serving.
Serves 6-8.

Roasted Pears in Sherry with Hazelnuts

*This simple and aromatic dessert is a perfect light treat after an autumn meal.
Try it with a dollop of vanilla frozen rice or soy dessert!*

INGREDIENTS:

5 pears, cored, peeled and thinly sliced (5)
2 tbsp lemon juice, freshly squeezed (30 ml)
⅛ tsp stevia powder (0.5 ml)
5 tbsp dry sherry (75 ml)
½ cup hazelnuts, finely ground (125 ml)

DIRECTIONS: 350°F (175°C); 30-40 MINUTES

Place the sliced pears in an 8-x-8-inch baking pan. In a small bowl, combine the lemon, stevia and sherry, stirring together to dissolve the stevia powder. Pour this mixture evenly over the pears and then sprinkle the hazelnuts evenly on top. Place the pan in a preheated oven and bake for 30-40 minutes. Remove from the oven. Spoon the dessert into four small dessert bowls and serve warm.
Serves 4-6.

234

Rhubarb Bars

*Rhubarb is a very easy crop to grow as it comes back each year bigger
and bolder. These bars are a delicious way to use up extra rhubarb.*

DIRECTIONS: 350°F (175°C); 35-45 MINUTES

Chop the rhubarb and place the pieces in a medium saucepan with 1 cup sugar, cornstarch and vanilla. Cook the rhubarb on medium heat, stirring constantly until it thickens and the rhubarb is cooked down into a sauce. Remove from heat and allow the sauce to cool completely.

To prepare the topping, combine the flour, baking soda, oats, 1 cup sugar, and soy margarine in a large bowl. Work the margarine into the flour mixture with a spoon or with your fingers to reach a crumbly consistency. Evenly pack ⅓ of the topping into a 13-x-9-x-2-inch oiled baking pan. Spread the cooled filling over the first layer, then sprinkle the remaining topping evenly over the rhubarb filling. Place in a preheated oven and bake for 35-45 minutes. Remove from the oven and allow the crisp to cool completely before cutting into squares or bars. *Makes 20 bars.*

INGREDIENTS:

FILLING:

3 cups rhubarb, cut into ½-inch pieces (750 ml)

1 cup organic sugar (250 ml)

2 tbsp cornstarch (30 ml)

1 tsp vanilla extract (5 ml)

TOPPING:

1 ½ cups flour (375 ml)

½ tsp baking soda (2 ml)

1 ½ cups large, rolled oats (375 ml)

1 cup organic sugar (250 ml)

¾ cup soy margarine (175 ml)

Chocolate Truffles

These soft bombs of chocolate are fabulous with their sweet, smooth center and cocoa powder coating. Experiment with your own flavor variations.

INGREDIENTS:

¾ cup vegan dark chocolate, chips
or chunks (175 ml)
¼ cup soy milk (60 ml)
¼ cup sherry (60 ml)
¼ tsp chili powder or flakes (1 ml)
2 tbsp cocoa powder (30 ml)

DIRECTIONS:

Place the chocolate in a double boiler on medium-low heat, stirring until the chocolate is thoroughly melted. Add the soy milk, sherry and chili powder, stirring until all of the ingredients are thoroughly combined and the mixture has thickened. Remove from heat, place the mixture into a bowl and refrigerate for 1-2 hours.

Place the cocoa powder on a small plate. Roll small balls of the chilled chocolate in your hand and then roll them in the cocoa powder. Serve. If the chocolate has solidified too much, allow it to sit at room temperature for a while until it softens enough to roll into balls. Makes 20-30 truffles.

Variations: Omit the chili powder and try adding ¼ cup of other liqueurs to the recipe instead of sherry. Or omit the alcohol and chili altogether and use ⅓ cup (80 ml) of soy milk, and just enjoy the chocolate flavor. Or try adding any of your own flavors such as ¼ tsp (1 ml) peppermint or almond extract, 1 tbsp (15 ml) lavender flowers, ½ tsp (2 ml) orange zest or finely chopped almonds or other nuts. Experiment and enjoy!

Alice's Hibiscus Ginger Spritzer

Lemon Lavender Spritzer

Ginger Orange Spritzer

Fresh Fruit Freezies

Blueberry Frozen Yogi Popsicles

Strawberry Spritzer

Hot Chocolate Mole

Alice's Hibiscus Ginger Spritzer

This is a creation from my friend Alice and it is an incredibly refreshing beverage.

INGREDIENTS:

15 cups water (3.75 L)

1 cup water (250 ml)

2 cups fresh gingerroot, chopped (500 ml)

3 cups dried hibiscus flowers (available in health food and herb stores) (750 ml)

½ tsp stevia, to taste (2 ml)

2 oranges, sliced into thin circles (2)

4-8 cups carbonated water (1-2 L)

DIRECTIONS:

Place 15 cups of water in a large pot and bring to a boil. Place remaining cup of water in a blender with chopped gingerroot. Blend for several minutes until most of the ginger has been relatively puréed. Pour the ginger and water into the boiling water in the pot. Add the hibiscus and cover, turning the mixture down to a simmer. Let it simmer for about an hour, then remove from heat and let sit overnight, preferably in the refrigerator. The next day, strain the ginger and hibiscus from the mixture and discard. In a small bowl, scoop about a half cup of the mixture and to this add the stevia powder. Stir it until the powder has dissolved and then pour it back into the main pot of liquid. If you prefer your drinks sweeter, add another dash of stevia and stir it in thoroughly. The mixture will have a very strong and spicy ginger flavor.

This beverage can be poured into glass jars and stored in the fridge for up to a week. I like to serve this as a punch at parties: pour the mixture into a large punch bowl, add orange slices and pour in as much carbonated water to suit your tastes. If you prefer to just drink a bit at a time, simply combine half a glass of the ginger hibiscus mixture with half a glass of carbonated water and add a slice of orange to your glass, if desired. I find the oranges add a nice fruity zing!
Serves 10-20.

Lemon Lavender Spritzer

This is a quick and refreshing drink for you and your guests to enjoy.
You can strain out the lavender when serving, if desired.

DIRECTIONS:

Place the lemon juice, stevia and lavender into a large jug and stir together thoroughly. Pour the sparkling water into the jug and serve. Garnish with slices of lemon rounds and tall sprigs of fresh lavender.

Serves 2-4.

INGREDIENTS:

2 tbsp lemon juice, freshly squeezed (30 ml)
⅛ tsp stevia powder (0.5 ml)
1 tsp dried lavender flowers (5 ml)
4 cups sparkling water, chilled (1,000 ml)
Several lemon rounds

Ginger Orange Spritzer

This is a quick and refreshing drink to make on hot summer days.

INGREDIENTS:

Juice of 2 oranges
⅛ tsp stevia powder (0.5 ml)
1 tsp fresh gingerroot, grated (5 ml)
4 cups sparkling water, chilled (1,000 ml)

DIRECTIONS:

Place the orange juice, stevia and ginger into a large jug and stir together thoroughly. Pour the sparkling water into the jug and serve. Garnish with slices of orange and tall sprigs of mint. *Serves 2-4.*

Fresh Fruit Freezies

We freeze a lot of the berries that we grow on our farm, and then process them into fruit freezies for sale at our market stand. You can use this recipe to create your own popsicles at home.

INGREDIENTS:

3 cups apple juice (750 ml)
3 cups berries, fresh or frozen (750 ml)
½ tsp stevia powder (2 ml)

DIRECTIONS:

Blend all ingredients in the blender until smooth, then pour into popsicle containers and place a popsicle stick in each one. Freeze for a few hours before serving. *Makes about 12 popsicles.*

Variations: Try using different juices, such as pear, cherry or grape juice instead of apple juice. Try using different fruits that are in season as well, such as peaches, nectarines, pears and plums.

Blueberry Frozen Yogi Popsicles

This mock-yogurt dessert can be made and poured into popsicle containers as a delightful treat for youngsters and adults alike on a hot summer day. You can also use it as an unfrozen yogurt substitute on top of granola or fruit crumbles.

DIRECTIONS:

Blend all ingredients on high for several minutes until a creamy and smooth consistency is achieved. Depending on your sweet tooth and texture preferences, add more or less maple syrup and apple juice. Pour into popsicle molds and freeze.
Makes 6-8 popsicles.

INGREDIENTS:

1 block tofu (approximately 1 pound) (1)
1 cup blueberries, strawberries, raspberries, peaches, nectarine or apricots, or any combination (250 ml)
½-¾ cup apple juice (125-175 ml)
Maple syrup, to taste

Strawberry Spritzer

This gorgeous summer drink is a beautiful rose color. It has a wonderful bubbly, refreshing taste and is great for children and adults alike on a hot summer day.

DIRECTIONS:

Place the strawberries, apple juice and stevia powder in a blender and blend until a smooth consistency is achieved. Pour the mixture into a large punch bowl or jug, then pour in the carbonated water. Stir together and serve in tall glasses or wine glasses. Garnish with rounds or wedges of fresh lime or sprigs of fresh mint.
Serves 6-8.

INGREDIENTS:

3 cups frozen strawberries (750 ml)
3 cups apple juice (750 ml)
⅛ tsp stevia powder (2 ml)
3-4 cups carbonated water (750-1,000 ml)

GARNISH: lime wedges or sprigs of fresh mint

241

Hot Chocolate Mole

*This thick and spicy hot chocolate will warm
up any soul on a wintery day.*

INGREDIENTS:

4 cups vanilla soy milk (1,000 ml)
1 tsp cinnamon (5 ml)
*⅛ tsp each chili powder, nutmeg, cloves
and dried ginger (0.5 ml)*
2 tbsp cocoa powder (30 ml)
Several dashes ground black pepper
1 tbsp vanilla extract (15 ml)
1 tbsp maple syrup (15 ml)
*¼ cup vegan dark chocolate,
chips or chunks (60 ml)*

DIRECTIONS:

Place all ingredients in a medium saucepan. Whisk together on medium heat until the chocolate is melted and the spices are thoroughly dissolved. Remove from heat and pour into mugs. Serve hot.

Makes about 4 cups.

PART III

Eating With Your Eyes

Natural Food Dyes

NATURAL DYES HAVE BEEN USED FOR CENTURIES for many different things including paintings on cave walls, dying skin, coloring wools and fabrics, and enhancing the appeal of foods. Natural dyes can be obtained from herbs, spices, seeds, fruits, vegetables and roots. Not all natural dyes are edible, however, and many that are used for naturally dying fabric are not suitable for food dyes.

The appearance of food plays a large role in a person's decision about what or how much of something to eat. Adding color to foods can transform a dish into a tantalizing color palette. Natural food dyes not only enhance the color and aesthetic value of a food, but some of them can also have health and nutritional benefits as well. If using natural food dyes, it is important to select a dye that both enhances the color of the meal and is compatible with the flavors of the meal. To that end, small quantities of natural dyes are usually used to avoid drastically affecting the flavor of a dish.

Consumers often demand consistency and uniformity in the color of a product, so artificial food dyes have become commonplace in numerous supermarkets. Many artificial food dyes have been linked to cancers and nervous system disorders and have eventually been banned, though thousands are still used in today's prepared foods.

Natural food dyes are one way to add color and festivity to your meals. However, if you do not wish to experiment with dyes, you can add color to your meals by choosing a selection of colorful vegetables or legumes that add a wide spectrum of color. Brightly colored sauces and soups can be incorporated into a meal to add contrast as well. Try using edible flowers or fresh herbs as garnishes, giving a wonderful splash of color and class to meals. Be sure to read the section on edible flowers and be careful to always correctly identify any plant or flower that you think may be edible. Never try a plant or flower that you are not absolutely positive is edible.

Here are some natural food dyes that can be used for coloring:

Yellow/Gold: turmeric powder, yellow onion skins, orange and lemon peels, saffron
Pink: beet powder, cranberries, strawberries, raspberries
Green: spirulina, chlorophyll
Red: annato seeds, paprika
Pale green: lime peel, spinach, parsley, cilantro
Orange/Brown: chili powder
Blue: blueberries, red cabbage (in acidic solution)
Purple: blackberries, red cabbage (in alkaline solution), red onion skins, purple grapes
Brown: coffee, black tea, coffee substitute, cocoa and carob powder

Some suggestions for preparing and using natural food dyes:

- Create a concentrated liquid solution from vegetables. For example, using beets, cabbage or onion skins, place 2 cups of the chosen vegetable product in a pot with an equal amount of water. Boil until vegetables are cooked, usually about 10 minutes. Strain out the vegetables, reserving the liquid. Place the liquid back in the pot and simmer to reduce the amount of liquid and achieve a more concentrated product. Use a few drops of the concentrated liquid as dye.

- Create a concentrated liquid solution from powders. For example, using turmeric, paprika or beet powder, place 1 tablespoon of the powder in 1 cup of water in a pot. Boil for 10-15 minutes, then strain out the powder through a cheesecloth. Place the liquid back in the pot and simmer to reduce the amount of liquid and achieve a more concentrated product. Use a few drops of the concentrated liquid as dye.

- Try adding powders directly into a recipe. Milder flavored powders, such as beet powder, can be used in this way. Be sure to only add a bit at a time when experimenting so as to not significantly alter the flavor of the food.

- Try juicing fruits or vegetables and adding the concentrated juices to a recipe to color dips, icings, sauces, breads, etc. Juices from berries, spinach, carrots and beets all have bright colors.

Some natural food dyes can be purchased online from a company called Nature's Flavors. The website at <www.naturesflavors.com> sells natural food colorings from vegan sources, and has a wide range of colors to choose from.

A Glossary of Edible Flowers

Edible flowers add a unique splash of color and class to food, as decoration, garnish or a main ingredient. They can transform an average meal into a visually stunning experience. However, flowers are usually quite fragile and need to be used immediately after picking, as they will not last long before wilting, even if refrigerated. When attempting to use edible flowers as part of a culinary dish, consider the flavors that you are combining. For example, you may not want to use chive blossoms on a cake, as the flavors may be incompatible.

I love adding edible flowers as garnishes on all kinds of foods. Putting tangerine gems and Johnny Jump-ups into ice cubes makes a wonderful addition to a punch. Decorating cakes, salads and platters of appetizers with an array of edible flowers and herbs adds a level of sophistication to a meal. I use many edible flowers and fresh herb garnishes for my Bed and Breakfast guests who enjoy the rainbow of colors in their morning meals.

There are some cautionary guidelines to consider when using edible flowers. First, you should assume all risk and be absolutely positive that you have correctly identified the plant you are using. Never try a flower that you are unsure of, as not all flowers are edible, and some are highly poisonous! When trying a new flower, sample the petals sparingly and only sample one kind at a time, as some people can have sensitivities or reactions to various plants that are harmless for others. If you have allergies, hayfever or asthma, avoid eating flowers.

With many edible flowers, only the petals are eaten, with the stamens, pistils and stems removed. These parts are often bitter, woody or generally unpalatable. When using flowers as a food garnish or decoration, be sure to only use edible flowers, as many people think that whatever is on the plate is edible.

Finally, growing your own flowers is the best way to ensure that you know what you are eating. Many seed companies offer seeds for edible flowers that you can order, or try your local farmers' market, as sometimes these specialty items are available. Never eat the flowers from a florist or nursery, as they have likely been sprayed. Similarly, avoid eating flowers by roadsides, as they have been contaminated by car emissions.

Following is a glossary of edible flowers:

Alliums (Allium spp.): The onion family, including leeks, onions, chives and garlic. All parts of these plants are edible. The flowers usually taste like the bulb. These small flowers vary from white to pink and purple, and can be used as a garnish in savory dishes or as a tasty addition to salads.

Angelica (Angelica archangelica): Some people have skin allergies to this plant, so be cautious. This flower has a celery-like flavor, and comes in several varieties with colors ranging from light blue to dark pink.

Anise (Agastache foeniculutum): This is an easy-to-grow perennial that bears lavender-colored flower spikes.

Anise Hyssop (Agastache anethiodorum): Both the flowers and leaves are edible. This plant is from the Mint family and is native to North America. It has the flavor of anise or licorice. The violet flowers bloom in July.

Apple Blossoms (Malus spp.): These edible flowers have a delicate flavor, though people are advised to limit the amount of flowers consumed as they may contain cyanide precursors.

Arugula (Eruca vesicaria): This plant is typically grown as a green for salads and cooking, though it can be left to flower. The flower has a nutty, somewhat spicy flavor, and is also an excellent addition to salads.

Bachelor's Buttons (Centaurea spp.): Also known as cornflower, these flowers come in a variety of colors including deep blue, white, red, pink and purple. The flowers have also been used as a natural food dye and are originally from Europe.

Basil (Ocimum basilicum): The leaves are most often used as an herb, fresh or dried. However, the small white to pink blossoms of basil plants taste like basil leaves and are an aromatic addition to salads or pasta dishes.

Bee Balm (Monarda spp.): Both the red flowers and the leaves are edible. This plant is in the mint family and tastes of mint and oregano.

Borage (Borago officinalis): These beautiful blue to purple star-shaped flowers make an excellent edible flower decoration for adorning cakes and pies. They are also wonderful served floating in punch bowls or cold beverages, or frozen into ice cubes.

Broccoli florets (Brassica oleracea.): These pale yellow flowers sprout up from unpicked broccoli heads and make a delicate garnish.

Calendula (Calendula officinalis): Also called Pot Marigold, these hearty, bright yellow to orange flowers are originally from Europe and make a splendid and vivid garnish for any dessert.

Carnations (Dianthus spp.): The white base of these multi-colored flowers is bitter and should be removed when adding to culinary dishes, though the petals are sweet.

Chamomile (Chamaemulum nobile): These dainty, small yellow flowers add spots of color as a garnish and are best used in conjunction with other flowers.

Chervil (Anthriscus cerefolium): This plant is a member of the carrot family and grows small, white flowers in an umbel shape. They add a delicate touch as a garnish and have an anise flavor.

Chicory (Cichorium intybus): Both the pale blue petals and buds of this plant are edible. Chicory is from the aster family.

Cilantro (Coriander sativum): These delicate white flowers taste similar to the culinary herb and add a nice flavor to salads.

Clover (Trifolium pratense): The pinkish purple petals of these flowers have a mild flavor similar to anise or licorice. Clover is a member of the pea family.

Dandelion (Taraxacum officinale): The bright yellow flowers of this member of the aster family are sweetest when picked young, growing more bitter with age. Often considered to be just a weed, these flowers add a bright garnish to a dessert platter.

Daylily (Hemerocallis fulva): The large showy flowers of this plant make a gorgeous centerpiece on top of an iced cake or as garnish around the edge of a dessert platter. They're almost too beautiful to eat! The tubers, shoots and buds of the daylily are edible as well, and the flowers come in a range of colors from yellows and oranges to reds and pinks.

Dill (Anethum graveolens): The tangy flavor of these yellow flowers is similar to that of the leaves and seeds, typically used as a fresh or dried herb for pickling.

English Daisy (Bellis perennis): The small whitish-pink flowers of this member of the aster family offer a dainty garnish, though often slightly bitter tasting.

Fennel (Foeniculum vulgare): The fennel plant is a member of the carrot family and has yellow flowers in the shape of an umbel. These add a delicate fringe around a dessert platter.

Fuchsia (Fuchsia X hybrida): These ornate purple and red flowers look gorgeous adorning a dessert, though their taste is considered unspectacular.

Gardenia (Gardenia jasminoides): These elegant white flowers are wonderfully fragrant and attractive as a garnish.

Garden Pea (Pisum spp.): Do not eat ornamental sweet peas as they are poisonous! However, edible garden peas have flowers ranging in color from white to deep pink and taste like peas.

Gladiola (Gladiolus spp): These showy flowers have little flavor and are used more as a garnish. Remove anthers before eating or use only the petals in salads or as a garnish. Gladiolas come in a stunning array of colors.

Hollyhock (Alcea rosea): These tall, showy flowers can be somewhat bitter but are excellent when used as a garnish, as they can be grown in a multitude of colors.

Jasmine (Jasminum sambac): These fragrant white flowers are native to India and traditionally used to flavor teas.

Johnny Jump-ups (Viola tricolor): These little purple, yellow and white violets are a wonderful addition to salads, cakes, ice cubes, punches or soups. They have a mild flavor and the entire flower can be eaten.

Lavender (Lavendula spp.): These fragrant purple flowers can be used as a garnish or added to recipes fresh or dried. Lavender flowers keep well when dried and have a strong floral flavor.

Lemon and Tangerine Gems (Tagetes tenuifolia): These small, bright yellow and orange flowers are easy to grow. Try them in ice cubes, on desserts or in salads.

Lemon Verbena (Aloysia triphylla): These small cream-colored flowers have the scent of lemon.

Lilac (Syringa vulgaris): Lilac flowers have a lemony floral taste and are incredibly aromatic as well. Bunches of light purple blossoms add a spectacular garnish around the edge of serving platters.

Marjoram (Origanum marjorana): From the mint family, the leaves of marjoram are traditionally used as a culinary herb. The flowers can be used in the same manner, as they have a similar taste to the leaves.

Mint (Mentha spp.): There are many varieties of mint, each with a strong mint flavor and hints of an additional flavor, depending on the variety (e.g. lemon mint, chocolate mint). The small flowers usually range from white to pink in color and carry the mint aroma with them.

Nasturtium (Trapaeolum majus): These bold and brilliant flowers can be eaten in their entirety and range in color from yellow to orange to deep red, depending on the variety. This is a commonly used edible flower that creates an eye-catching addition to salads and soups, and also works as a garnish. Both the flowers and leaves of this plant are edible and have a spicy flavor.

Oregano (Oreganum vulgare): The small white to pink flowers can be used as you would the herb, as they have a similar flavor.

Pansy (Viola X wittrockiana): Pansies come in a variety of colors, and the entire flower is edible. Use as a garnish on cakes, desserts or in salads.

Pineapple Sage (Salvia elegans): These bright red tubular flowers attract hummingbirds and add a colorful splash to salads. The flowers are sweet.

Red Clover (Trifolium pretense): This perennial herb has dense, round flower heads that range in color from red to purple. Use fresh in salads or dry the flower head for later use.

Rosemary (Rosmarinus officinalis): These pale purple flowers have a similar taste to the leaves commonly used as a culinary herb.

Roses (Rosa spp.): All varieties of roses are edible and they come in a wide range of colors. Sprinkle petals into salads, on desserts, or the sides of plates as a garnish.

Sage (Salvia officinalis): These white to blue flowers have a similar flavor to the leaves most often used as a culinary herb. Great in salads or roasted vegetables.

Savory-Summer (Satureja hortensis): This culinary herb is often used with bean dishes, and is a great companion plant for beans in the garden as well. Use flowers as you would the herb.

Snap Dragon (Antirrhinum majus): Although these flowers are edible they are not particularly palatable, as they are often bland or bitter, depending on the variety.

Squash Flowers (Curcurbita pepo spp.): Zucchini blossoms taste of raw squash. The stamens should be removed before eating. These bright yellow to orange showy flowers are an excellent garnish.

Shungiku or Edible Chrysanthemum (Chrysanthemum coronarium): The leaves of this plant are often used for salad greens and the pale yellow flowers are a wonderful garnish. I like to pull off the petals and sprinkle them in our salad mix.

Sunflower (Helianthus annus): These showy favorites come in a variety of colors from yellows to deeper reds. The petals can be used as a garnish.

Thyme (Thymus vulgaris): The small white to yellow flowers of the thyme plant have a similar flavor to the leaves used as a culinary herb.

Violets and Violas (Viola spp.): These small flowers come in a variety of colors and are a beautiful, cheery addition to salads, soups, desserts and drinks. Violets are a popular edible flower. **CAUTION: African Violets (a common houseplant) are not considered an edible flower!**

References

Barclay de Tolly, Amy and Peggy Trowbridge. *Home Cooking: Edible Flowers* [online]. [Cited June 2005]. About, Inc., 2005.
http://homecooking.about.com/library/weekly/blflowers.htm

Creasy, Rosalind. *The Edible Flower Garden.* Periplus Editions, Boston, Massachusetts, 1999. 106 pp.

StarChefs. *Edible Flowers* [online]. [Cited June 2005]. StarChefs, 1995-2005.
http://starchefs.com/edible_flowers/html/index.shtml

Stradley, Linda. *Edible Flowers* [online]. [Cited June 2005]. What's Cooking America, 2004.
http://whatscookingamerica.net/EdibleFlowers/EdibleFlowersMain.htm

Wilkinson, Cathy. *Edible Flowers: Desserts & Drinks.* Fulcrum Publishing, Golden, Colorado, 1997. 84 pp.

Wilkinson, Cathy. *Edible Flowers: From Garden to Palate.* Fulcrum Publishing, Golden, Colorado, 1993. 250 pp.

Recipe Index

Sweet Loaves, Brownies, Cobblers, Crumbles and Oddballs

Beverages and Frozen Treats

Index

About the Author

LAURA MATTHIAS has worked as a field biologist for over a decade, studying rare and endangered plants and animals. Her background in biology led her to an interest in organic food production. She operates Phoenix Organic Farm B&B, an 11 acre property in Victoria, BC. The property is home to organic gardens and a farm market stand where she sells her fresh produce. An increasing amount of her produce is sold to restaurants whose growing demand for fresh local food keeps farmers like her in business. Laura also operates a bed & breakfast on the farm, offering gourmet breakfasts made from organic ingredients and farm fresh produce. Her commitment to environmental consciousness extends to her suites where she uses organic shampoos and soaps, as well as biodegradable cleaning and laundry supplies. A long-time vegan, she has researched the nutritional value of foods and has cooked vegan food as a personal chef for clients with dietary sensitivities.

If you have enjoyed *ExtraVeganZa* you might also enjoy other

BOOKS TO BUILD A NEW SOCIETY

Our books provide positive solutions for people who want to
make a difference. We specialize in:

ENVIRONMENT AND JUSTICE • CONSCIENTIOUS COMMERCE • SUSTAINABLE LIVING
ECOLOGICAL DESIGN AND PLANNING • NATURAL BUILDING & APPROPRIATE TECHNOLOGY
NEW FORESTRY • EDUCATIONAL AND PARENTING RESOURCES • NONVIOLENCE
PROGRESSIVE LEADERSHIP • RESISTANCE AND COMMUNITY

New Society Publishers

ENVIRONMENTAL BENEFITS STATEMENT

New Society Publishers has chosen to produce this book on Enviro 100, recycled
paper made with **100% post consumer waste**, processed chlorine free, and old
growth free.

For every 5,000 books printed, New Society saves the following resources:[1]

42	Trees
3,775	Pounds of Solid Waste
4,153	Gallons of Water
5,417	Kilowatt Hours of Electricity
6,862	Pounds of Greenhouse Gases
30	Pounds of HAPs, VOCs, and AOX Combined
10	Cubic Yards of Landfill Space

[1]Environmental benefits are calculated based on research done by the Environmental Defense Fund and
other members of the Paper Task Force who study the environmental impacts of the paper industry.

For a full list of NSP's titles, please call **1-800-567-6772** *or check out our website at:*

www.newsociety.com

NEW SOCIETY PUBLISHERS